UPON THE EARTH

FOUNDATIONS OF THE CHRISTIAN MISSION
Studies in the Gospel and the World

FOUNDATIONS OF THE CHRISTIAN MISSION
Studies in the Gospel and the World

UPON THE EARTH

The mission of God and
the missionary enterprise
of the churches

by

D. T. NILES

McGRAW-HILL BOOK COMPANY, INC.
NEW YORK   TORONTO   LONDON

Library of Congress
Catalog Card Number : 62—15292,
46560

MANUFACTURED IN U. S. A.

Contents

The quotations from the Bible are taken from the Revised Standard Version except where otherwise stated

"I know that my Redeemer lives, and at
last he will stand upon the earth"
(Job 19: 25).

"I came to cast fire upon the earth"
(Luke 12: 49).

"On earth as it is in heaven"
(Matthew 6: 10).

Foreword

A BOOK by D. T. Niles needs no introduction, but because he has asked me to write one I do so with great pleasure. There are three reasons why this book is important and deserves to be read and pondered by many.

The first is that it is a book about the greatest of all subjects—the mission of Christ and His people. Jesus said "I came to cast fire upon the earth". To be a Christian is to be part of that fire —to burn for His sake and to share in setting the world on fire. Sometimes it seems as if the fire were burning low, or as if it were just one of the flickering flames that only make enough light to cast up big and menacing shadows. Here is a book that will not only talk about the fire; it is a book which is part of the fire and will—pray God—help to make it blaze.

Secondly, this book is part of a unique effort of co-operative thought by Christians of many nations and many churches. We have become rather accustomed to "Agreed Statements" produced by international conferences. They have an important part to play in the development of Christian thinking, but they have severe limitations. They are apt to conceal more than they reveal. And they are often dull reading! The Department of Missionary Studies had wrestled long with the problems of ecumenical missionary study before it reached the plan of which this book is one of the fruits. The plan is described in detail in Dr Niles' introduction. It involved the active participation of a great number of people in five continents and the writing of two books, one by Dr J. Blauw of the Netherlands[1] and the other, the present work of Dr Niles. The writing of this book, illuminated and stimulated by the thinking of a truly world-wide company of Christians, is both the closing of one stage of the discussion and the invitation to a new stage. All who have been involved in this discussion hope that the publication of this book will stimulate a wider circle of Christian people

[1] *The Missionary Nature of the Church*, 1962.

7

to think, to ask questions, and to seek to carry into the day-to-day work of churches and missions boards the insights to which we have been led in these studies.

Thirdly, this book is important because of the man who has written it. When the study plan on "The Word of God and the Church's Missionary Obedience" was developed, there was never any doubt about who should be asked to write this book. D. T. Niles combines in a unique manner the insights and experiences that were needed for the job. He is both a theologian and an evangelist. There are theologians who can write about evangelism but have not the gift of so presenting Christ to men that they find in Him their Saviour. And there are effective evangelists whose theology is an easy target for attack. Niles is an evangelist who is also a profound thinker, a theologian who can commend his Saviour effectively to others. Moreover, he is at home at both ends of the foreign missionary operation as it is normally understood. He knows the "feel" both of older and of younger churches from inside and he can speak with authority to both. And, finally, his ministry is both local and ecumenical. Perhaps this is his most important qualification to speak to us at this moment. Those who see and hear him only in the context of great ecumenical conferences and discussion may not guess that he has maintained at the same time throughout his ministry the strongest and deepest local ties, as evangelist, teacher, pastor, counsellor, in his own Church and in the community where he was born and lives. What he says in an ecumenical setting has been tested again and again in the ordinary responsibilities of a local congregation. He knows what he is talking about and he has earned the right, as few men have, to be heard.

For every reason, therefore, this book deserves to be read and pondered. I venture to say that most readers will need to read many of its paragraphs more than once—not because they are obscure but because they are deep. The effort will be rewarded. All of us who have been involved in this study are grateful for this book.

LESSLIE NEWBIGIN, Bishop

Preface

THIS book is addressed to all who bear the name of Christ. It seeks to raise with them questions about a subject of elementary but far-reaching importance: a subject, therefore, on which books have been written since the earliest days of the Church.

What is the nature of the Church's mission to the world?
Where does the justification for this mission lie?
Whose is the responsibility to carry out this mission?
Why are "missions" from land to land an essential feature of
   the Church's missionary obedience?
Which are the factors that contribute to a sense of missionary
   urgency?
Whence arises the necessity to maintain "missions" as an
   identifiable part of the Church's activity?
Whither will an adequate missionary strategy lead "mis-
   sions" to-day?

The immediate need for the writing of this book was the awareness, on the one hand, that many reasons demanded a major re-appraisal of the "foreign" missionary enterprise of the Churches, if not of the Church's evangelistic mission itself; while, on the other hand, it was quite obvious that such a re-appraisal done by experts for experts would not meet the need where it had to be met.

If there is a loss of confidence in "mission", that loss does not primarily arise because the methods of the missionary enterprise seem outdated or even perverse. It stems from a loss of conviction about the Christian faith itself. That is why this book is addressed to the members of the churches in general and not simply to missionary administrators or advocates. "Missions" must be recognized as one of the real implications of Christian discipleship as such.

The phrase "foreign missions" has practically gone out of

9

use, but "missions" remain, and it is essential to know what they signify in terms of the totality of the faith. Only so can criteria be set up by which the forms of missionary administration and the modes of missionary endeavour may be judged and moulded. There are many things about "missions" which demand discussion and revision, but no such discussion can be fruitful, or such revision effective, except as "missions" are seen in relation to the total mission of the Church and that, in turn, in relation to the total mission of God. "Missions" must cease to be a speciality, and be seen instead as an integral part of churchly obedience.

This means that the ordinary Christian and every Christian has so to face the missionary implications of his faith as to recognize that a description of the mission of the Church is, in a true sense, but a description of the Church's day-to-day life. Too often a discussion of "missions" is made to depend too exclusively on a discussion of the nature of the Church. This is inadequate, since the Church's life can be understood only in relation to the world to which it is sent and in which it is set. The Church is the home of the Christian; it is the world which is the home of all men. So that true perspective demands that the discussion take place in terms of the inclusive reality within which the Church's mission to the world is contained and its nature and limitations determined—the Kingdom of God.

God's work in the world and the pressure of His grace upon persons are both the context of and the provocation for the Church's mission and the "missions" of the Churches.

The first five chapters of this book deal with the Christian faith in general, and seek to raise the questions which Christian discipleship must face. In the second half of the book are raised the specific issues concerning "missions". This sequence is inevitable in order to maintain the integral relation between missionary obedience as such and Christian obedience as a whole. All Christians must face the question "Why not be a missionary?" because to be a Christian is to be a member of a missionary community and to become a participant in the activity of a missionary God. The apostolic privilege belongs to all who are Christ's, and each has to decide in what form and what measure to share in the Church's missionary task and destiny. So that no responsible answer to the question "Why not be a missionary?" is possible except as it is rooted in an obedient answer to the more primary question "Why not be a Christian?" If the missionary is a symbol of the Christian faith it is because all Christians share in the Church's missionary task and the missionary enterprise belongs to the very nature of the Gospel.

It has already been said that this book is not by an expert for experts. It is intended to be read by anyone who bears the name of Christ and who seeks to understand in some measure what that involves both in privilege and in responsibility. To such a reader a word of advice may not be out of place. He will probably find it best to omit, in the first instance, a reading of the Introduction and go directly from the Preface to Part 1 and then on to Part 3. The Introduction will need to be read before tackling Part 2. In this part questions are dealt with which may not be of immediate interest to many, but which nevertheless an increasing number must give their minds to if the mission of the Church and the missionary enterprise of the Churches is not to become an esoteric affair.

Three chapters of this book are based very largely on my own writing elsewhere. The chapter on "the Self-hood of a church" is based on my John R. Mott memorial lecture delivered at the E.A.C.C. assembly in Kualalumpur and published, along with the other lectures there delivered, by the British S.C.M. Press under the title *A Decisive Hour for the Christian Mission*. The chapter on "the World of Religions" is based on one of my Lyman Beecher lectures which were published by Harper and Brothers and the Lutterworth Press under the title *The Preacher's Task and the Stone of Stumbling*. And the chapter on "the Westernity of the Base" draws largely on my contribution to a symposium published by William Collins entitled *Twentieth Century Christianity*. Acknowledgment is here made to these publishers for their kind permission to use this material.

It will be found that throughout the book the term "younger

churches" is used. This has become the accepted term to designate those churches which are the result of the modern missionary enterprise of the Churches of the West. Clumsy, and sometimes misleading, as this term may be, I could not think of another which would be more suitable.

One last word, and that is about the title of this book. Two considerations have led to the choice of this title, *Upon the Earth*. First, the central thesis of these chapters is that the earth is the true correlate of the Gospel and that, therefore, the goals and problems of this earthly life in all their complexity are the true addressees of the missionary endeavour. "Thy Name be hallowed, Thy Kingdom come, Thy will be done—On earth." Secondly, the earth is the scene not only of Christ's coming in the flesh but it will also be the object of His coming in glory. Salvation will be the culmination of His plan for all humanity, indeed of all creation, and not simply the collecting together of saved souls. The symbol of the end of redemption is an eternal city where men will find themselves restored to one another as well as to God.

"I came," said Jesus, "to cast fire upon the earth." That fire must become a conflagration. That is what the mission of the Church is about. "My redeemer lives," said Job, "and at last he will stand upon the earth." Those words express the Church's confidence too. Like Job, the Church is facing in all lands a time of severe testing and there are many false comforters. Everywhere the Church needs to lay claim to the faith by which it lives and which it asserts in the face of its own wretchedness.

> "The earth is enough and the air is enough
> For our wonder and our war ..."[1]

George: May I introduce myself? My name is George Jefferies. I work in Hongkong as a missionary, and I am just returning from my furlough in England. I suppose you joined the ship at Marseilles?

[1] G. K. Chesterton, *The House of Christmas*, Burns and Oates Ltd.

William: That's right, thank you. I'm William Arkwright, and I am going out to India to teach in a Christian College. I am coming from the States, and this is my first journey abroad.

George: We have another companion at this table—Sundar Priyanath. He seems to be late this morning. No, here he comes. Sundar, we have an addition at our table. Let me introduce William Arkwright to you.

Sundar: Good morning.

George: William is from America and is going to India to teach in a college there.

William: I am going to Lucknow. I have just finished my course in Union Theological Seminary at New York.

George: Sundar is returning to India after attending the Peace Congress in Prague.

William: That is interesting. When I was at Union we had a visit there from a group of communist students in Russia. It was a very revealing discussion that we had with them.

Sundar: What do you mean by "revealing"?

William: Let me put it this way. It was disconcerting to find that the Russians were more sure of the future success of communism than we were concerning the Christian hope.

Sundar: How was that? What became of the Christian certainty concerning the end?

William: Somehow, we never did manage to talk out of this certainty. In fact, the whole conversation with the Russians was in their idiom. We were all the time trying to meet their case from their point of view.

George: But isn't that right? Must we not seek to state the Christian message in the language of the hearer?

Sundar: Yes. But we always get into a quandary when we seek to set out the Christian message as an answer to the questions people ask.

Bola: Excuse me, friends, but can I join in this conversation? I overheard you from the next table and I am so interested in what you are talking about. My name is Bola Idolo from Kenya. I am returning from a course of law studies in Germany. I get off at Port Said, to attend a student conference there.

Sundar: Yes, join us by all means. I was answering a question about how to state the Christian message. Is it not true that, when we have formulated the problems and decided the terms in which the problems must be handled, we have already distorted the relevance of the Christian faith to human life? It seems to me that the first Christian task is to allow the Christian faith itself to question the human questions.

Bola: How right you are. I am sure you have heard about our problems in Kenya and about the crucial importance for the whole political and economic future of Kenya of seeing a way through the vexed questions of land tenure and food production. All discussions had practically arrived at a stalemate, when the Christian Council of Kenya summoned a conference of African and European farmers to discuss these questions under Christian auspices. The decisive difference was made by these auspices; the Christian faith determined the form in which the old questions were to be faced, and because the form of the questions was changed a way forward was cleared for the finding of answers.

William: But how do you face the problem of misunderstanding? The World Council of Churches organizes a consultation in South Africa on the question of race, and the consultation succeeds in re-stating the question within a Christian context: immediately the politicians begin to pressurize the churches. Church leaders in my country plead for "open" politics but have to face the opposition of those who would make the cold war the determinant in the political decisions of our government. The Church in Germany decides to hold its Kirchentag in Berlin and the East German government calls it political provocation. The issue boils down to this: that men are prepared to listen to the Christian message if it answers their questions, and are glad to set it aside if it does not; but that they get angry when Christianity begins to question them.

Sundar: You can also get a situation in which the Church in a particular place can itself refuse to be questioned. In Ceylon, for instance, there has been for the last five years a growing estrangement between the Sinhalese and the Tamils centering in a controversy about the policy of the government to make Sinhalese the only official language of the country. As far as I have been able to follow the developments, while the Church in Ceylon, which has in its membership both Sinhalese and Tamils, has repeatedly called for conference and consultation to resolve the conflict, it has not itself discussed the issues and pronounced upon them.

Bola: Our minister told us that the word "salvation" in the Bible has the root meaning of "spaciousness". This must mean that in Jesus Christ life will be rid of every narrowing and restrictive circumstance. Somehow that is not the picture which the actual life of the Christian community in Africa suggests. The Gospel is proclaimed for the salvation of souls and not of life itself! As the saying goes: Why scratch where it does not itch? The Christian Church must deal with "where it does itch".

Sundar: That there is a Christian message is simply the result of the fact that God became man in Jesus Christ and that, by the resurrection, He remains man. So is determined the very structure and destiny of human history. Man's situation in the world is the result of Jesus being part of it. Men speak about man's existential situation; they forget, or prefer not to see, that this existential situation is given by the incarnation of Jesus Christ. The initial task of Christian witness is to uncover this fact and make it explicit.

William: The Incarnation is certainly the decisive event, but the life of Christian witness begins in a meeting with the risen Lord. Our Christmas is always Christmas after Easter.

George: I work as a missionary in Hongkong. Somehow, in that tumultuous city, we don't seem to be able, by our preaching, to do what you say we ought to do.

Bola: Just preaching is not enough. The questions, that need to be raised, need to be raised by the Christian community and the way it lives. There is a very real sense in which the uniqueness of the Christian Gospel is tied up with the uniqueness of the Christian community. If the Christian Church in the lands of Africa does not, by its very presence, cause men to ask the right questions about God and man and human life, then the preaching of the Gospel is bound to remain an affair on the outside.

Sundar: Yes, and where the language of a country is one that is rooted in a non-Christian culture, this business of the questions being raised by the life and ways of the Christian community is of special importance.

Bola: Some people speak glibly of Christ being the answer to the problems of men. Christ is not the answer. The answer is that which Christ provided—a Church, a body of people set in the world as His Body, living His risen life and continuing in the world the ministry of His incarnation. "To brother all the souls of men": that would give to life true spaciousness.

William: Let me back-track a bit. Why did we not, at Union, in our conversation with the communists, give evidence of the fighting certainty of our faith? Do you think it was because in our minds we had identified, almost unconsciously, our hope for the future with the successful prosecution of the Church's missionary enterprise? If so, that is where we went wrong, for "successful missions" is no more a category that we are able to apply to the future. To put it bluntly, it no longer seems possible to think in terms of a progressive conversion of the world. And, because this is so, we tend to lose our nerve.

George: Modern missions arose in a Christendom situation in the West and, without reflection, assumed that the end of missions will be a Christendom situation throughout the world. This kind of thinking is not possible any more. Both facts and theology demand that we re-state the case for missions in terms of God's total mission towards the world as a whole. The Church ...

Sundar: Please excuse me for interrupting, but you remind me of a point that Dr Devanandan used to make in his lectures on Hinduism. He used to say that in the many forms of renewal which we find in Hinduism to-day, we must learn to perceive the creative hand of the living Spirit as He is engaged in bringing into being the new creation. The crucial issue in all evangelistic work is so to claim for God in Christ everything which is truly His, that those who have received His gifts will also receive Him and become His disciples.

William: Principal Hwang of Taiwan, in a lecture which I heard him deliver in New York, spoke of that verse in the book of Job where God is said to work "on the left hand". I am not sure that the actual verse he referred to carries the meaning he intended, but his point was clear. He was emphasizing the mission of God as a vaster concept than the mission of the Church. "There is only one mission," he said, "the mission of God. The Church is in this mission." The Church carries forward the purpose of the incarnation, but the incarnate Lord cannot be limited by the Church. The Church's life and witness is held within His vast enterprise.

George: This way of talking about the world and God's work in the world is not always easy to understand. We are told that the world lies in the evil one, we are also told that God loved the world. This means that we cannot attribute everything that happens to God. We must be prepared to reckon also with the demonic. It is true enough that God is bringing into being the new creation, but it is still too early to discern between wheat and tares.

William: Cannot we say that we are puzzled, in seeking to understand what happens as the result of the missionary thrust, not only because we cannot distinguish now between wheat and tares, not only because the proclamation of the

Christ itself arouses the anti-Christ, but also because there is taking place in the world a double preparation? In the book of Revelation we read of the Bride as well as of the guests at the wedding banquet, we read of the river of life as well as of the nations for whose healing it flows.

Sundar: A person viewing the missionary task is as it were standing at a cross-roads where three roads meet and cross. The sign board of the first road reads—All men, the whole world, the whole creation, all things. The sign board of the second road reads—Each man, he who believes, he that is chosen. The sign board of the third road reads—the part shall consecrate the whole. The significance of the junction is that here these three roads meet.

Bola: That is why emphasis must fall on the Christian Church. Not only is the mission of the Church within God's mission, it is also the inner structure of that mission. It is impossible to speak of the new creation in a general way without recognizing that the Christian community is itself God's new creation.

Sundar: True, but too often it is only theologically true. In actual fact the Christian community in place after place, and in situation after situation, bears feeble witness to the truth of the new creation. Take the Church's missionary enterprise itself as an example. Is not the significance of the mission of the Church blurred because what men see are the missions of the Churches? There is no task more necessary right now than that of re-defining the missions of the Churches in terms of the mission of the Church. We speak so easily about our time as the ecumenical era. We must make clear what this involves for the mission of the Church both in theological definition and in actual missionary administration.

William: A more basic need is to justify the Christian conception of time in terms of a scientific world-view. The Christian mission has no justification apart from the faith that the end of time has begun, but it is this very faith which people find difficult to grasp.

Bola: This connection between the developments of human history and the mission of the Church, this connection between the being of the Church and God's design for the new creation, this connection between the preaching of the Gospel for the salvation of men and the power of the Gospel for the transformation of the earth—here, it seems to me, lie the issues which need to be made clear.

George: I am a missionary. Somehow I believe that the missionary task itself, by the way it is performed and by the motives which sustain it, will set forward its own explanation. Paul talks about the incalculable wealth of Christ, the picture in his mind being that of a rich country stretching to the far horizons waiting to be explored. The whole Christ for the whole world—yes, but also the whole world in order that the riches of the whole Christ may become man's inheritance.

Introduction

THERE is a history behind the writing of this book. The issues with which it deals came to prominence at the Willingen meeting (1952) of the International Missionary Council (I.M.C.), and the decision to have these issues systematically discussed was made at the subsequent meeting in Ghana (1958). The method adopted to discuss them was to call a series of consultations on them in which theologians, missionaries, missionary administrators and local church leaders took part. These consultations, officially called by the I.M.C., were held in New York, Geneva, Bangalore, Singapore, Hongkong, Brazzaville, Accra, Salisbury and Marangu; and unofficial consultations convened locally were held at Johannesburg, San Jose, and Christchurch.

These consultations were asked to address themselves to the question which was formulated in the following way: "What does it mean in theological terms and in practice in this ecumenical era for the Church to discharge its mission to all the nations?" As part of the preparative material for these consultations, Dr J. Blauw of the Netherlands Missionary Council was asked to write a book setting forth, in the light of the most recent biblical scholarship, the teaching of the Bible concerning the theological basis and meaning of the Church's mission. This book has now been published under the title *The Missionary Nature of the Church*. The World Council of Churches and the International Missionary Council also convened a consultation of theologians in Bossey in July 1961 to which the first draft of the present book was submitted for discussion and comment. In addition to making their comments on the draft, the Commission produced its own statement, which has been published by the World Council of Churches under the title *The Missionary Task of the Church—Theological Reflections*.

Important, however, as all these consultations have been,

and important as is the attempt to reflect theologically on the Church's mission, it is essential to remember that theology does not itself provide the justification for missions. It rather elucidates the justification which already exists in the Church and which has been driving Christians to be missionaries for centuries. In other words, we are involved in this study in a theological interpretation of the Church's actual missionary existence. To neglect this dimension of historical positivism in the discussion is to fall a prey to an attitude of theological criticism which is unfair to the actualities of the mission as it is and as it has been. "The missionary enterprise," says Wilhelm Andersen, "has not come into being through conscious theological reflection on the self-revelation of God in Jesus Christ, but through the descent upon certain men or groups of men—we cannot express it otherwise—of a compulsion of the Holy Spirit to undertake the proclamation of the Gospel overseas."[1]

Coupled, however, with this warning concerning the nature of this inquiry must go also another warning which points in the opposite direction. It is one thing, in a theological reflection on the Church's mission, to take account of the actual missionary enterprise; it is another thing to feel bound by the theological categories in which that enterprise was conceived and executed. There is truth in a contention of Professor Hoekendijk that, if there is one change above all else which is necessary in missionary thinking, it is to replace a Church-centred orientation of missions by a Kingdom-centred one. Speaking of this Church-centred orientation, which he sees as dominant since the Jerusalem meeting (1928) of the I.M.C., he says:

> Its whole horizon is completely filled by the Church. The missionary now hardly leaves the ecclesiastical sphere. He tries to define his whole surrounding world in ecclesiological categories. The world has almost ceased to be the world and is now conceived of as a sort of ecclesiastical training ground. The Kingdom is either confined within the bounds of the Church or else it has become something like an eschatological lightning on the far horizon.[2]

[1] *Towards a Theology of Mission*, S.C.M. Press, p. 13.
[2] *International Review of Missions (I.R.M.,)* July 1952, p. 324.

Commenting on this thought of Professor Hoekendijk, Dr Max Warren says:

> By laying this continual stress upon the Church and its establishing everywhere as the "end" of the missionary enterprise, we have manoeuvred ourselves into a position where the survival of the Church as we have created it has become scarcely less important than its previous establishment.[1]

"The Church as we have created it"—that is the nub of the problem. Only in the perspective of the Kingdom of God do we really see the Church as God has created it, and are set free to serve that Kingdom as members of that Church.

QUESTIONNAIRE

In the several consultations which were held, a basic questionnaire of ten questions was used with slight variations. This helped to reveal the actual issues which people were wrestling with who were concerned with the subject of "missions", and the significant experiences and convictions from which guidance could be drawn for the providing of answers. The questionnaire used was as follows:—

(1) What is the connection between God's sovereignty, the Lordship of Christ over the world, and the mission of the Church to all the nations?

In view of the biblical assertion that it is Christ who is the Word of God to man, and that it is God who draws man to Himself through the Holy Spirit, what is the place of our witness?

(2) How does the obligation to mission evidence itself in the life of the individual Christian? With what authority does he engage in the missionary task and how does he receive the sense of urgency?

How is the missionary vocation to be understood? Who is a missionary? How can the terms "evangelist", "witness", "missionary" be distinguished?

[1] In a paper presented at a Conference held at Toronto, Oct. 17-18, 1958.

(3) Is the missionary character of Israel in the Old Testament inherent in its existence as the chosen people? If so, how was it defined and challenged?

How did the Apostolic Church conceive and discharge its universal mission? How are the churches of Asia, Africa and Latin America to participate in the world mission of the Church?

(4) What is the nature and validity of the Christian claim that there is salvation in "none other Name"? Is there salvation outside the Christian Church?

What is the relation of the mission of the Church to the Kingdom of God? What is the nature of the encounter between Christianity and other religions? Is this encounter actually taking place—with Islam in Africa, with Hinduism in India, with Buddhism in Burma, and so on?

(5) Is the missionary movement of the Church, specifically involving the crossing of national and cultural frontiers, an essential part of the Church's life; or does the Church in one land receive missionaries from another as a temporary measure until it is able to do without them?

Are "missions" which cross national and cultural frontiers a theological necessity or a historical contingency? Is there a relation between the eschatological and the geographical character of the Christian mission—the ends of the earth and the end of time?

(6) What is the meaning of the term "nation"? In what sense, if any, can a church be a national church? Is the object of missions the formation of churches among the several nations? What does it mean in theological terms and in practice, in this ecumenical era, for the Church to discharge its mission to all the nations? Must missions be totally recast in ecumenical terms? How?

Relate the movement towards world organized confessionalism to the movement towards Church Union in different countries. Does disunity among the Churches hinder the mission of the Church? In what way are the separatist churches in Africa important? Have we anything to learn from them?

(7) How can the whole organized missionary and evangelistic activity of the Church be carried out so that it does not
hinder but stimulates the manifestation of the Holy Spirit in
the daily life of Christian communities and persons?

What type of laymen does a spontaneously missionary church
pre-suppose?

(8) When is the life of the Church an obstacle to mission?
How can we distinguish between the essential character of
Christian community and particular cultural patterns of
Church life and structure?

When Christians are so unlike their Master, how can we call
people to join their fellowship?

(9) What effect has the emergence of autonomous churches
had on missionary initiative and responsibility? What effect
should it have? Does the missionary obligation require for its
fulfilment work directly among non-Christians, or is it equally
fulfilled by fostering a missionary spirit in other churches, and
by participating in their life?

Review the present relationships in your area between
churches and mission boards in their bearing upon the missionary task of the Church as a whole.

(10) Do the Churches in their missionary outreach offer a
total Christian world-view; or do Christians in your area, in
times of stress and perplexity, in fact if not in intention, fall
back upon the world-view of their traditional culture? Is the
actual impact of Christianity in your area experienced chiefly
as a new law or as gospel?

There is not only a Christian Gospel to be proclaimed but a
Christian wisdom to be taught. How may "missions" discharge this responsibility?

SUMMARY OF CONSULTATIONS

What were some of the things said in the course of discussing
these questions? There were certain common factors which
were felt in all the consultations to be of such crucial importance

that it would be a fair summary to group what was said under those headings. To enumerate them, they were:

    (a) Criticism concerning missionary foreignness
    (b) Questions about missionary justification
    (c) Issues relating to missionary unity
    (d) Problems of missionary frustration
    (e) The spread of the sectarian spirit
    (f) The voice of the African revolution
    (g) The challenge of resurgent religions

Missionary foreignness. Here was a criticism of missions as it stemmed from the birth of new nations in so called mission lands. The form in which Christians in China often stated these criticisms was felt, in many of these consultations, to be a pointed way of expressing thoughts held more generally in most churches of Asia and Africa.

This Chinese criticism can be fairly summarized in five propositions. The Gospel preached was socially reactionary, concentrating the issue on individual salvation, so that social and political behaviour became a mere consequence of personal dedication to Christ. The Church had a class character, was socially conservative and represented a cultural imperialism; the results of which were that Christians became denationalized and the ways of life of the missionary community became the pattern for the local church. The policy that the Church should be above politics bred in large measure political irresponsibility. Foreign missionaries were agents not only of foreign churches but also of foreign governments. The foreign missionary had too much influence in, if not control of, the Chinese church. An illuminating illustration of this last criticism is given by Dr Charles West who was a missionary in China.

> One of the critical tasks [he says] of mission is to develop a brotherhood with the Christians in the land to which the mission goes in the handling of money which comes from abroad. This proceeded in many missions, at any rate the ones that I knew about, by way of appointing a Chinese treasurer for the mission. Yet, our Chinese brethren always knew that we could get access

to money or could influence the process by which money came. Our dominance continued no matter what the external arrangements were.[1]

Of course, this is but one example of what is meant by control. In oriental lands the forms of courtesy which have to be observed towards guests make this assumption of power only too easy.

An example of the fact that this Chinese criticism voices a more generally held point of view in the lands of the younger churches is a statement drawn up by a Sinhalese Baptist Minister explaining the Buddhist attitude to Christianity in Ceylon. He says:

> There has been a psychological aversion to Christianity on the part of the Buddhist public on the ground that it is a foreign religion, couched in alien paraphernalia, introduced to this country by foreign missionaries. It is also regarded as a powerful ally of Western Culture and of Western Imperialism. To say the least, there is a great deal in our attitude, conscious and unconscious, in our worship, in the terms we use and in our religious practices, which lends colour to these criticisms. Another motive behind the resurgence of Buddhism is concerned with the supposed danger which the impact of Christianity has on our national culture. This impact, according to our critics, is so strong and harmful, that if the Christian Church is allowed to continue its way any longer, there might be a sort of cultural disintegration in our land. This fear is seriously entertained by many.[2]

Missionary justification. All these five propositions seem to add up to only one: the Church which the missionaries founded in China was not truly Chinese. The issue here is not whether this criticism is fully justified but that it is made, and that it is highlighted by the form in which "missions" are generally criticized also in the West to-day.

There are those who look at China, for instance, and say, Missions are not useful anyway. All forms of Christian service

[1] From a speech delivered at the Ecumenical Institute, Bossey (1959).
[2] From a paper submitted by the Rev. S. J. de S. Weerasinghe to the United Bible Society (1961).

are only ameliorative; while the issues of personal religion seem to make so little difference to national development. The real needs of the nations of Asia and Africa and Latin America are hardly touched by missions. There are others in the West who raise the question in a more elementary form. "Why missions anyhow! Are not all religions adequate to serve human needs, and cannot the weaknesses of the various religions be met by religious collaboration?" Professor Toynbee is the latest *guru* of those who take this line. At the consultation in New York, I asked a mission board executive what effect support for missions had on the convictions of the home-church with respect to the person of Christ. His answer was, "A belief in the relative uniqueness of Jesus Christ is sufficient to support missions. That is as far as the missionary understanding of many missions-supporters goes."

To many, in the Churches of the West, it seems as if, in any case, the day of missions is over. Some take the line, "The younger churches do not need our help any more. Look at the quality of those from the younger churches whom we have met." Others take the line, "The missionary frontier is every-where, the geographical frontier has not special importance, to become a missionary to another land can be an escape from immediate responsibility to one's own." "After all, a basic factor in the present situation is the failure of nerve among Christians in the West regarding the worth of their own achieve-ments in social and personal life. A great deal must happen in the West before the religion which underlies its culture can be exported with confidence." To quote Bishop Newbigin:

> It is impossible to exaggerate the importance of the fact that, at the moment when the scientific culture which was formed within the western Christian tradition has achieved world-wide expan-sion and dominance, its unity with the supernatural faith in which it was begotten has disintegrated. The typical and domin-ant scientific man of the West is to a large extent alienated from the Christian tradition.[1]

[1] From an address given to the North American Advisory Committee of the I.M.C. (Nov. 14, 1958).

And then there are those—many of them young people in the Universities—who feel the compulsion to live on the frontier between a situation in which the Church recognizably exists and an adjacent situation in which the Church does not: but who are seeking to find ways of getting to this frontier without becoming involved or implicated in the machinery of missions. Consequent on the conference convened by the World Student Christian Federation at Strasbourg (1960) on the Life and Mission of the Church, there appeared two statements, one issued by the Federation itself and the other written by the General Secretary of the International Missionary Council. Two paragraphs, one from each statement, are given as illuminating the attitude to missions of Christian students to-day.

Most of us were impressed by the sharpness of the present student and youth reaction against institutionalism, not only in Missionary Societies and Churches but also in Student Christian Movements and in the Federation itself. It was more than clear from the reaction of the majority of participants in Strasbourg that their criticisms, sometimes so violent that they were quite unfair, proceeded not from any lack of concern for, and sense of membership in, the Church, but from a genuine desire to see its mission carried on more faithfully and effectively. For them the rigidity of organizations and institutions is one of the major obstacles, if not the greatest, to the missionary enterprise of the Church.

There is a quite shattering degree of unanimity that the traditional missionary pattern cannot provide the pattern of obedience for our day. This is not argued; it is assumed. I think we have to take it that the present generation of students derives its "image" of foreign missions not from what is put out by mission boards, but by what is told them by the Asian and African students who sit beside them in the lecture room and the laboratory. Any pattern of missionary effort which captures this generation of students will have to be marked by at least the following features:—freedom from connection with Colonialism; facing real "frontiers"; standing where the other man stands; unity. The question of unity is one that is felt deeply. My impression is that this group of students feels the scandal of our divisions more deeply than I had thought.

This questioning about missions by Christians in the West as well as by Christians in the so-called "mission-lands", however, is seen as a crisis only when there is added to it the radical questioning which the development of the ecumenical movement produces. Commenting on the questions, first drawn up for use in the consultations, Dr Keith Bridston, the secretary of the Faith and Order Commission of the World Council of Churches, remarked:

> The existential question seems to me to be the quite practical one arising out of the fact that the ecumenical movement seems to be making past motives, mores, and moorings of the missionary movement anachronous. The more this study can be directed to the direct institutional organizational crisis in the missionary movement which is a real crisis in the post-war circle of younger missionaries, the more it will be listened to.

Dr Kraemer puts the issue thus:

> The great new fact in the total Christian world situation since the second world war is undoubtedly the ecumenical movement, and its intimate association with the apostolic calling and outreach of the Church. It is of paramount significance that it has with one stroke paved the way for full participation by the younger churches in the ecumenical encounter and conversation, and that it has confronted missions with the previously ignored and evaded fact that missions are by nature and calling ecumenical, that it is the Church of Christ which must be planted and expanded, and not the Reformed Church, or the Lutheran Church, or the Methodist Church, etc. In other words, the era of "confessional" missions is ended. This is an agonizing issue for Western Christians, but also for some of the younger churches.[1]

One problem very evident at the Willingen meeting of the I.M.C. was the tension between the view that the entire purpose of the Church was mission and the view that the Church has a mission but that its own existence was a prior reality possessing its own validity. Does it not seem that the sharpness of this tension is simply because of the dividedness of the Church? As long as the prior existence of the Church is a divided existence,

[1] *History's Lessons for Tomorrow's Mission*, W.S.C.F., p. 205.

so long will it be necessary to insist on the reality of this prior existence for the wrong reasons. The Church's mission is one mission to an undivided world, so that it will be only as the Church's unity in mission is recovered that the prior existence of the Church itself can be persuasively demonstrated.

Missionary unity. Thus is raised the whole nexus of problems concerning the need to establish and maintain the Church's unity in mission through the missions of divided Churches. These problems are not all of the same kind, but they belong together as expressing the same concern.

How may the missions of divided Churches maintain that posture of self-questioning which will keep them open to the possibilities of obedience to the demands of the Church's unity in mission? At a time when the powerful Churches of the West are using their resources to organize confessional loyalties on a world scale, what must the younger churches do to strengthen in their own lands their fellowship across denominational lines, and to help the older churches to overcome the temptations that are incident to any organization of power? What is the theological validity of those non-ecclesiastical parts of the Church (Y.M.C.A., Y.W.C.A., W.S.C.F., independent missionary societies, etc.) which, because of their desire for mission, feel that it is better not to be a "church"? Missionary Societies once independent have been brought into close relationship with separate churches: how is this development to be safeguarded from strengthening denominationalism? Can mission programmes of separate Churches be merged before the Churches themselves are prepared to unite? What is the best way of helping the younger churches to take a more effective and substantial part in the world mission of the Church?

The fact that already there are more than one hundred Asian missionaries, sent by their churches, working in lands other than their own, has made this last question of practical urgency. The following alternative possibilities are under serious examination:—that a denomination like the Methodist Missionary Society, for instance, which belongs to the Methodist Church in

Great Britain, become the missionary society of all the Methodist Churches historically related to the British Methodist
Church; that each autonomous church in the world establish
its own missionary society and that these societies help one
another primarily within but also across denominational lines
with personnel and finance; that missionary endeavour be
organized at the world confessional level; that in the lands of
the younger churches, missionary procedures and policies be of
an interdenominational character from the very beginning,
organized either on a national or regional basis.

The simple problem is that the demands of the world mission
and the essential unity of the task are becoming too great for
divided Christendom, with the result that there is, on the one
hand, an awakened zest in the search for churchly unity which
can be local in its manifestation and therefore powerful at the
place of need; while, on the other hand, there is the attempt to
set up bureaucratic procedures which will minimize the effects
of the Church's disunity and give it the possibility of unity in
action even though it falls short of unity in its life of Word,
Fellowship and Sacrament.

Missionary frustration. Into all this questioning about
missions and their future there is introduced an element of
tragedy when one considers the problems that torment the
actual missionaries on the spot. These problems need to be
stated both from the point of view of the missionaries as well as
from the point of view of missionary administrators. (I asked
the executives of four long-established missionary societies—
one in Great Britain, one on the continent in Europe, and two
in the U.S.A.—what their main problem was in missionary
administration to-day, and each of them said—for they were
interviewed separately—"the frustrations experienced by the
missionaries we have sent".) Among the situations in which the
missionaries find themselves under frustrating pressure the
following are often mentioned.

The relationship between "church" and "mission" is not
everywhere sufficiently clarified, so that the missionary finds

himself in a state of insecurity, not knowing where authority resides. Missionaries in many lands find themselves assigned to tasks which give them little scope to fulfil their evangelistic calling. "To-day the gravest embarrassment of the missionary societies," says Dr Warren, "lies in the actual unwillingness of the younger churches to set them free to perform the tasks for which they properly exist—the pioneering of those new frontiers, not necessarily geographical, which have not yet been marked with a cross."[1] Then there is the fact that many missionaries suffer from an unresolved and to them unresolvable tension—a tension between their awareness that by their very presence they seem to be impeding the growth of local leadership and initiative, and their conviction that they are needed where they are even if the church which they have come to serve is passive towards them. Also, the missionary finds himself faced with a task which by its very nature is an impossible one, and he finds himself inadequately prepared both theologically and spiritually to support its impossibility. On the one hand, the task is to identify himself with the people among whom he has come to live; and, on the other hand, it is to remain what he is so that he can truly give himself. "To denationalize a missionary," says Dr Warren, "which is what a good deal of current talk about identification virtually involves, may be to reduce his ability to serve to the very minimum."[2] Commenting on this statement Count van Randwijck observes, "Missionaries are expected to put off their old nature, including all its typically Western sins. Anything going beyond this is unbiblical romanticism."[3]

The issue about "identification" is related also to the fact that, in the countries of the West, the Gospel has been so domesticated within their culture that the missionary too obviously sees an Asian or African culture as alien to the Gospel. How is he, except as he himself attempts "identification", to help the people among whom he works to respond to

---

[1] Quoted in Ghana Assembly Report, I.M.C., p. 94.
[2] *I.R.M.*, Oct. 1953, pp. 389-390.
[3] Ghana Assembly Report, I.M.C., p. 86.

the Gospel in their own cultural idiom? And, finally, to all these problems are added the purely external problems which missionaries have to face—the education of their children, the political attitudes of the countries to which they go to the countries from which they come, the adjustment of their living standards to the living standards of their national colleagues, the imaginativeness or lack of it in the pastoral care they receive from the churches which they have come to serve, and so on.

All these problems faced by missionaries are the problems also of missionary administration, though some further questions need articulation from the point of view of missionary administrators themselves. The central problem of missionary administration, as it revealed itself in the various consultations that preceded the writing of this book, was that of "partnership" between sending and receiving Church. Not only was the problem that the Whitby formula "partnership in obedience"[1] did not envisage partnership in the lands of the sending Churches, but also that the true partners at both ends happened to be minorities. The missionary administrators in the sending Churches represent an understanding of and an attitude to "foreign" missions which is much in advance of the general convictions of their own people. Also, in the receiving Churches, there is a church-conscious vigorous minority who are the necessary partners of the missionaries but who do not share the common attitude of complete openness to "foreign" missions which is still the characteristic of most Christian people in the receiving lands.

Another issue, basic to the concept of partnership, is that, with the emergence of autonomous churches, it is necessary to devise new procedures by which true partnership in decision-making can be maintained between sending and receiving churches. When a missionary Church is reduced to the bare function of recruiting-agent of personnel and finance to support another Church, then the heart of the missionary connection has been betrayed.

[1] I.M.C. Assembly held at Whitby, Canada, 1947.

The sectarian spirit. A good way of obtaining perspective on these vexed questions concerning the relation between "Church" and "mission" is to look at the far more critical problems raised by the increase of sectarian missions. These missions remain uninhibited by the growth of the younger churches. They are simply concerned with converting people to Christ and gathering them together into worshipping communities. The up-building of a Church in a land, so that that Church can be the Church for the nation, is a concept that sectarian missions reject as not even worthy of consideration. The Church remains invisible and does not, therefore, give any trouble.

And yet, those Churches within the ecumenical movement which engage in mission must face the questions raised by those aspects of sectarian missions to which their strength belongs. In the words of R. K. Orchard, "we must be aware of the contrast which is often drawn (no doubt too crudely but with an uncomfortably sharp point) between the 'conservative evangelical' missions and their direct and uninhibited line in evangelism and the 'church' missions with their preoccupation with inter-church relations and their lost directness in mission."[1] Where, as in Latin America for instance, the established church is itself seen as an evangelistic problem, the question is complicated further still.

Bishop Newbigin tells the story of how, during his visit in Latin America, he went to see the work among the Jungle Tribes. He asked in a village, "How many Christians are there here?" The answer was, "Well, I know So-and-so is a child of God, and I think So-and-so is, but I am not quite sure about the others." The only visible form of the Church was a series of precious but fragile personal relationships with a single missionary. This individualistic emphasis certainly has its strength. On a continent where sinful human nature and cheap grace are both taken for granted, it has produced a striking testimony to the power of the Gospel to lift the moral life of people. But, at the same time, it has thrown out of focus the nature of the Church as the community of faith. At an informal meeting in

[1] From a paper prepared by him for private circulation (1958).

Buenos Aires someone told a story of a Roman Catholic who was astonished to learn that evangelicals believed in God. When the laughter had died down, Bishop Barbieri said: "I do not think this is simply a laughing matter. We have to ask, why it is that people can have such fantastic ideas about our beliefs? Is it because we have concentrated so much on the things which, against the Roman Catholic, we deny; rather than on the things which, with them, we confess?"

The sectarian attitude has its consequence in the area of Christian co-operation also. It prevents the recognition that at the heart of co-operative organizations between Churches there should always be the element of mutual encounter between them on the level of faith. Where Christian co-operation is mainly conceived as co-operation in certain common, non-controversial tasks, or for representing the evangelical case to Governments, or for withstanding Roman pressure, then the essence of the ecumenical movement has been missed. The issue here is not simply one concerning Christian unity. It is the issue concerning the life of the Christian community in the world. Even a vital individual Christian experience cannot be sustained apart from active participation in the Church's mission to the world in its several needs. A very able and sympathetic Roman Catholic, who conducts missions all over Chile, made the remark that he was constantly meeting people who had been converted from a nominal Roman Catholicism to a living Pentecostalism, but were now completely lost to any kind of Christian faith at all.

There is only one adequate answer to sectarianism, both in its strength and in its weakness, and that is realized ecumenism. The Church is not only One, the Church is not only divided, but the Church is also a gift where its unity is given to God's people amidst their divisions. This given unity must receive appropriate forms. It must also be put at the service of the Church's mission there to find and to give evidence of its true nature. As far as the autonomous Churches in "mission" lands are concerned, the endemic problem is that in so many places so little is happening on the evangelistic frontiers. An autonomous

Church has the authority to order its own life, but there must be some way provided for a due disobedience to that authority where the Church is not true to its mission. A broad-based evangelism alone, because the evangelizing activity is a manifestation of the Church under judgment, can prove an adequate solvent of the actual condition of a Church and a sufficient power for its renewal.

The voice of Africa. The general line taken in the consultations which has been outlined so far holds true for the consultations held in Africa as well. But it is appropriate, for the purpose of this introduction, to give independent expression to the African accent. The African revolution not only challenges many missionary policies and procedures as they apply to Africa but it makes urgent the need for drastic changes in the life and thought of the people of those lands from which missionaries to Africa come.

To read the record of the African consultations was to receive certain very strong impressions. The first and strongest impression was the vigorous repudiation of any remaining apartheid between "mission" and "church". Wherever there was any tendency for the mission to remain a separate organization, or for missionaries to think and act as a group apart from the Church, this was deeply and rightly resented. In several places some of the missionaries, generally the younger ones, said in effect: "We are temporary people, who are here to give some special contribution which we have, and when we have given that we should leave. We are just the scaffolding; you are the real African church." The answer always was: "This is a completely false idea. The only proper way for you to think of yourselves is as part of the one Church. We do not want an African church, we want a Christian church in Africa, and we want you to be part of it." Separatist sects have arisen in Africa partly or mainly because the churches under mission control did not give proper authority to African leadership. But those who remain in the "established" churches are those who have faced this issue and seen a vision of the Church which is truly supra-racial.

Hence the vehemence with which they repudiate the idea implicit in the term "African Church".

Many of the African leaders appealed for missionaries who would really commit themselves for life to the Church in Africa. What was repeatedly said can be put in the words: "Send us missionaries who will live with us, work with us, die with us, and lay their bones here in Africa. We do not want missionaries who come to shake hands and say goodbye." In more than one place it was asked: "Why must missionaries go to their former homeland to retire? Why do they not retire here?" A question which hit very hard, especially in the Congo, arose from the fact that many missionaries left during the 1960 troubles. The question was asked, "Who is the authority who has told them that they are not wanted?" By implication the question was whether missionaries come and go with the colonial power.

Yet this demand for identification was emphatically not defined in terms of living conditions etc. Mr Sithole, the well-known political leader and author of the book *African National-ism*, said in one of the discussions: "There are two ideas of identification; one is what I may call anthropological identification; the other is identification in Christ. It is the latter we are concerned with." The idea of missionaries deliberately going to live in the slum quarters of an African city was vehemently resented. At one consultation there was a vigorous debate following upon a speech of Bishop Trevor Huddleston in which he spoke of the Good Samaritan who "went where he was", and said that we must go down into the ditch where men are and stand beside them. The reply was that there is no good going and standing in a ditch; the only reason for going there is to pull the man out and lift him up on to the back of the donkey. This (in Africa) was interpreted to mean that you give him a decent salary and a good house. The idea that you do any good by going yourself to live in a bad house didn't evoke any assent.

In certain places the idea of "Africanization" was strongly rejected. Clearly it was felt by some to be a sort of reversed paternalism. Once more the white man thinks he knows what is best for other people. It was strongly said that no African wants to feel that he has been put into a position of authority because he is an African; he wants to feel that he has been put there because he is the best man for the job.

There was deep awareness of the danger hinted at in some places, but explicitly pointed out by one of the ablest of the Kikuyu leaders, that the present emphasis on specialist and technical aid, as a big part of missionary work, may lead to a new sort of colonialism and destroy the possibility of real mutuality and equality. It means stressing again the things in which the white man is strong, and under-emphasizing the things in which the white man is weak. Essentially the missionary must come as a bearer of the Gospel. When he does that, he will be both a giver and a receiver. He will not be handing something down to the Church; he will be sharing in its deepest life. And, if he is primarily a bearer of the Gospel, then all his other gifts will find their proper place.

On the subject of the foreign missionary task of the African churches the response was patchy, but fairly encouraging. What was impressive was the fact that the first bearers of the Gospel in many parts of Africa were not the white missionaries, but African Christians whose very names have been almost forgotten. All efforts should be made to recover the facts before it was too late and to see that these stories were properly written up so that they could become part of the mental background of all African Christians, and others too. This is a vital part of that re-minting of the word "missionary" which is so badly needed.

All these points summarizing the discussion in Africa about the relation between church and mission are important, but in a sense what is more important is the emotional power with which they are charged when they are seen in the light of the over-all questions which Africa is asking. Is Christianity in the West translatable into political terms in Africa? How can Africa's search for Negritude find its answer and its limitation in the Gospel? Can the black African be trusted to be just to the white who also is an African?

39

Resurgent religions. All these challenges faced by the missionary enterprise are challenges incident to the development of the
enterprise itself. With these must be reckoned the challenges
posed by the great religions of the world in encounter with
which the Church's mission must be fulfilled. In their own
estimation, these religions have to-day passed beyond the stage
of meeting the judgment of the Christian Gospel; they are
engaged in claiming for themselves a uniqueness and universality with which the Christian evangelist must come to terms.
Christianity is certainly not to-day, if it ever was, the only
missionary religion. For the Church's mission the basic question
always remains: What is the essential significance of the particularity of Jesus Christ?

In meeting this thrust of the religions, however, the demand
upon the Church is not simply that it should be aware of the
nature of the uniqueness of its own faith. That is paramount.
But it is fruitless unless there goes with it the willingness and the
ability to see all men in Christ, even men in their religions, so
that seeing them thus one may converse with them about their
Saviour. Let three illustrations emphasize this truth and point
out its implications.

In his book *Sandals at the Mosque*, the Rev. Kenneth Cragg
pleads for the Christian presence amid Islam and "for a theology which is on the frontiers of religions in their mutual
existence."[1] His thesis is well summed up in his own words.

The call of the minaret to Muslim prayer becomes a call for the
Christian to exacting tasks. If we respond to him with his own
seriousness we shall not silence or suppress the meanings we have
learned in Christ to the very things for which he pleads or for
which he speaks. How shall we take the meanings of Christ into
the summons from the mosque? For mission is grounded in
relevance and the bearer of relevance is never the alien.[2]

Dr Charles West comes at the problem from quite a different
angle.

[1] *Sandals at the Mosque*, Oxford University Press, p. 21.
[2] *The Call of the Minaret*, Oxford University Press, ix, 183-185.

A religion [he says] remains as religious system a closed alternative to the acceptance of God in Christ; so that the point of contact between the Gospel and men of other faiths is the free word of God lived in the Christian community. Since, however, the non-Christian is in the tragic situation of being confronted with the historical and secularizing consequences of the coming of Christ before he has heard about the Lord who makes life in such conditions hopeful and creative, it is the ministry of the Christian to help his non-Christian neighbour step by step to define the outlines of a secular culture with its human goals and limits.[1]

The missionary encounter takes place within the world of other faiths into which the Christian must enter and be present, it takes place within the secular world with its common human problems, it also takes place in Christ as Christian and non-Christian meet in Him who makes all things new.

All new creation [writes Dr P. D. Devanandan] can only be from God. The fulfilment of God's design for His whole creation is already the active ingredient in the renewal that is taking place in the hearts and minds of men of all faiths as well as of no faith. This means that there is a new task awaiting the Christian Church. The time has come to reckon with men and not simply talk about religious systems.[2]

CONCLUSION

Even a cursory reading of this introduction must show how wide is the ground to be covered in this study and how immediate are the questions which have to be dealt with. But, as far as this book itself is concerned, it will be found that it does not deal in any detail with the many issues which have been indicated. Indeed, to do so would need a series of books, and such books there are. The purpose of this book is simply to outline a general framework of thought within which these issues can be seen in their relation to one another, and so help to overcome for Christians in general that specialization of treatment of these issues which leaves so many of them on the outside.

[1] From an address delivered at the Ecumenical Institute at Bossey (1961).
[2] From an article issued by the Information Department of the W.C.C. (Aug. 14, 1961).

It must be remembered that the study project of which this book is one result has also included the writing of Dr Blauw's book entitled *The Missionary Nature of the Church*, to which reference has already been made. Dr Blauw's book is the more important of the two. It is most suited for recalling those facts which must ultimately determine policy. The present book will serve its purpose if it helps to create in the Churches those convictions about the Christian faith, and to undergird for Christians that personal commitment to discipleship, which will make compelling the various challenges that are implicit in the missionary enterprise in our day and generation.

Part 1—THE FAITH

Jesus Christ is the Deed of God. Every action of God, anywhere performed, is in Him and unto Him. He works in the power of the Holy Spirit who is God continuously active in the world. He will consummate God's design.

The Holy Spirit creates and indwells the Church, setting it between the times as the promise and herald of the end. The end has begun and will be fulfilled. The end is the glory of God completely manifest in and through His whole creation.

The modes, therefore, in which men seek satisfactions for their needs, and the forms in which they ask their questions about life's meaning, contain a double challenge. On the one hand, they cannot determine either the Church's message or ministry, but decide only what the Church must do to make its message heard and its ministry persuasive. On the other hand, they constantly interrogate the Church and preserve it from secular irrelevance.

The message itself, its delivery and its demonstration, are given by the Christ and sustained by the Spirit.

Thus the way in which Christian faith is anchored in the Triune God is also the way in which the Christian Church is invested with its mission. In God's action the Church's mission finds its authority, and in His activity its compulsion.

I

THE MINISTRY OF JESUS TO PERSONS

Wherever I go, God makes my life a constant pageant of triumph in Christ. (2 Cor. 2: 14, Moffatt)

PAUL can never forget that first victory of Christ in his life when, on the Damascus road, he was met and subdued. Christ had said to him then, "Saul, it hurts you to kick against the goads" (Acts 26: 14). When an ox was yoked to the plough, a cross-piece with little spears on it was set in position behind so that, should the ox refuse to obey but kick, it would be reminded that it was already yoked. So it was with Paul. At a time of which he did not know, Jesus had claimed him as His own, and set His yoke upon him. Grace had found him even when he did not know that he had been found. And now, his Lord was telling him, "Saul, you are mine. Why not bear my yoke gladly? Why hurt yourself kicking against the goads?"

When the Lord's word came to Jeremiah, it brought him too the same message: "Before I formed you in the womb I knew you, and before you were born I consecrated you; I appointed you a prophet to the nations" (Jer. 1: 5). Jeremiah had not known, but he was already God's. God had set His yoke upon him.

Simon and Andrew had gone to the sea to fish, but actually they had gone to meet Jesus—He had decided that (Mk. 1: 16-17). The woman of Samaria came to draw water but she found Jesus—He made the appointment (John 4: 7). Matthew went to his office only to be faced with a new claim, "Follow Me" (Matt. 9: 9). Jesus had arrived.

The Previousness of Jesus

The Gospel of Jesus Christ begins with God's incursion into human history. He came. So also the Gospel begins for every man. He comes. And when He comes many, if not all, of the fixed points of one's life get jolted out of position. Where there was conviction, there arises doubt; where there was desire, there is a feeling of satiety; a new restlessness creeps into one's life; one's needs and ambitions either become obsessive or lose their force; life becomes haunted by mystery. Into this situation the Gospel is proclaimed; those who know Jesus speak about Him; and their witness brings conviction to a man here or a woman there that what is being described, that the person being proclaimed, is the key to their own mystery, the source of the unidentified voice that for so long has been heard in their lives. And then happens, what happened to Saul, the act of surrender: "Lord, who are you?"

This previousness of Jesus in the lives of men and women is the fact of central importance in understanding how He ministers to persons. He comes, He arrives—at His own time, in His own way, by His own initiative. That man was made in the image of God (Gen. 1 : 27) is not simply a once-for-all event. It is the promise that God will be with each man whom He has made, so that each man may have the image-relation fulfilled in his life, so that each man may live the life of response to God. The "Imago Dei" is God's foundation-covenant with man.

What a joyful thing it is that God's image in man is man's unbreakable relationship with God. For otherwise men will be bound by what they themselves are, each man will be at his own mercy, and no one may reap except what he sows. But now, by God's grace it is open to men to reap what God has sown. The grain of wheat has fallen into the ground and died and borne much fruit (John 12 : 24), and that fruit is for men freely given, lavishly bestowed, and no one is left out. "So wide," said Charles Wesley speaking of God's grace, "so wide it never passed by one, or it had passed by me."[1]

[1] Charles Wesley, *Methodist Hymn Book*, 77.

Jesus and a Man's Needs

When this fact of the previousness of Jesus is understood, there is understood also a second fact which characterizes His ministry to persons, the way in which He ministers to them in their needs. When Jesus meets men, He meets them in their several situations; He comes to them as they are, and, whether He satisfies their immediate needs or not, they find Him satisfying. To have met Christ is to be able to say, "Thou, O Christ, art all I want, more than all in Thee I find."[1] Indeed, it is to be able to say even more than that. Paul could say, "Whatever gain I had, I counted as loss for the sake of Christ. Indeed I count everything as loss because of the surpassing worth of knowing Christ Jesus my Lord" (Phil. 3: 7, 8).

This does not mean that Jesus, in His ministry to men, is not interested in their needs. It was He who taught us to pray, "Give us this day our daily bread." He who cares for the sparrows cares for us (Lk. 12: 6), He who clothes the grass will clothe us, He who decks the lilies will fill our lives with gladness. Our anxiety need not be about these things (Matt. 6: 25). To be ministered to by Him is to be relieved of this anxiety, it is to learn to tell Him our needs and then turn our minds to the doing of His will: and, in the doing of it, find also that our immediate and material needs begin to re-arrange themselves in our lives. Iron filings set in a magnetic field take up new positions.

But what can we really expect will happen about our immediate and material needs? Are they only marginal to His interest in us? By no means! He is the God who answers prayer, who does for us above all that we can ask or think (Eph. 3: 20). He who gave His Son, will He not with His Son give us all things? (Rom. 8: 32). The point is not that He will not meet our needs, but that, even though He cares, some of our needs go unmet and for so long. Why this should be so we rarely understand, except that we always find that it is precisely in that kind of situation that He makes Himself abundantly real

[1] Charles Wesley, *Methodist Hymn Book*, 110.

to us. So we repeat without qualification the binding truth already enunciated, that whether Jesus meets men's immediate needs or not, He satisfies them with Himself. It cannot be otherwise. God must satisfy or He cannot be God.

Job sought an answer to the problem of his suffering. He received no answer. But, poignant as his question was, he was content simply with a vision of God. "I had heard of thee," he says, "by the hearing of the ear, but now my eye sees thee; therefore I repent" (Job 42: 5-6).

Habakkuk pleads with God for the blessing of Israel. They were His people and heir to His promises. But, in the last analysis, Habakkuk is satisfied with God alone.

> Though the fig tree do not blossom,
>   nor fruit be on the vines,
> the produce of the olive fail
>   and the fields yield no food,
> the flock be cut off from the fold
>   and there be no herd in the stalls,
> yet I will rejoice in the Lord,
>   I will joy in the God of my salvation.
>   (Hab. 3: 17-18.)

The psalmist is bewildered by his own suffering and sorrow in contrast to the prosperity of the wicked, but his bewilderment vanishes when he enters the sanctuary of God. Sorrow remains, but God remains also. "Whom have I in heaven but thee?" he sings, "there is nothing upon earth that I desire besides thee. My flesh and my heart may fail, but God is the strength of my heart and my portion for ever" (Ps. 73: 17, 25, 26).

Paul is stricken with some ailment of the body. He identifies it as caused by Satan. He prays that it be removed. It is not, and he learns to be satisfied with God's grace alone (2 Cor. 12: 7). Paul is anxious to visit the church at Thessalonica. The devil, he says, has prevented this visit so far. But, his desire not realized, he is yet content to leave his plans in the hands of his Lord (1 Thess. 2: 18).

That is what it always adds up to when one's needs and desires go unfulfilled, whatever be believed as the reasons for such unfulfilment. God is enough. If need be, God by Himself, without any of His gifts or blessings, is enough. In fact, even with His blessings, if He Himself is not given and received no want is truly met.

> Thy gifts alone cannot suffice,
>   Unless Thyself be given;
> Thy presence makes my paradise,
>   And where Thou art is heaven.[1]

To be brought to this conviction, to be led into this experience, to be secured in this state of mind: that is the primary ministry of Christ to persons. To have been ministered to by Christ is to have found Christ and to have rejoiced in Him.

There is an incident recorded in the Acts of the Apostles (16: 19-34) which not only illustrates fully the point we have been seeking to make but also leads us to the next point in our thinking. Paul and Silas have gone to Philippi. At the end of their day's work they find themselves in prison. The jailer has been charged to take special care of them, so that he puts them into the inner prison and fastens their feet in the stocks. In the middle of the night, the jailer wakes from his sleep in a panic. He finds the prison doors open. He concludes that the prisoners have escaped. What has happened he does not know. What explanation will he give to the magistrates in the morning? He will certainly lose his job, he may even lose his life. It would be more honourable to commit suicide. He draws his sword. But Paul calls to him and says, "Do not harm yourself, for we are all here." The jailer rushes to Paul and asks him the question that is uppermost on his mind, "Sirs, what must I do to be safe?"— to be safe in the morning when the magistrates come. Paul says to him, "I do not know, but I can tell you what will keep you safe whatever the magistrates do and whatever the morning brings. Believe in the Lord Jesus, and you will be safe, you and your whole household. Jesus can keep your wife and children safe even if you should lose your job or perhaps your life itself." Safe, whatever happens—that is salvation: But you must believe.

[1] Charles Wesley, *Methodist Hymn Book*, 560.

Jesus and a Man's Faith

When does the Christian life begin? When did it begin for any of us? It began when, in the mercy of God in Jesus Christ, He claimed us as His own (Rom. 1: 6); when He set out after us who had wandered into the far country (Lk. 15: 4, 13); when He put His yoke upon us even without our knowing it (Matt. 11: 29); when He loved us while we were yet in sin (Rom. 5: 8). That is when our Christian life began. That is how it begins for any man. But, because it begins thus, it remains a source of strife and of rebellion and restlessness until men believe. God invades a man's life, and he must either contend or surrender.

Believe, and you will be safe. There is no other way to be safe either with God or from God. Jesus keeps God safe for men when life's sorrows and perplexities would rob them of their sense of His presence. Jesus also keeps men safe in God's presence when their sins become unbearable in the light of His holiness and their worthlessness strikes terror into them as they draw nigh to Him (Heb. 12: 22-24).

> Jesus sought me when a stranger,
>   Wandering from the fold of God;
> He, to rescue me from danger,
>   Interposed His precious blood.[1]

When God seems far away; when our eyes, dim with tears, are unable to see His face; or when our souls burdened with sin shrink from Him; then it is that we realize what Christ is able to do for us. We hold to Christ and, when the crisis is past, realize that in holding to Him we were all the time holding to God. In sober truth Jesus is Emmanuel—God with us (Matt. 1: 23).

But how is this experience brought about? How do men come to belief? The straightest way of answering this question is to ask, how did it happen at all that there arose a religion called Christianity? Jesus had lived and died, but so had many

[1] Robert Robinson, *Methodist Hymn Book*, 417.

prophets before Him, and they were all part of the tradition of the Jewish faith. A new religion came to be centred around Jesus only because He not merely lived and died but also rose again from the dead. The apostles preached the Resurrection (Acts 1:22). That was the distinguishing mark of all that they said. So that it is obvious that if the resurrection of Jesus Christ is not the central truth in a man's religion, that religion is not Christianity.

Some years ago, I was conducting a series of evangelistic meetings at Point Pedro, a small town in Ceylon. The chairman of the meeting, on the first night, was a Hindu friend of mine who had studied in the same school as I. I made the point that the resurrection of Jesus Christ is the differentiating truth of the Christian message. When I had finished the chairman said: "I too studied in the same school as Niles, but in my scripture class I never learnt that the resurrection of Jesus Christ was all that important. He may have risen from the dead, but the important thing for us is what He taught." Was the chairman of that meeting right? Or, were the early disciples right in insisting that Christian discipleship began when a person believed not simply that Jesus was risen from the dead, but believed in the risen Jesus. To believe is to belong, and one cannot belong to a dead person. To belong is to be accepted, and the heart of the Christian faith is the affirmation that Christian discipleship begins with this transaction.

To believe is simply to meet the risen Christ and acknowledge Him as Lord: and, because He is risen, He can be met. When He was in the flesh, He was bound by space, time and mortality. Now that He is risen, He is free from these limitations. It is the resurrection that crowns the incarnation and fulfills the promise of Emmanuel—God with us.

Have you met Him? If you have, then you know how you came to recognize and accept His hand upon your shoulder, His yoke upon your neck, His goad behind your feet, His call within your heart. You know yourself as His possession and Him as possessor. Any other form of the Christian religion is to treat Jesus and His teachings as man's possession. To do this is to think of Jesus simply as helping men in their religious life, as providing for men means whereby they can attain to God or, at the lowest level, as securing for them God's blessings in and for this material life. To be possessed by Christ, on the other hand, is to find oneself delivered from religious preoccupations and involved in the secular life, because that is the life in which He, the risen Lord, is involved. He must reign (1 Cor. 15: 25) until all enemies are subdued and those who are His must be agents of His rule. Obedience constitutes the direction of Christian striving. As for the beatific vision, He will give it as His final gift. Now we are the children of God, bound by His purposes, engaged in His work: at the end we shall see Him and be like Him (1 John 3: 2).

A few days before I wrote this chapter, I attended a seminar on Hindu practices conducted by a Hindu. We were a group of Hindus and Christians at the seminar. "Man must realize God," the leader said, and proceeded to show how all religions provided helps towards this realization. "Different persons," he said, "according to their spiritual attainments and mental aptitudes, find different things helpful. Christianity is simply one religion among many to those engaged in the religious search." But, is the religious search what Christianity is about?

Jesus and a Man's Obedience

To put it crudely, the heart of Christianity is not concern for the soul but concern for the world; not forms of life in the world, whether in terms of religious practice or moral behaviour or responsible citizenship, in order to attain to God; but a way of life in the world consequent on being possessed by Him. The end-event of the Christian life is not simply salvation of the person but a new heaven and a new earth (Rev. 21: 1), each person's salvation being his share in this new creation (Rom. 8: 20f.). Into this sharing Christ invites those who believe in Him. That was why He laid hands on them. That was why He led them to faith. To be the people of God is to be His people in the world and for it, until that world is fully obedient to its Lord. "We have received grace and apostleship," said Paul, "to bring about obedience ... among all the nations" (Rom. 1: 5). The great commission as recorded in Matthew's Gospel is rooted in Christ's authority in heaven and on earth; and its intent is to disciple the nations, teaching them to observe His commands (Matt. 28: 18-19).

My life is a pageant of His triumph, He invaded my life, He made me surrender it, and now I find myself committed to His obedience. This obedience too is a pageant of His triumph, for not only has it no substance apart from the establishment and extension of His rule in the world, but its very possibility is the consequence of His constant victory in my life—victory over my sin and faithlessness, over my doubt and blindness, over my sloth and waywardness. The triumph is His, therefore the obedience is mine.

What happens when we meet the risen Jesus that it results in such a life of obedience? What is the effect of His ministry to us as persons when we meet Him? He Himself has given us the answer. "I am come," He said, "not to be ministered unto but to minister and to give my life a ransom for many" (Mk. 10: 45). Behind that word "ransom" is the whole content of the Jewish sacrificial system. On the day of Atonement, the goat that was led out into the wilderness (Lev. 16: 21f.) was the one that had been made SIN on behalf of the people. Jesus was made SIN on our behalf (2 Cor. 5: 21). When God became man, it was not accomplished in one event.

He did not abhor the virgin's womb,
He became human flesh,
He was baptized with the baptism of sinners.
He was friend of all men.
He was numbered with the transgressors.
He was forsaken on the cross.
Eloi, Eloi, lama sabachthani—
My God, my God, why hast thou forsaken me?
God has arrived, at last at the place of sinful man.

The Incarnation was complete. Henceforth, men could partake in this life lived for them and, partaking in it, find freedom from their sin. The vine had been planted in the earth and the branches could abide in the vine (John 15: 5). The Lamb of God was slain and His blood would cleanse from all sin (1 John 1: 7).

Jesus was not only the offering that, on the day of Atonement, carried the sins of the people; He was also the sacrifice sealing the covenant, and sacramentally effecting the mingling of the life of man with the life of God. (Blood was the symbol of life to the Jew, so that when he offered blood he was offering life and not death.) "This cup," said Jesus, "which is poured out for you is the new covenant in my blood." "This bread is my body broken for you" (Lk. 22: 19-20).

The risen Christ whom men meet is the crucified Christ. When they come to Him, He ministers to them with His crucifixion. "It is necessary," He said, "for the Son of man to be crucified" (Mk. 8: 31). It was necessary for man. There is now for man a place to which he can go to meet God by God's appointment, a place where every disguise is left behind, (Matt. 20: 17f.) and man can come to God as man truly is. "On the cross," said Paul writing to the Colossians, "Jesus stripped every principality and power of its disguise and so triumphed over them" (Col. 2: 15). Similarly does Christ triumph over us when we come to Him. In His presence we stand naked. Our respectability is filthy rags, the ways in which we have rationalized our sins are arrant hypocrisy, our goodness is dross and not gold: but in our nakedness we are accepted. We learn to say, not simply, "Forgive me my sins"; but "God, be merciful to me a sinner" (Lk. 18: 13); and, even as we pray, we find ourselves pardoned and received; and, as the sign and seal of our pardon, engaged in His service.

Repent and believe: that is the demand. To believe is to meet the risen and crucified Christ, and by that meeting to belong to Him. To repent is to have one's mind set at cross-purposes with one's sinfulness. The full import of the demand for repentance is often missed because the word "sin" has lost in common

THE MINISTRY OF JESUS TO PERSONS

speech its reference to God. In my language—Tamil—the word that is used for sin means anything that reduces a man to a pitiable position. In the Bible, sin is what brings God to a pitiable position. It affronts His honour, rejects His love, spurns His gifts and, at the end, crucifies His Son. To repent is to change direction. It is not simply a question of confessing one's sins to God when sins have been committed, but so to be anxious about God that one dare not hurt Him. Love for Him falls athwart one's desire to sin and saves one from sinning.

Jesus and a Man's Freedom

There is, however, one more term in the demand. Repent, believe and be baptized (Acts 2: 38). Baptism is into the name of Jesus, and that means the whole community who bear and witness to His name. Christ's ministry to persons includes the way in which He takes them and makes them responsible members of a community where respect for each man's personality is a rule without exception, and where the autonomy of every person is denied without qualification. In surrendering myself to Him, I find myself unable to maintain a dignity and freedom that is my own. Only in Him am I able to be free, only in Him am I able to maintain my position as a person. When I reflect upon this situation I find one consequence of it which revolutionizes my whole being. I find that the natural societies to which I belong cease to have any absolute authority over me. Nation, state, race, tribe, family—I can say of them all, "I now know no man after the flesh" (2 Cor. 5: 16). How true the claim of Jesus is: "If the Son makes you free, you will be free indeed" (John 8: 36)—but only with the freedom of one who is baptized, of one who bears the mark of Jesus (Gal. 6: 17), of one whose life is the life of a whole people, of one whose tasks are the tasks of the King!

Let me explain what it means to be set free by Jesus by using, as an illustration, the practice of astrology in my own country, although to many this may be of only exotic interest. It is common practice in Ceylon to have the horoscope cast of children when they are born. People also go to the astrologer, from time to time, to ask him what the future holds for them. About two or three years ago, a professor of Law in one of the Western universities came to my town in Ceylon to consult an astrologer. He had been recommended to this astrologer by a lawyer friend of his from Ceylon. The astrologer looked at his palm, was given his date of birth, and he went into his study to make some calculations. Then he came out holding in his hand an old manuscript selected from the bundle of manuscripts that formed his library. He read from this manuscript. It said that his consultant was a lawyer, a professor in a university, and so on and so forth. You have no brothers or sisters, the astrologer read, since your mother fell seriously ill at your birth and could not have any more children. It was all there, all the major details of his life. "And, will I become head of the faculty of Law in my university?" he asked; to which the astrologer replied, "According to what is written here, not for another six years." That six years is not yet over, but those who know the circumstances say that it looks as if this prediction will come true.

My purpose in giving this story is not to discuss astrology. It is to share the conviction that the bondage to which we are born is more far-reaching than we imagine. A causal universe must also be in large measure a pre-determined one. So that, in speaking of the freedom with which Christ sets men free, we are speaking of something that concerns the very core of man's being, the very substance of his life. The proclamation of the Gospel is that in this causal universe God is directly present, and that, in the last analysis, man's life, however conditioned, is open to God's immediate control. A causal universe can also be an open one. It is neither arbitrary nor mechanical, it is responsive to the purposeful activity of God, and also of men. Such is our world. Angels go up and down the ladder set between it and God (Gen. 28: 12). God Himself came down that ladder to be man among men. Prayer guards this open door between heaven and earth (Rev. 4: 1). It holds the promise that men may be free. Man has to choose between the bondage of his humanity and the freedom of his sonship, and that is the ultimate choice. So to choose and so to be chosen is the sign of Christ triumphant.

Jesus and a Man's Holiness

In the text with which we began, Paul uses the word "pageant". Here is a word that puts emphasis on two facts. There is the fact of that which is done; there is also the fact that what is done, is done to be seen. A pageant is no pageant without an audience. In another place, Paul expresses a similar idea. He speaks of the apostles as having become "a spectacle to the world" (1 Cor. 4: 9). This conception of the Christian life as a spectacle to be watched, as a pageant to be seen, is integral to the truth that the Christian life is the life of Christ as it is lived in His disciples. It is part of His ministry that they, to whom He ministers, become evidence to others that He is Lord (2 Cor. 3: 3). To keep this evidence clear, to make it persuasive and compelling—that is the Christian concern for the holy life. It is an essential part of Christ's ministry to us that He wakens this concern in us, preparing for us "good works" (Eph. 2: 10) that we may walk in them.

Christ ministers to men by making Himself their minister. He comes to them where they are and meets them in their need. They meet Him who is risen from the dead and in that meeting are conquered by Him. They meet Him who was crucified for them and claim in Him their ransom. They find faith and repentance in His name, and into His name are baptized, becoming members of His Church. Here their lives are invested with a purpose and claimed for His obedience. It is an obedience to be manifested by the holy life which it will beget, and by which in turn it will be begotten.

It is no accident that the writer of the epistle to the Hebrews (12: 1-13) makes the Christian's call to holiness a part of his call to run the race of faith. "Surrounded as we are," he says, "by those who have run this race before us, let us run our lap of the race freeing ourselves from those obstacles which prevent us from running, and stripping ourselves of those sins which make us stumble." But how do we do this? "God Himself will do it for you," he says, "because God will discipline you with His chastening and teach you holiness." "Don't lose heart," he admonishes, "if this chastening is unpleasant at the time, for when it is over you will see that it has produced in you the fruit of real goodness. Therefore, take a fresh grip on life and brace your trembling limbs. Don't wander away from the path but forge steadily onward. On the right path the limping foot recovers strength and does not collapse."

This positive purpose and content of holiness, however, has been unfortunately forgotten in a great deal of modern discussion about it. It has become associated in the minds of many with a whole series of negatives. "The modern puritan," said G. K. Chesterton, "has the vandalism of his forebears without their passion." But, worse than this, holy living means to many people simply a mode of life in which the secular is guarded within strict limits by the sacred. I shall never forget, sitting in one of the commissions of the General Committee of the World Student Christian Federation held at Tutzing, in which commission "the call to holy living" was being discussed, when a Japanese girl exclaimed in dismay: "Please, I don't want to be holy."

Part of the problem here is not only that holiness seems to consist of too many negatives, but also that its positives are often claimed to have general application. Irrespective of the spiritual and moral needs of the person concerned, or of the circumstances in which he has to bear his witness, the same prescription for the holy life is offered. For much of this prescription the reason adduced is the injunction of Paul that the weaker brother should not be made to stumble. Why not teach the weaker brother not to stumble where he need not and should not! (1 Cor. 8: 13.) The disciplines of holy living must be relevant to each case, and serve the particular need of a particular person or a particular situation.

I cannot resist the temptation to use here a story that I heard only recently. The story may be well known, but let me use it because it is so apt. A man was visiting a friend. That evening, when the friend returned from his office, his visiting friend saw him greet his wife with a kiss and say to her, "It has been a lovely day, darling." After dinner he kissed his wife again and said, "It has been a wonderful meal, dear." In the morning, as both friends left together for the city, the wife was kissed again: "Goodbye". On the way to the city the visitor said to his friend, "Do you do this kissing always?" The answer was "Yes—I have done it all these twenty years that we have been married and it is the secret of our happiness." That evening, the man who had gone to visit his friend came to a decision: he would do the same. And so, when he got home from his office, he took his wife into his arms and kissed her. The wife broke down in wild sobbing. "What is the matter, dear?" he asked: to which she replied, "Everything has gone wrong to-day. Our son has got the measles, our servant has run away, the milk is spilt and the meat is burnt, and now you come home drunk."

No—the same prescription will not do. Indeed, holy living cannot be prescribed for at all. It is neither a moral endeavour nor a religious discipline. And, still less is it that form of piety of which the late Rev. W. R. Maltby, President of the British Methodist Conference, remarked that it was as if one "oozed synthetic unction". Holy living is simply the natural concomitant of a witnessing life.

In the very passage from which our opening text is taken, Paul gives his explanation of what it is. "We Christians have the unmistakable scent of Christ," he says, "discernible alike to those who are being saved and to those who are heading for death. To the latter it seems like the very smell of doom, to the former it has the fresh fragrance of life itself"[1] (2 Cor. 2: 15-16).

Certainly, there is a discipline—the discipline of the soldier who will not partake in civilian pursuits (2 Tim. 2: 4), the discipline of the athlete who keeps his body under control (1 Cor. 9: 25), the discipline of the man who is in such earnest that he is prepared to pluck out his eye or cut off his hand

[1] J. B. Phillips, *The New Testament in Modern English*, Geoffrey Bles, London; The Macmillan Company, New York.

rather than with eye and hand be cast into hell (Matt. 18: 8-9).

This pageant of the holy life the world must see. This fragrance of the divine country the world must smell. We may not claim that Christ is having His way with us until we become part of that pageant, until we waft to those who associate with us the scent of that land where we habitually ought to dwell.

Conclusion

Let me close this chapter with a story. In a village called Kiran in a remote part of the eastern province of Ceylon, a man was stabbed to death some two years ago. He left behind a widow and four little children. The result of sorrow and shock was that the two youngest ones fell quite seriously ill. The mother was distraught. At about that time, the Ashram in Jaffna extended its work to Kiran and built there a Christian temple. A worker took up his residence there. This mother, a Hindu, began visiting the Christian temple. She would bring her two little children with her. She wept before God. She sought His aid. The children slowly recovered, and the mother came to the Ashram Sevak and asked for baptism. The Sevak put her off saying, "Wait for some time more." After a few months, she insisted on being baptized, and her two younger children. The older two had by that time begun to attend a Hindu school and were in its hostel. The mother and her two children were baptized. Soon, the older children were in trouble, for they refused to apply holy ash to their foreheads as was the custom in their school. They were under instruction from their mother not to do so. The headmaster of the school sent for the mother. "Have you become a Christian?" he asked. She said "Yes". "Why did you do that?" To which she replied, "Jesus met me in my need. He healed my children." "And, how much money did the Christians give you to change your faith?" "Nothing," she said. "They too are poor at the Ashram. I earn a little, selling home-made food, and with what little I earn I support myself and my children and also, from

time to time, give some money to the Ashram." The headmaster excused the two boys from wearing holy ash. Now, on
every Friday, there is a large group from the village who come
to the Ashram temple for prayer. This woman brings them.
They are all Hindus, but her faith has been infectious and her
witness persuasive.

A Christian temple is built in a remote village. It becomes
the method of the previousness of Christ in a woman's life.
Sorrow and need bring her to her meeting with Jesus. His hand
upon her life gives it a new direction and purpose. By His
mercy she is ministered to by Hindu and Christian. She is set
free from the bondage of her circumstance and made glad by
her passion to bring others to Him. She takes her place among
those who bear the name of Jesus, and finds her satisfaction in
ministering to the saints. The aroma of her life is known in her
village.

If you are then risen with Christ, reach out for the highest gifts
of heaven, where your Master reigns in power. Give your heart to
the heavenly things, not to the passing things of earth. For, as far
as this world is concerned, you are already dead, and your true
life is a hidden one in Christ. One day, Christ, the secret centre of
our lives, will show himself openly, and you will all share in that
magnificent dénouement. (Col. 3: 1-4; J. B. Phillips.)

2

THE WORK OF THE HOLY SPIRIT IN THE WORLD

"Did you receive the Holy Spirit when you believed?"
And they said, "No" (Acts 19: 2).

"COME"—"Come and see": that was the Lord's first invitation to His disciples (John 1: 39). "Go"—"Go and preach": that was His last command to them (Mark 15: 16). This reversal of direction is a constitutive part of the Christian life.

The story, which the gospels tell, begins with Bethlehem when God in Jesus came to dwell with men. But that story comes to a definite end where the gospel writer says, "He parted from them" (Luke 24: 51). He himself had said to them a few hours before His death, "It is to your advantage that I go away, for if I do not go away the Counsellor will not come to you; but if I go, I will send him to you" (John 16: 7). Mary of Magdala, when she met her risen Lord, clung to His feet. He said to her, "Mary, do not hold me, for I have not yet ascended to the Father" (John 20: 17). Of course, the story continues; but with the coming of the Holy Spirit, it moves out of the villages of Galilee and towns of Judaea into the highways of life. It is with this movement that we are concerned in this chapter.

When Paul came to Ephesus, he found some disciples there. They had been baptized into the baptism of John, but they had not even heard of the Holy Spirit. Paul baptized them again into the name of the Lord Jesus, "and when he had laid hands upon them, they received the Holy Spirit and spoke with tongues and prophesied" (Acts 19: 1-6).

Peter and John came to Samaria. There were some disciples there who had already been baptized into the name of the Lord Jesus. But they had not received the Holy Spirit. Peter and

John laid their hands upon them and prayed for them that they might receive the Holy Spirit, and they received Him. (Acts 8 : 15).

Nicodemus came to Jesus to talk with Him about the signs He did (John 3 : 1f.), and the way in which God was with Him. Jesus said to Nicodemus, "You cannot see the signs of the Kingdom, you cannot see them as signs, unless you are born anew. This birth is by water and the Spirit. John baptizes with water, I baptize with the Spirit."

Jesus said to His disciples (Acts 1 : 4, 8), "Depart not from Jerusalem but wait for the promise of the Father. Before many days you shall be baptized with the Holy Spirit. And when the Spirit has come upon you, you shall be my witnesses in Jerusalem and in all Judaea and Samaria and to the end of the earth."

The Experience of the Spirit

What do these incidents add up to? Is it not clear that they show the absolute importance of the coming of the Holy Spirit into the lives of Christ's disciples, and that it is by the Spirit alone that men see and understand the signs of the Kingdom of God in the life and ministry of Jesus, as well as find power and authority to proclaim these signs to the world? On the day of Pentecost, the disciples spoke with tongues (Acts 2 : 3). The Gospel became a Gospel for all the nations. Whenever the Holy Spirit comes into the life of a person now, nothing less takes place. He is swept into that movement which would take the Gospel to the uttermost parts of the earth. It is said that, when the apostles laid their hands on those who believed, with prayer for the Holy Spirit, the Spirit came: so He comes even now when the mission of the Church claims a person, lays its hand upon him, and he surrenders to that claim.

The Christian faith is more than a Jesus religion. It is concerned with the consequence to men of who Jesus is.

Jesus is ascended on high. He sits at the right hand of the Father. His Kingdom is exercised upon earth. He must rule till all God's enemies are subdued.

Jesus is risen from the dead. He is alive on earth. He is constantly seeking the lost, upholding the faint-hearted, strengthening the weak, spreading His love abroad in the hearts and lives of men.

The Holy Spirit is come to lead those who believe to participation in power in this on-going ministry of Christ. He is come also to prepare believing response to Christ among those who have not as yet accepted Him.

It is said that, when God made the heavens and the earth, the Spirit of God was moving over the face of the waters (Gen. 1: 2). Because of that movement of the Spirit, chaos responded to the creating Word of God. When the angel brought his announcement to Mary (Lk. 1: 35), it is said that the Holy Spirit came upon her and the power of the Most High overshadowed her. That was how Mary brought forth Jesus.

That is how it always is. It is the Spirit in our hearts that teaches us to say "Abba! Father!" (Rom. 8: 15.) It is when the Holy Spirit comes that we even learn to pray as we ought (Rom. 8: 26). "Grieve not the Holy Spirit" (Eph. 4: 30) is Paul's warning. The Holy Spirit has come. He is preparing a response to the Gospel, here, there and everywhere; and He is seeking to lead the Church in its mission into those places and to those persons whom He has so prepared. The Holy Spirit guided the first Council of Jerusalem (Acts 15: 6f.) to fashion a policy that would meet the kind of preparation among the Gentiles which He had already effected. The Holy Spirit would not allow Paul and Silas to go to Bithynia (Acts 16: 6, 7) but took them instead to Troas where Paul received the call to take the Gospel to Europe. Paul went, on his last visit to Jerusalem, bound in the Spirit, not knowing what should befall him there (Acts 20: 22). What happened to him there took him ultimately to Rome, the centre of the empire.

The fact is that the possibility of Christian obedience is bound up with the experience of the Holy Spirit. He directs the campaign in which the Christian is a participant, so that without Him the Christian life simply becomes a religious exercise.

The issue is never only, "Do you believe in Jesus Christ?"; it is also, "Have you received the Holy Spirit?"

To avoid serious misunderstanding let it be insisted that the way in which the distinction is here made between Jesus Christ and the Holy Spirit should not lead anyone to theorize about distinctions within the Godhead, as if man can understand or explain what the life of God is like. The distinction is drawn only because it is an important distinction when we are considering God's work of salvation. When God dealt with human history that was how He dealt with it, so that it becomes determinative for us and our obedience. However, it affords no basis on which altars can be set up to three gods. There is only one God about whom, when men approach Him, they find that their obedience has three decisive moments in it. I accept Jesus Christ. I receive the Holy Spirit. I am a son of the Father. But, when Jesus Christ is accepted, we find that He and the Father are one (John 10: 30). When the Spirit is received, we know that the Lord is the Spirit (2 Cor. 3: 17). When we seek to live as children of the Father, we see that it is only Jesus who is able to establish us in this relation (John 14: 6), and that it is only the Spirit who is able to maintain us therein (Rom. 8: 27). There is one God in three persons, not an identity of the three but a unity of them, a unity which reflects itself in the Christian experience.

Jesus said to Nicodemus, "The wind blows where it wills, and you hear the sound of it, but you don't know whence it comes or whither it goes; so it is with everyone who is born of the Spirit" (John 3: 8). An electric fan can circulate the warm air in a room. Many church activities and even some evangelistic missions achieve little more. It is a different matter when one is able to go out where the breezes blow and feel the breeze on one's face. To receive the Holy Spirit, one must stand where the Spirit blows. There, where God is so obviously at work, is the place to be caught by the Spirit of God. To come into close association with a person alive in the Spirit is to come where one may catch contagion. The symbol of the Spirit is not only wind but fire. Some men are so aflame with the Spirit that to draw near to them is to be where the sparks fall. A Christian congregation is a failure if, in its midst, the Spirit does not break out into flame and fire; if, there, those who do not have the Spirit do not receive Him. Jesus said, "If you, who are evil, know how to give good gifts to your children, how much more will the heavenly Father give the Holy Spirit to those who ask him?" (Lk. 11: 13). To any other prayer God's answer may be "No"; but, to the prayer for the Holy Spirit, God's answer is always "Yes".

When our Lord said to His disciples, "Wait for the Spirit", this, then, was what He asked them to wait for. They needed the Holy Spirit in order that in their own lives they may be filled with the presence of Jesus Christ. They needed the Holy Spirit in order that they may be led to follow their Master in His continuing ministry in the world. And they needed the Holy Spirit so that each may find the locus of his own obedience. "When the Spirit comes," said Jesus (John 14: 26), "He will bring to your remembrance the things I have taught, He will take what is Mine and declare it to you, He will make Me glorious in you" (John 16: 14).

The Launching of the Mission

But when our Lord said, "Wait for the Spirit", He meant also, "Wait until the mission of God is launched in the world". In their different ways, Christmas and Pentecost both celebrate the coming of God to become part of human history; to be involved in it. The coming of God in Jesus Christ determined what man's history shall be. The coming of God in the Holy Spirit regulates the tides of this history.

I was discussing this point with a friend of mine when I was preparing this chapter. He was a person greatly influenced in his thinking by the writing of the mystics of all religions. He said to me, "It is generally thought that the postulate of a personal God is a concession to the religious instinct. In your thinking you seem to make God even time-bound." My answer was "Yes: but probably not in the sense in which you mean it. God

66

is time-bound until time itself will be redeemed and set free. He entered into time, and that entrance is the basis of our hope in cosmic redemption." "But the incarnation," my friend countered, "was only for the purpose of revealing God." I said, "No. By the incarnation certainly, God is revealed, but the incarnation is not just a revelation. It is what it means—the entrance of God into human life in order to be part of it. The Avatars of Hinduism are not incarnations in this sense. They are revelations. They are interventions in human affairs and in human lives. Jesus is God incarnate. That is why the Christian faith announces not only an incarnation but a resurrection—a continuous participation of God incarnate in the movement of human history. That is also why the Christian faith announces an end-event when this action of God entering into time will have reached fulfilment, and time itself is no more because death is swallowed up in victory" (1 Cor. 15: 54). "All this is dogma," my friend said. "What is the experiential proof?" "The experiential proof," I replied, "lies in receiving the Holy Spirit. God's entrance into history is a double entrance. He becomes part of it in Jesus Christ. He makes this part embrace the whole through the Holy Spirit. Jesus Christ is the content of the Gospel—the good news of what God has done. The Holy Spirit is the missionary of the Gospel. It is He who makes the Gospel explosive in men's lives and in human affairs."

"Until Jesus was glorified," says John (7: 39), "the mission of the Holy Spirit could not be launched." But when Jesus was glorified, the Spirit came. He came to lead men to see the glory of God in the face of Jesus Christ (2 Cor. 4: 6). Acceptance of the Christian witness must be prepared for by the Holy Spirit in the lives of men. Apart from that preparation, they will neither understand nor believe. Ask any convert and he will tell you that he is unable to explain how he came to believe. C. S. Lewis gives to the story of his conversion the title *Surprised by Joy*. It is always a surprise when one suddenly sees life according to a new pattern, when, within the soul, one's knowledge of Jesus catches fire and becomes a living awareness, when the will accepts the mastery of Christ and is satisfied.

What of Unbelief?

But what of unbelief? No consideration of the work of the Holy Spirit can avoid this question. In the teaching of Jesus there are two emphases which determine the perspective in which this question must be viewed. He spoke of those who were known as believers but whom the Lord would not acknowledge (Matt. 7: 23). He also spoke of those who were known as having said "No", but who turned out to be those who had done "Yes" (Matt. 21: 28-30). The elder son who stayed with his father finally stayed outside the home, while the younger son who left his father finally found his place within the home (Lk. 15: 11-32). "The men of Nineveh will arise at the judgment with this generation and condemn it" (Lk. 11 : 32). "Many that are first will be last, and the last first" (Mk. 10: 31).

The second emphasis in the teaching of Jesus on this question is that on the Holy Spirit as the author of true discipleship. The scribes and the Pharisees persistently rejected Jesus and opposed His work, but His judgment upon them is pronounced precisely at the point where they attributed His work to the devil (Matt. 12: 24; Mk. 3: 30). "A word against the Son of Man," He says, "will be forgiven; but whoever speaks against the Holy Spirit will not be forgiven" (Matt. 12: 32). Unbelief is a refusal to say "Yes" to Jesus Christ, but such refusal may be based on a rejection of Jesus Christ because of who He is. It is this rejection which is the sin against the Holy Spirit, for by the Holy Spirit Jesus has been made known and yet rejected.

Any reflection, then, on unbelief as one meets it in the course of one's Christian ministry of witness must be a reflection in the shadow of the last judgment which will be an event of many surprises. It will also be a reflection on the work of the Holy Spirit as He witnesses to Jesus Christ and draws men to Him. In His last discourse in the upper room, Jesus speaks of the work of the Holy Spirit as that of convincing the world of sin because they do not believe in Him, of righteousness because of His death, and of judgment because by His triumph the ruler of this world is judged (John 16: 8-11). Here becomes evident the inextricable link between the person and work of the Holy Spirit and the person and work of Jesus Christ. The Holy Spirit works as it were by applying Jesus Christ to the souls and consciences of men. Who can say where and in whom this work is being performed?

How does He work? He works through the ministry of the Church, which ministry He surrounds with His previousness and impregnates with His presence.

The life and mission of the Church is the result of the coming of the Holy Spirit into the world. Because of Him, the Church is engaged in the proclamation that Jesus is Lord. By the Holy Spirit alone is the announcement born that Jesus Christ has come in the flesh (1 John 4: 2). He thrusts the Church out to make this proclamation, He empowers the Church to make it under all circumstances, He effects in the Church a demonstration of it, He gives to men the gifts of repentance and faith by which they accept the Lord who is proclaimed and confess Him.

But here precisely is the problem that not all who hear demonstrably believe, so that the question is raised: What of unbelief? An answer, to be true to the New Testament, must say two things, the one said under the shadow of the last judgment and the other said in the light of the warning about sin against the Holy Spirit.

Can we put into words what needs to be said in the shadow of the last judgment? At least one instance can be given, that which it is necessary to say when the question of belief and unbelief is discussed with respect to the uniqueness and particularity of the Christian Gospel and its relation to other faiths. This discussion always runs into difficulty precisely because the relationship being discussed is never a static one. The Holy Spirit is at work. He is eliciting response in the hearts and minds of men to the working of God upon their lives. Their lives are lived within their faiths, sometimes as those who accept them and sometimes as those who do not. Into this situation, the Holy Spirit brings the witness of the Church to the Lordship and Saviourhood of Christ. This witness evokes the response of faith. It sometimes meets with rejection. It often-times results in raising questions in the minds of the hearers and leaving those questions there. The Holy Spirit takes all these ways in which people respond to the Gospel, and uses them in His own ministry of leading them to confess Jesus as Lord; or even where that confession is absent, of making Christ's Lord-ship a felt pressure upon their lives. The whole business is too complex for neat answers. We cannot meet a dynamic situation with rigid orthodoxies; we can only recognize it through lives of sensitive obedience. It cannot be otherwise since the mission of the Church is a mission within the mission of the Holy Spirit.

But just because this is so, the other word is of equal impor-tance: that it is the Gospel proclaimed which causes the double movement of faith and unbelief. Mark sets forward the story of Jesus in this very form, a story culminating in the Cross. In John this double movement centres in the figure of Judas. "So, after receiving the morsel, he immediately went out; and it was night" (John 13: 30). In the light of the Gospel, unbelief is the terrible tragedy of sin.

Is there, then, nothing more to say? There is, because the world's hatred, which the Gospel precipitates, itself creates the suffering Church which is for the world's redemption; and the coming of the Holy Spirit will bring to bear His own witness to Christ on the Church's witness to Him (John 15: 18-27). Also there is more to say because the world's hatred is not a surprise to God (John 15: 19); it was known in His great wisdom always.

The classic discussion in the New Testament of the problem of unbelief is that by Paul in his letter to the Romans concerning the unbelief of Israel (Rom. 9: 11). At the very outset of his argument Paul moves away from the unbeliever as his starting point. Not all Israel were faithless, there were those who believed (Rom. 9: 27). Besides, this faith was possible to all because all heard the good tidings (Rom. 10: 18). Why, then, did they not believe? The answer has to be in terms of the actual consequences which their unbelief produced. Because of the unbelief of Israel the Gospel went to the Gentiles and, by their acceptance of it, became manifest as God's offer of free salvation to all men (Rom. 11: 32). So it became clear that Israel's unbelief itself was held within the wisdom and design of God (Rom. 9: 18), while the promise implicit in the faith of those in Israel who believed has also been fulfilled (Rom. 11: 33).

The inner significance of this argument of Paul becomes luminous when we read what he has to say in the previous chapter. "The hope is," he writes (Rom. 8: 21, 14, 11, 19), "that in the end the whole of created life will be rescued from the tyranny of change and decay, and have its share in that magnificent liberty which can only belong to the children of God. They are God's sons who follow the leading of God's Spirit. Within them lives the Spirit that raised Jesus from the dead, bringing to their whole being new strength and vitality. The whole creation is on tiptoe to see the wonderful sight of the sons of God coming into their own." A direct connection is here made between the liberty of the sons of God—those who are in Christ—and the liberation of the whole cosmos. Faith and Hope jump from the redeemed community to the redemption of all things, a jump which is possible only because the in-between situation of belief and unbelief is comprehended within the mystery of God's plan of salvation.

The Holy Spirit is the agent of the New Creation, the new heavens and the new earth, which He creates in Christ. And, because this is so, the Church comes to see its own meaning as the community of the Holy Spirit, becomes aware of the encompassing ministry of the Holy Spirit by which its own ministry is sustained, and understands the task of its own up-building in relation to the great work of salvation.

In speaking about salvation, the thrust of the Christian hope is to include "all": it is in speaking about the Church that the selective principle applies. A direct consequence of the Church's mission, when men find faith in Christ, is that the mission itself is strengthened. The mission is intended to produce mission-aries, the evangel must produce evangelists. Bishop Azariah introduced the practice in his diocese of people confirmed placing their hands on their heads and saying, "Woe to me if I do not preach the Gospel" (1 Cor. 9: 16). That is what the confirmation service is about: prayer for the Holy Spirit that one may live the witnessing life. But it is just here that the selective principle applies (John 15: 2). The army of Gideon had to be reduced, the vine needs to be pruned, the confessed and confessing people of God in the world will necessarily be a remnant. It is of the Church that it is true that "many are called but few are chosen" (Matt. 22: 14).

In the work of the Holy Spirit, then, there is the quality not only of comprehension but also of selection, not only of wideness but also of narrowness: a contradictoriness which ought to be no surprise for anyone whose faith is grounded in the Bible. For, as the Bible makes plain, the work of God is always characterized by universality of intention as well as particularity of method. Israel is for the nations, the Church is for the world. When the Gospel is proclaimed there are the few, who are led by the Spirit to faith, who become members of the community whose task it is to proclaim the Gospel. When the Gospel is proclaimed it becomes also within the ministry of the Holy Spirit the power of God for the salvation of the world.

There is only one Saviour, Jesus Christ (1 Tim. 2: 5), and all who are saved will be saved by Him. There is only one end-event towards which all things move, their re-creation in Jesus Christ (Eph. 1: 10). There is only one finale to the story of man (Rev. 21: 23, 26), and that will be its fulfilment in the eternal city where God and His Christ are the light by which men will walk and into which the treasures of the nations will be gathered. The ministry of the Holy Spirit in the world is to recall the world to its moorings, to re-establish it on its true foundation, to make actual the once-for-allness-for-all-men of what God has done for man in Jesus Christ. "The Holy Spirit is My witness," said Jesus (John 15: 26). "He will claim on My behalf all truth that belongs to Me (John 12: 13-15). He will own on My behalf the light wheresoever the light may be. I am the Truth, I am the Light—the light that enlightens every man" (John 14: 6; 8: 12; 1: 9).

This argument must now be concluded, and yet no way of concluding it seems to be wholly satisfactory. Paul concludes his argument with a shout of praise: "O the depth of the riches and wisdom and knowledge of God!" (Rom. 11: 33): God has unlimited resources of grace and mercy. He also remains wholly free so that no one has rights over Him. His people have no claims on Him above those of others. But this is only one half of the conclusion of the argument. The other half lies in the fact that this shout of praise is the shout of the people of God, those who have found their sonship in Jesus Christ. They witness to the fact that for all men God has provided a place of reconciliation, a mercy seat, a visible Saviour and a visible company which is the saved and saving community.

Let our Lord's own parable concerning the last judgment say the last word. The sheep and the goats are separated (Matt. 25: 40). So, at the last, will God's judgment separate men. And the judgment turns on the question, Had they accepted Him? But, as the parable makes clear, the form in which He had presented Himself to them for their acceptance was the form of one despised and rejected of men. There is no salvation except in Jesus Christ, but who shall decide how and in what guise Jesus comes to men and claims their acceptance!

The Nature of the Church's Mission

There we must leave it, and turn to a search for an understanding of the nature of our own obedience, of the meaning and significance of the mission of the Church. First of all, the Church's mission is to be the people of God. Redeemed by Christ and raised from death in Him by the Holy Spirit, the Christian community exists as the result and the demonstration of the facts of the Gospel. "You are the light of the world," Jesus said (Matt. 5: 14). The Christian community cannot escape this responsibility. In the night, it has to be the moon reflecting the light of the sun. In the day, it has to be the mirror in which men can see themselves. Its task is to make plain the way of life, to reveal life and to direct it. The proclamation of the Christian Gospel must arise from a demonstration of what it means. The Christian must be a witness of what he proclaims, he must be an evidence of it. "We are," says James, "the first specimens of His new creation" (Jas. 1: 18). It is true that the treasure will always remain in earthen vessels (2 Cor. 4: 7), but the treasure will be there. There will be proof that the door of heaven has been opened and that God has come among men. "If a man loves me," said Jesus, "he will keep my word, and my Father will love him, and we will come to him and make our home with him." Emmanuel is the promise "God with us" (John 14: 23). To us who believe in Jesus Christ, it is the promise of God's presence and companionship; to those who do not yet believe in Jesus Christ, it is the promise that the presence of God will be mediated to them. God has made us priests (Rev. 1: 6); we are no priests unless we mediate God to the world.

"Men are not so foolish," said Jesus (Matt. 5: 15), "as to light a lamp and put it under a bushel. Neither is God less wise. When He lights a lamp He puts it where it will give light to the whole house." The sanctuary is the place where the lamp is lit, where it is filled with oil, where its wicks are trimmed. It should never become the place where the lamp is left. The lamp is meant for the world outside. It is not a sanctuary lamp but a street light that the Church represents. An ecumenical conference, called by the World Council Youth Department and held in Berlin in May 1960, was reported on in the Ecumenical Press Service.[1] The report says that there was a session at the Conference when the participants were asked to write press articles on "Peace" arising out of Paul's letter to the Ephesians. One conference member is said to have remarked, "I should prefer to write a book on systematic theology. It is easier." Of course it is. Systematic theology is an exercise within the precincts of the temple. Press articles demand converse with wayfarers on the road.

The Church, it is commonly said, is a divine society. It is. But its divine nature lies in the actuality of its mission as the

[1] *E.P.S.* No. 19, 20 May, 1960.

herald and carrier of the divine. The divine nature of the Church is in its dynamics. It is, and remains wherever it is, the place where men find God; whether they find Him as One who is troublesome or satisfying, as effecting their obedience or causing their rebellion.

Secondly, the Church's mission is to be the people of God everywhere—in every situation, in every land and nation, in all areas of life. The Church anywhere represents the gathering of the first-fruits (Rev. 14: 4, 15) which is the promise of the final harvest. That there be first-fruits everywhere, that in every city of earth there be a colony of heaven (Phil. 3: 20): that is the task of the Holy Spirit through the mission of the Church. The unfinished task of evangelism is the task of bringing the Gospel to those who have not heard it, of building the Christian community within a people among whom such a community does not exist, of maintaining the Christian witness amidst current problems and tensions in all areas of human relationships, of exerting the pressure of the Christian way of life on those who do not yet accept it.

There is a sense in which, until all men are confessing Christians and all life is lived in the Christian obedience, the task of evangelism is not over. But the task to which the Church is committed is not so much the finishing of it as the beginning of it. It is the beginning that is yet unfinished. When the leaven is hid in the meal (Lk. 13: 21), the beginning of the task is over. But there are so many situations in which the leaven is not yet so hid. Where the seed is sown (Mk. 4: 26), the beginning of the task is over. But there are hundreds of thousands of villages in Africa and Asia alone where the seed has not yet been sown. Where the city is built (Matt. 5: 14), the beginning of the task is over. But there are many places in which the Christian city has not yet been built. "The gospel must first be preached throughout the whole world as a testimony to all the nations; and then the end will come" (Matt. 24: 14). The end cannot come where the beginning is not over. To be the people of God everywhere, that is the mission. To go to the ends of the earth, that is the task. As we think of it cannot we hear the word of the Lord that came to Israel long ago (Deut. 2: 3): "You have compassed this mountain long enough. Go north"?

For a whole generation they had lived on the slopes of that mountain. It was their home. They had left Egypt, a crowd; here on this mountain they had been welded into a nation. Why could they not continue to live here? They could not, because they were a pilgrim people. The promised land lay north of where they were. They had to strike their tents and set off again on the march.

This mission of the Church is to be the people of God. It is to be the people of God everywhere. It is also to be the people of God on a journey. A Church at rest is no Church. I was present one day at a discussion conducted by Dr Nolde on some aspect of international affairs. During question time he was asked, "And for what solution are you prepared to settle?" His answer was, "For none." "The Christian community," he said, "cannot settle for any answer. We shall press for the best possible compromise in the present situation, but we shall also press for a complete change in the situation itself." This is a good illustration of what it means for the Church to be a pilgrim people.

A pilgrim people is bound to have a set of values which are different from those held by people who have settled down. It will tend to accumulate less luggage, it will not be over-concerned with creature comforts, it will enjoy its food provided for the journey. When I was studying in the Theological College at Bangalore, I was to go one day with three of my friends to visit the waterfalls at Shimoga. We had planned to leave early in the morning. Sandwiches for the trip were prepared, and we had our thermos-flasks filled with coffee. Unfortunately for us, at the very last moment, the picnic had to be called off. We decided to eat the sandwiches and have the coffee for breakfast. I can still recall how flat those sandwiches tasted and how insipid the coffee. On the picnic they would have been wonderful, on the breakfast table they were awful.

The sacraments of the Church, the worship of the congregation, the study of God's word, the practices of religion in the home and in one's personal life—all these are food for the journey. So many neglect them because they do not need them. Theirs is a sedentary life, and all this food is unnecessary. And even what food they take they do not relish. A beautiful cloth and flowers on the breakfast table will not make much difference. Even "Music while we eat" is quite irrelevant. The sandwiches are for the road. Get up and get out. Go north.

This challenge to the Church to take to the road implies also another consequence. It means that the Church can never be satisfied with its forms of obedience. What the Church is to-day in our several countries is the result of the obedience of our fathers in the faith. But their obedience cannot necessarily be ours. In one of the discussions in the Negotiating Committee for Church Union in Ceylon, a suggestion was made by one of the Anglican representatives that a paragraph be included in the Scheme of Union expressing repentance for the past sin of division. "I shall never repent," said a Congregationalist, "for the action of the pilgrim fathers." We don't have to. It is not necessary for the past to have been wrong in order to make repentance now necessary. Repentance is our essential response to new tasks and new commands. There is no entail on the Church's past. A great deal has to be left behind. That is what it means to be a pilgrim people, that is what is involved in being called to take to the road.

In the Gospel narrative the challenge of Jesus, that those who would follow Him must take up the cross and follow Him (Mk. 8: 27-37), appears before there is any mention of the cross on which He himself must die. What meaning then could it have conveyed to those who heard Him? It would have only suggested to them that they must be prepared to die at the hands of the Romans, a likelihood contingent on Jesus leading an insurrection. Explaining this difficulty, Dr Findlay quotes a traveller familiar with Bedouin life as saying that in the Aramaic the word "cross" simply meant something sticking up from the ground and that it was used generally to describe a tent-peg. Even now, this traveller remarked, the Bedouin sheikh when he orders a move, says to the women of his harem "take up the cross and follow me".[1]

Peter has confessed Jesus as the Christ, Christ has said that He must suffer and die and rise again. Peter has protested that this cannot be and been rebuked by the Master. Then Jesus says to them all, disciples and multitude: "You cannot follow me by staying where you are. You must break camp. You think that your security lies in the well trodden paths of yesterday. I tell you that it lies only in following Me along the unknown paths of to-morrow and sharing there both my passion and my victory. If you seek to save your life you will lose it. And what will it profit you if by staying behind you gain the whole world and lose your own soul?"

It is said of Abraham that he obeyed not knowing whither he went (Heb. 11: 8). The unknown is the pilgrim's goal and obedience, it is also his hope and his heritage. And what a magnificent thing the unknown will be when finally the pilgrim arrives! A city with foundations, whose builder and maker is God! And, all along the way, what an exhilarating experience to find that, while one leaves behind that which one has made his home—whether spiritually or materially—and takes to the road with fear; God provides safety for the journey, sustenance for the road and a foretaste of one's inheritance. "In His hands," sang the psalmist (Ps. 16: 11), whatever those hands will dispense, "are joys for evermore."

"It is not enough," I heard Dr Hoekendijk say at a conference, "to speak of the Church as engaged in a mission. It is essential to realize that the Church is a mission." To use a phrase of Bishop Newbigin, "the Church is an expedition." And, because it is an expedition it creates consequences for other people, for those in whose midst this expedition has been launched. These consequences, too, are part of the Church's task in the world.

The consequence for others of having a pilgrim people in their midst is that such a people will exert a peculiar pressure on the forms of common life. Theirs will be a worldliness that is

[1] J. A. Findlay, *A Portrait of Peter*, Hodder & Stoughton, p. 130.

holy. They will live the common life as those who are soon to leave it behind. Also, they will cause even those who are not on the pilgrimage to serve it. The Church loses one of its greatest opportunities of fulfilling its mission when the Christian community seeks to be self-contained. This is an insistent temptation for the small Christian groups that are scattered throughout the large lands of Asia and Africa. A pilgrim people must maintain their differentia as pilgrims, but they must belong to the society among whom their journey is set. This common association is of the heart of the business.

By far the greater part of the Church's mission is to bring to bear on people the pressure of the Christ. So will their living be influenced by Him even when they are not Christians by commitment. In the Western world, there is a Christian national past in the lives of the nations on which such pressure can depend; in the lands of the younger churches such pressure must depend on the normality of the relationship between Christians and their fellow citizens in all walks of life. The Christian community has always to be a witnessing community, but its intention to convert to Jesus Christ is never a conditioning factor in its relationships. It qualifies but does not condition: and, because it qualifies, the Church becomes in human affairs the instrument of the inescapability of the Christ.

So be sure you do not refuse to hear the Voice of God! He has made a promise, saying: "Yet once more will I make to tremble not the earth only, but also the heaven". This means that in this final "shaking" all that is impermanent will be removed, and only the unshakable things will remain. Since then we have been given a kingdom that is "unshakable", let us serve God with thankfulness in the ways which please him, but always with reverence and holy fear. ... Our God is a burning Fire (Heb. 12: 25-29; J. B. Phillips).

3

THE KINGDOM OF THE FATHER IS FULFILLED

Our Father, Thy name be hallowed, Thy kingdom come, Thy will be done (Matt. 6: 9-10).

WILL this prayer, which is the constant prayer of the Church, find fulfilment? Will the time come when His name, by which every family in heaven and on earth is named (Eph. 3: 15), is honoured among them; when His children will rejoice to hear His name and keep it sacred? Will the Father's Kingdom come, the Kingdom of glory, when all strife with sin shall be over and the rule of Christ shall have accomplished its purpose? (1 Cor. 15: 24, 25.) Will the Father's will be done on earth as it is done in heaven; will His design for His whole creation (Col. 1: 20) be achieved?

The New Testament answer to these questions is an unequivocal "Yes": a confidence derived from its determining faith that to the end God will be God, and that at the end God's purpose will triumph because it is God's. "The Son of God, Jesus Christ, is not Yes and No; but in Him it is always Yes. All the promises of God find their Yes in him" (2 Cor. 1: 19, 20). "You shall know that I am the Lord," says God to Israel in exile (Ezek. 11: 10). That is always God's final message to men—His word of warning to them in their self-confidence, His word of hope to them in their despair.

The hope to which the Gospel witnesses is not the result of any realistic calculation of present trends, nor of any prognosis based on an assessment of the problems that lie ahead; rather it is a hope offered as a hope to live by, a certainty in the future on which one can count and by which one can guide one's life. Peter, writing to his fellow Christians under pressure to deny their faith, proclaims to them "a salvation ready to be revealed in the last time" (1 Pet. 1: 3-5). It is a salvation to depend on, a hope to be sustained by. "We have been born anew," he announces, "to a living hope through the resurrection of Jesus Christ from the dead, and to an inheritance kept in heaven for you." This kept inheritance is what the hope is about.

The Promised Inheritance

The Old Testament story is controlled by this fact of an inheritance.

God had promised an inheritance to Abraham. Once the promise was made, the inheritance was sure. It was there. For many years Abraham had no children, but an heir was certain because there was the inheritance.

The people of Israel were in bondage, but they would be free because their inheritance was waiting for them. For many years they wandered in the wilderness, but they would come at last and possess the promised land because it was promised.

Israel's faithlessness to God had brought them into exile. They lived in exile for many years. But they would return to their inheritance again because that inheritance was theirs.

In the New Testament, too, it is the inheritance that is always determinative. "Faith," says the writer to the Hebrews (11: 1f.), "is the title deed of our inheritance." It is that which has controlled through the generations the pilgrimage of faith. What is this inheritance? It is a new creation, a complete renewal of all that God has made;

We wait for new heavens and a new earth in which righteousness dwells (2 Pet. 3: 13). And he who sat upon the throne said, Behold, I make all things new (Rev. 21: 5).

It is the restoration in man of God's image, the offer to man even now of his new nature to be;

It does not yet appear what we shall be, but we know that when he appears we shall be like him (1 John 3: 2).

You have put on the new nature which is being renewed in knowledge after the image of its Creator (Col. 3: 10).

It is the reconstitution in Christ of the broken peace of the world. God's plan is

a plan for the fullness of time to unite all things in Christ, things in heaven and things on earth (Eph. 1: 10).
For in him all things were created and in him all things hold together (Col. 1: 16, 17).

This inheritance is also the eternal city, man's final dwelling place, in which death shall have been conquered and man's fellowship with God reclaimed.

And I saw the holy city, new Jerusalem, coming down out of heaven from God; and I heard a great voice from the throne saying, Behold, the dwelling place of God is with men. And death shall be no longer (Rev. 21: 2-4).

It is the return of the risen Christ, triumphant, to His union with His bride, the Church; and to the completion of the salvation of the world which He has wrought.

Little children, abide in him, so that when he appears we may have confidence and not shrink from him in shame at his coming (1 John 2: 28).
The Spirit and the Bride say, Come. And let him who hears say, Come. Surely I am coming soon. Amen. Come, Lord Jesus! (Rev. 22: 17, 20).
For there is one God, and there is one mediator between God and men, the man Christ Jesus, who gave himself as a ransom for all, the testimony to which was borne at the proper time (1 Tim. 2: 5, 6).

This promise of the end which will certainly happen, however, is not left hanging in the air as a kind of deus-ex-machina event to give a happy ending to a tangled drama. The end promised is already begun. "You are those," says Paul, "on whom the end of the ages has come" (1 Cor. 10: 11) so that we wait for its fulfilment with confidence. When our Lord began His ministry in Galilee, He announced a Kingdom that had arrived. "It has come near," He said, "it has come within reach. Stretch out your hand and touch it" (Mk. 1: 15). The coming of the Kingdom was the coming of the King.

It is always difficult to present convincingly the message of the Christian hope but the task is made needlessly difficult by clinging to the language of apocalypticism when the New Testament itself points the way to Christocentric eschatology. Christ has come and, therefore, while we do not know when the end will be, we do know that the end is now. Now is the day of salvation. Everywhere, the preaching and the hearing of the Gospel is the sign of the eschatological presence. The presence of the work of anti-christ and of false christs also bears the same witness (Mk. 13: 9-23).

This King who has come, the Gospel announces, was born by the Spirit. It is essential to see how closely the Gospel intertwines the action of the Son with the activity of the Spirit if one is not to miss the richness of the biblical teaching on the Kingdom. The Spirit came on Jesus when He was baptized. The Spirit led Him into the wilderness to think through the meaning of His mission. The Spirit of the Lord was upon Him as He began His ministry. He came to men in the power of the Spirit. And, when He had completed His mission by His death on the cross, the Spirit raised Him from the dead. Now, from His Kingdom on high, He has sent the Spirit into the world, that in the Spirit He may continue His work in the world until it is over, the Spirit Himself fulfilling in the world the ministry He began through the Christ. In the daring phrase of Paul, "the Lord is the Spirit" (2 Cor. 3: 17), so that past event, present experience and future hope hold together as that one act of salvation by which human life is upheld.

The Gospel announces a new creation—already in Christ the new creation has begun (2 Cor. 5: 17)—He is the new Man in whom all things will be renewed (Col. 3: 10), in whom those who believe have the first-fruits of the Spirit (Rom. 8: 23). The Gospel promises the restoration in man of God's image—already in the face of Christ the glory of God has been revealed (2 Cor. 3: 18), so that we beholding that glory may be changed into His likeness. The Gospel declares the hope of a healed humanity—already Christ has broken down the middle wall of partition between those who were far and those who were nigh (Eph. 2: 14). The Gospel proclaims the certainty of eternal life (1 Cor. 15: 55, 56)—already death has been conquered by Christ, and the saints are already with Him in glory (1 Thess. 3: 13).

"Now is the judgment of this world, now shall the ruler of this world be cast out": those are the words of Jesus (John 12: 31). And, because He has said, "Now", we are able to say "Already". The end is certain because the end has begun; it is certain also because from this beginning the end is increasingly thrusting itself into every crevice of life. "Sealed with the promised Holy Spirit, which is the guarantee of our inheritance" the Holy Spirit works "until we acquire possession of it, to the praise of his glory" (Eph. 1: 13, 14).

It is obvious, is it not, that if this be the teaching of the New Testament on the end-event as it has happened and as it will be completed, then the consequence of this truth for the mission of the Church and the obedience of the Christian is tremendous? Let us see what these consequences are.

A Mission with Compulsive Urgency

Throughout its history the mission of the Church has never commended itself as simply a good thing to undertake. Whenever and wherever it has been felt, it has been felt as an urgent necessity. Why?

Firstly, because the mission of the Church arises from the work of the Holy Spirit, so that he who is swept into this work finds himself in the power of another. We do not need to sustain ourselves by our conviction about the mission of the Church. To engage in that mission is to be sustained by the mission itself. Urgency belongs to the mission, so that the Church's sense of urgency is only derivative. When on D-day the allied forces landed on the French shore, every Frenchman became involved in an urgent undertaking. The urgency of the mission is simply due to the invasion of the Christ.

84

Secondly, the mission arises from the fact that because Jesus has died for all men, all men have died (2 Cor. 5: 14), and they will remain dead until they are raised by the Holy Spirit to participation in the risen life of Christ. The mission of the Church is to proclaim this resurrection—its necessity and possibility—and to be the locus where the risen life of Christ can be found and experienced. The Gospel is not lest men die but because they are dead. It is a proclamation which answers the question: "Son of man, Can these bones live?" (Ezek. 37: 3.) Such a proclamation is necessarily urgent. "If you believe in the resurrection of Jesus Christ," said an unbeliever to a Christian, "shout it out from the house tops."

Thirdly, the mission is to men whose response is being prepared by the Holy Spirit. That preparation demands that it be availed of. "In season and out of season," said Paul (2 Tim. 4: 2); which means all the time and as widely as possible. Let it not happen that I was the neighbour to someone who was ready for the Gospel and that I passed him by. Since the essential ministry is the ministry of the Holy Spirit and the risen Christ, the Christian mission has necessarily to be performed with watchful urgency. Oftentimes the disciple does not know where the Lord is waiting for him, so that Christ's disciples have to spread themselves and be everywhere.

Fourthly, the mission is to make the pressure of Jesus Christ on the lives of men and of the world inescapable and insistent. This calls for strategy in the performance of that mission. Strategy means an over-all design, plans that must be carried out, decisions that must be obeyed. The mission is the mission of the Church, so that each individual Christian and every separate group find themselves under urgent command not to let down their fellows.

And lastly, the mission is also God's method of saving those who have believed. The disciple is saved as he participates in the operation of the Gospel. "The word of the cross" (our witness to it and our proclamation of it) says Paul, "is the power of God to us who are being saved" (1 Cor. 1: 18). "Being saved"—that is the correct tense in which to express the

Christian's experience of salvation. The movement of the Gospel is a continuous one, and what happens to the believer happens within this movement. No wonder Paul said, "I will explode if I do not preach the Gospel" (1 Cor. 9: 16).

A Mission within the Working of the Spirit

The important thing to recognize here is the fact that that which determines the Church's mission remains independent of it. The Bridegroom comes and so the virgins go to meet him (Matt. 25: 1f.). Some go prepared for any emergency, others do not; but the coming of the Bridegroom takes no account of the situation of these virgins. The Master returns at an hour on which He decides. The servants may be awake or asleep (Mk. 13: 35), they may have done their duty or neglected it; when the Master comes He will deal with it all. The supper is ready and will not go to waste. If those who are invited will not come, others will be brought to the supper (Lk. 14: 16f.). The supper will be held nevertheless.

This means that those engaged in the mission must be prepared to encounter in their work the results of God's free initiative, the previousness of Jesus Christ in every situation, the all-encompassing work of the Holy Spirit within which the mission of the Church is set. "The fruit of the Spirit" wherever it may be found "is love, joy, peace, patience, kindness, goodness, faithfulness, gentleness, self-control" (Gal. 5: 22). Paul uses the singular "fruit" because all these fruits are from the same tree, they also belong together. Wherever, then, by His fruit we see that the Spirit is at work, there we must press the claims of the Gospel with strong confidence. "No one speaking by the Spirit of God ever says 'Jesus be cursed!' and no one can say 'Jesus is Lord' except by the Holy Spirit" (1 Cor. 12: 3). The working of the Spirit is often evident in people's lives before they confess "Jesus as Lord". Indeed, it is because this is so that the Church's mission to proclaim Jesus as Lord becomes a pressing one. Only in Jesus is the fruit of the Spirit secure, to Him alone the glory of that fruit belongs, in His service it must

86

be used. To accept Him as Lord is to put Him in possession of that which is His (John 1: 11). Often the question is asked, "Are you saved?" The question that rather needs to be asked is, "Do you know that Jesus Christ is your Saviour?" It was His vineyard that the Son came to claim (Mk. 12: 6). It was a usurper that the Strong Man came to dispossess (Mk. 3: 27). It was at His feast that the Master challenged the right of the guest to appear without the wedding garment (Matt. 22: 12).

But, in speaking of the mission of the Church as fulfilled within the larger context of the work of the Spirit, it is not enough to see this mission as required by the fruit of the Spirit. It is essential, too, to see this mission as determined by the gifts of the Spirit. These gifts decide not only the special tasks of each recipient but also the ways in which all of them must work together. The gifts are the gifts of the one Spirit for the one task. When the disciples sought to forbid a man who was casting out devils in the name of Jesus because he did not belong to the disciples' band, Jesus said to them, "Do not forbid him, for he that is not against us is for us" (Lk. 9: 49, 50). The common task determines a shared discipleship. To stay separate or to make separate is either to deny that the gifts are of the Spirit, or to claim that once we have received a gift we can treat that gift as ours.

A Mission with a Call to Unity

A third consequence, then, which the nature of the Kingdom imposes on the Church's obedience is a call to unity that cannot be neglected. This call to unity is a call to be true to the wholeness of the Gospel and of the task. According to the testimony of the Acts of the Apostles there were three primary elements in the ministry of the early Church. They preached the Gospel, healed the sick and cast out devils. It will not do, therefore, for us to say, we do preach the Gospel, we run hospitals and devils don't exist. The ministry of healing that Jesus entrusted to His Church does include the work done in hospitals, but it is infinitely more. It is that ministry of the Church (Jas. 5: 14, 15) by which those who are sick are brought into conscious participation in the healing life of Christ. Hal Leiper, facing death because there was nothing more that doctors could do for him, wrote this in his last letter to his friends: "My conviction that spiritual healing through prayer and worship is a given part of our obedient ministry, lay and clerical, has grown. It is as right in the Church as is preaching and teaching. It does not find validation in success any more than baptizing or preaching."[1] The exorcist ministry that Jesus commands is of equal importance. It is certainly part of that ministry to rid the minds of men of the fear of devils. It is also part of that ministry to deal with the demonic elements in human life. But it is a necessary part of it also that devils be cast out exactly as Jesus cast them out in His day (Matt. 17: 20-21). The power that comes by fasting and prayer and the word of command pronounced in the name of Jesus is still normative experience for the Church. It is recorded (Acts 4: 29f.) that the first disciples prayed saying, "Lord, grant to thy servants to speak thy word with all boldness, while thou stretchest out thy hand to heal, and signs and wonders are performed through the name of thy holy servant Jesus": and that when they had prayed, the place in which they were gathered together was shaken and they were all filled with the Holy Spirit. Obedience to the wholeness of the Gospel is the Church's way to spiritual power.

The call to unity is also a call to shared discipleship. The point is often made, in discussing Church Union, that different Churches are custodians of different gifts, and seek to bear witness to different truths. This contention would be pure nonsense if it were not for the ecumenical movement which has broken down the isolation of the Churches and has given to them the possibility of being together. Truths separated from one another became distorted and even false. Indeed, those who have worked on actual Church Union negotiations will testify how they saw for the first time the tremendous potency of a truth they had known and held dear for a long time only when that truth was seen in relation to some other truth that

[1] From a copy of his letter sent to his friends, after his death, by his father.

someone else from another Church was expounding. The present growing conviction about the ministry of the laity is a case in point. As long as the doctrine of the priesthood of all believers was a battle cry it remained comparatively barren of results. But now that it has come to be seen in relation to the doctrine of the Church and its sacraments, the doctrine of the world and its salvation, the doctrine of work and of vocation, it has become one of the most powerful truths in the Church. Unity is a condition of power, unity is also a condition of truth.

Unity is a condition of integrity too. I studied in the United Theological College at Bangalore in India. We were Methodists, Presbyterians, Congregationalists, some Lutherans and members of the Mar Thoma Church. Whenever the teaching of the New Testament on the Church was given to us, each one of us assumed that this teaching was about our Church. I never realized the significance of this unconscious dishonesty until I became a member of the Church Union Negotiating Committee in Ceylon. It was there that all of us discovered that we did not have a theological understanding of our Churches in their separation. We certainly could get by in our discussions by using such categories as "the marks of churchliness", "the validity of orders", "vestigiae ecclesiae" etc., but we all knew that, as long as those who bore the name of Christ could not belong to the same household, there was a loss of integrity. That the churches are the Church is the gift of His sovereign grace, but shall we sin that grace may abound? (Rom. 6: 1.)

A Mission with Consequences for Personal Discipleship

Man's inheritance as God has provided it, the New Testament affirms, is a joint inheritance. We are joint heirs with Jesus Christ (Rom. 8: 17), we share our inheritance with the saints (Eph. 1: 18), we are joint heirs of God's grace (1 Pet. 3: 7). The joint-family system in the countries of Asia gives the exact feel of these phrases. The property belongs to the whole family, it cannot be partitioned, no member of the family can control or enjoy his share separately: the whole belongs to all and anyone who decides to break the unity of the family must forego his part of the inheritance.

This inheritance belongs, in the first place, to creation as a whole. "Go into all the world and preach the gospel to the whole creation," is what we read in the ending to Mark's Gospel (16: 15). "That men are brought into the life of the sons of God must mean that all creation is delivered from bondage," says Paul (Rom. 8: 21). "Cultivate the earth and subdue it" (Gen. 1: 28) was God's first command to man. His demand now is that men so live and work in whatever occupation or profession they may be as to make effective God's will in His creation. Personal religion is only thus far and no further. Christian discipleship involves the disciple in responsible living in the world.

Man's inheritance belongs also to mankind as a whole. As in Christ there is and will be a new creation, so also in Christ there is and will be one new man (Eph. 2: 15), one reconciled humanity. Someone has said, "Do not send anyone to hell, for in the end you will need him to enter heaven with you." The mission of the Church to reclaim all men for Christ is the simple outcome of this truth. Will all men be reclaimed? That is not our side of the problem. Our side of the problem is that so much depends on us who are disciples of Jesus Christ. Again, it must be said that personal religion is only thus far and no further. Christian discipleship involves the disciple in finding men for Christ.

What is true in terms of all creation, what is true in terms of man, is also true in terms of the Church itself. The Church is One and there is only one inheritance. Writing to the Corinthians, Paul says, "Chloe's people inform me that you are quarrelling. By 'quarrelling' I mean that each of you has his party cry, 'I belong to Paul', 'And I to Apollos', 'And I to Cephas', 'And I to Christ'. Has Christ been parcelled out?" (1 Cor. 1: 11f., Moffatt). A new creation, a new man, a new household: there is no escape from the discipline of joint ownership and joint inheritance into an exclusive reliance on personal religion. How important it is, then, for us to realize that precisely what has happened to us as persons is what has made us messengers of the Kingdom! Reconciled, we have been made agents of His reconciliation (2 Cor. 5: 18, 19); saved, we have been called to be heralds of His salvation (1 John 1: 1-4); loved, we are the first-fruits of His love to all mankind (Rev. 14: 4).

God and man, the Gospel and the world, the Holy Spirit and the new creation: these are the true correlatives as we have them in the Christian faith. They determine the axis of the Christian life and set the context of Christian discipleship. In one of Charles Wesley's hymns there is a striking verse in which the full circle of the Christian commitment is traced.

> That I Thy mercy may proclaim,
>   That all mankind Thy truth may see,
> Hallow Thy great and glorious name,
>   And perfect holiness in me.[1]

Thy mercy, Thy truth, Thy name—for all mankind—and I, both to proclaim it and to be perfected in holiness!

Paul puts the matter into one sentence: "Christ in you bringing with him the hope of all the glorious things to come" (Col. 1: 27, J. B. Phillips). "In you"—that is what everything depends on. "Christ in you"—He in whom the full nature of God chose to live (Col. 1: 19). And, because Christ is in you, "Yours is the hope of all the glorious things to come." What are they? They are the maturing of your own character as Christians; the fulfilment of the Church's mission in the creation of the new man of God's design; and the accomplishment of that great reconciliation which God has planned in Christ of everything on earth and in heaven by virtue of the sacrifice of the cross (Col. 1: 20). "So naturally," says Paul following up his great affirmation, "we proclaim Christ! We warn everyone we meet, and teach everyone we can, all that we know about him,

---

[1] Charles Wesley, *Methodist Hymn Book*, 562.

so that, if possible, we may bring every man up to his full maturity in Christ. This is what I am working at all the time, with all the strength that God gives me" (Col. 1: 28-29, J. B. Phillips).

A Mission in the Certitude of Hope

But, will everyone be saved? How may the certitude of Christian hope be expressed in relation to the Church's mission? That God will accomplish His great design purposed in creation and redemption and sought by Him through the countless years is certain because God is God (Rev. 11: 15); and yet, because man is man, the haunting question remains, Will each man attain to his inheritance, will all men find eternal life?

There are those who insist that no genuine and urgent conviction about the mission of the Church is possible unless one is able to say positively: Some will be saved and others will be damned, and they will be damned who, having had the opportunity in this life to accept Jesus Christ as their Lord and Saviour, nevertheless reject Him (John 3: 18). It is certainly true that those who are able to state the matter in this way do have a sense of urgency about their evangelistic and missionary responsibility; but the issue must nevertheless be pressed as to whether the whole drift of the teaching of the New Testament allows for so simple and simplified a conviction. Surely there are a series of exclamation marks which the New Testament puts in the face of too categorical an answer to the question raised! First, is there any real substance in the claim that God's great design for His whole creation will be fulfilled unless that claim includes the assertion that it will be fulfilled for each person? (Lk. 15: 4.) Second, where in the New Testament is the span of this earthly life set out as the measure of the limits of God's grace? Third, who shall say that the evangelistic presentation of Jesus Christ will necessarily be for anyone, who hears that presentation, the moment of his decision for Jesus Christ? Does not the Master offer Himself for acceptance by some of His children (Matt. 25: 31f.) in ways and forms that are of His own choosing and which may not ever carry the label "Christian"?

The New Testament will allow no diminution of the fact that there is only one Saviour—Jesus Christ (Acts 4: 12); nor will it allow any compromise of the fact that salvation is by faith in Him (Rom. 1: 16); but it foils all attempts to enclose these facts in tightly-thought systems of belief (John 1: 4, 9) or to make them at home within the boundaries of the visible Church.

This theological situation has led some to make an attempt to get round this problem by making the sovereignty of God the sole maxim by which the work of God's salvation is explained. God's purposes must find fulfilment since God is God and cannot fail. Also it is impossible to assert on the New Testament evidence that all men will somehow be saved. So that the conclusion is irresistible that God's purpose cannot be to save all men. God has chosen whom He will save and Jesus died for this elect only. This position is certainly consistent as a theological proposition, but it sets out a theology which blasphemes the name and nature of the Father of our Lord Jesus Christ. It is never permissible to use the doctrine of the sovereignty of God as a premise from which logical deductions can be made. Every time that Paul exclaims in his epistles "God forbid!" he is dealing with a logical deduction from the doctrine of the sovereignty of God which is logically correct but theologically false. Like the doctrine of the Trinity, the doctrine of the sovereignty of God is always a conclusion at which the believer arrives and never a starting point for theological specution. When William Carey first mooted the idea of preaching the Gospel to the people of India, he was met with the rejoinder, "Young man, if God wants to convert the heathen He will. You sit down." That may have been good logic, but it was atrocious theology. Both the doctrines of the Trinity and of the sovereignty of God are doctrines which signalize the end and limitation of human reason in its thinking about God. They are resource for faith and not data for reason.

But cannot this question about "all or some" be settled by

reference to the obvious teaching in the Gospels contained in those sayings of Jesus where He speaks of "the few"—the few who will find the straight and narrow path (Matt. 7: 14), the few who will be chosen out of the many who are called (Matt. 20: 16)? In these sayings, and many others like them, our Lord is speaking about the movement of the Kingdom which He has come to inaugurate and the few who, at all times, will yield to its pressure and share in the tasks. The words "salvation" and "eternal life" have also this meaning of participation in the life and activity of God in Christ in the world (Mk. 10: 21).

"This is eternal life, that they know thee the only true God, and Jesus Christ whom thou hast sent" (John 17: 3). "The servant does not know what his master is doing; but I have called you friends, for all that I have heard from my Father I have made known to you. You are my friends if you do what I command you" (John 15: 15). "Good Teacher, what must I do to inherit eternal life?" "Go, sell what you have and give to the poor; and come follow me" (Mk. 10: 17, 21).

In this sense "salvation" is actually the experience of the few. But the question still remains concerning the final end of all (John 10: 16). Will all finally arrive in the Father's Kingdom?

The seer of Patmos makes the following announcement as part of his closing vision:

> He who is seated upon the throne said, "See, I am making all things new!" Then he said to me, "It is done! I am Alpha and Omega, the Beginning and the End. I will give to the thirsty water without price from the Fountain of Life. The victorious shall inherit these things, and I will be God to him and he will be son to Me. But as for the cowards, the faithless and the corrupt, the murderers, the traffickers in sex and sorcery, the worshippers of idols and all liars—their inheritance is in the Lake which burns with fire and sulphur, which is the Second Death" (Rev. 21: 5f.; J. B. Phillips).

This announcement says no more and no less than that there will be no change in God's demands of men even at the last. No man need go astray or waste his opportunities for godly decision by hoping that at the end there will be a sentimental letting down of standards on the part of God.

Twice in the Gospels it is recorded that Jesus was asked the specific question with which we are dealing here, and His answers on both these occasions provide all that we can know or need to know. At the end of His conversation with the rich young ruler, Jesus said, "How hard it is for those who have riches to enter the kingdom of God!" Whereupon those who heard Him said, "Then who can be saved?" (Lk. 18: 18-27). Wealth gives to a man the possibility of meticulous observance of the law, it also provides him with the means of serving God. If, then, the wealthy will find it hard, who is going to be saved? Jesus answers, "Salvation is God's possibility and not man's." On the other occasion (Lk. 13: 23f.) Jesus was on His way to Jerusalem and someone said to Him, "Lord, will those who are saved be few?" Jesus answered, "Few or many, you strive to enter by the narrow door, and enter while there is still time, for once the door is shut it will not be opened for you again." Salvation is indeed God's possibility, but it also remains man's responsibility; and there is no way of so fusing these two truths together as either to minimize man's responsibility or limit God's possibility. With God all things are possible, but for man damnation remains a possibility also.

The Imperative

If, then, the theological hiatus here revealed cannot be eliminated, it is necessary to challenge the position that no genuine and urgent conviction about the mission of the Church is possible unless one is able to say positively, "Some will be saved and others will be damned." In fact, as one reads the Acts of the Apostles, it becomes abundantly clear that the early Church derived its sense of missionary imperative from this very theological hiatus. It was certain that God was on the march fulfilling His design for the world and for men and that, therefore, the Church had to be on the march too. It was itself part of God's design, so that urgent mission was part of its very nature. On the other hand, sin was everywhere holding men as thralls so that the task was urgent of setting them free. The Acts of the Apostles is the story of men who felt the pressure of a victory that was certain as well as of a combat that was critical. They never seem to have been plagued by the question, "How can the combat be critical if victory is certain?" May it be that we, for whom this question has become so important, find it so because we are neither certain of the victory nor are involved to the death in the combat? (2 Pet. 3: 4; Heb. 12: 4.) May it not also be that somehow we have got ourselves into a position in which we feel the need to convince ourselves that the task to which we are called is indeed urgent, when our real need should be to be so committed to the task that we are unable to escape its compulsion.

The New Testament does not allow us to say either Yes or No to the question: "Will all men be saved?" and by preventing us from doing this it forces on us the question; "Will you fulfil your share of the task to which God has called you in the Church—the task of making Jesus known and loved, confessed and obeyed, by all men in every area of life?" When God speaks to be obeyed, it is His word that is decisive and we must find it so. We must learn to accept what God says because it is God who says it. To expect God to furnish us with other reasons for obeying Him is to seek to take up a position with respect to God that He cannot allow. When Jesus said to Matthew "Follow me" (Lk. 5: 27-28) He gave Matthew no reasons. There was no attempt to tell Matthew: if you remain in your present job these are the consequences, if you follow me these other consequences will ensue, so that you can see that following me is the better and wiser course. No; when Jesus speaks, His word stands alone on its own authority.

Is it not obvious, if the Church is an expedition and if I am a member of the Church, that then I am myself part of the expedition? The expedition is not a task I undertake, it is something I become: and when I become it, I find that I am part of a movement which is both urgent and compelling. The point I am trying to make can be summarized thus: the imperative of the Church's mission arises from three facts—the certainty of God's victory, the crucialness of man's predicament, and the completeness of the Christian's commitment to his Lord. All three belong together, each generating its own type of urgency and authority, and at different moments of his obedience the Christian will find one or other of them that which is compulsive.

There is a final point to be made in seeking to state the eschatological truth in connection with the Church's mission. It is that one must not succumb to the temptation of believing that at the end Jesus will come in such a way as to extort faith or stampede men into belief. It is "the same Jesus" (Acts 1: 11) who will come who walked the streets of Palestine in the flesh and accepted the humiliation of the Cross. So that when He comes He will be as patient of men's freedom and as careful of men's personal dignity as when He sojourned among them. It is true that, when He comes in glory, all men will know who He is, for He will come unveiled.

> He is coming in the clouds
> and every eye shall see him,
> even those who pierced him,
> and his coming will mean bitter sorrow
> to every tribe upon the earth.
> (Rev. 1: 7; J. B. Phillips.)

And yet, whether this sorrow will be repentance or remorse, that final event will not by itself decide. Faith will still have to be free and God's grace will still have to be patient. But, can it be that anyone will reject Him even at this last? That is a speculation to which the New Testament does not lend itself. It simply says, He will come, and therefore let each man get ready to meet Him. No one can escape that meeting where finally each man will be judged by his Saviour.

So arose for the New Testament Church, and so arises for us the prayer which undergirds the Church's task and sets the direction for its mission: "Come, Lord Jesus, come quickly" (Rev. 22: 20).

Therefore let us go forth to him outside the camp, bearing abuse for him. For here we have no lasting city, but we seek the city which is to come. Through him then let us continually offer up a sacrifice of praise to God, that is, the fruit of lips that acknowledge his name. Do not neglect to do good and to share what you have (Heb. 13: 13-16).

4

MEANWHILE, THE CHURCH

As often as you eat this bread and drink the cup,
you proclaim the Lord's death until he comes (1 Cor.
11: 26).

"UNTIL he comes"—that is the *terminus ad quem* (the
goal); "the Lord's death"—that is the *terminus a quo*
(the source): and between these two events lies the
total ministry of the Church to the world. The verb translated
"proclaim" is translated by a word in the Tamil Bible which
means, "to make public". It underlines the truth that the life
and activity of the Church concerns Jesus and the world. The
Church's task is to make Him public: to publish His name, to
set Him out in the market place, to destroy any attempt by any
one to make Him a private possession. He is every man's heritage, each man's treasure, the Master and Owner of all.

This relation of Christ to the world is established through
His death. At the heart of the Church's life are the two sacraments of holy baptism and holy communion. Through baptism
in the name of Jesus the believer dies to sin and is raised to
eternal life. The death of Jesus becomes death effective for him,
so that the risen life of Jesus becomes effective for him also
(Rom. 6: 2-4). He dies into Christ and, therefore, lives with
Him. In holy communion the believer partakes in the risen life
of Christ. The bread and the wine are for him Christ's living
body (John 6: 52-56). So that, in partaking of Christ, he finds
himself participating in Christ's continuing ministry in the
world, the ministry of making His death the effective source of
all men's salvation.

In baptism the believer dies once, and once for all, and his
life henceforth is life in Christ; in holy communion the believer

99

lives continually by the life of Christ, his privilege thenceforth being to die for his Saviour. The Lord's death cannot become public in any other way except by the sacrifice and self-denial of those who belong to Him. Writing to the Colossians, Paul says, "though it is true that I am suffering on behalf of you who have heard the Gospel, yet I am far from sorry about it. Indeed, I am glad, because it gives me a chance to complete in my own sufferings something of the untold pains which Christ suffers on behalf of his Body, the Church" (Col. 1: 24, J. B. Phillips).

In his second letter to the Corinthians (4: 12), Paul makes quite explicit the nature of this ministry of death, "Always carrying in the body the death of Jesus," he says, "so that the life of Jesus may also be manifested in our bodies. For while we live we are always being given up to death for Jesus' sake, so that the life of Jesus may be manifested in our mortal flesh. So death is at work in us, but life in you."

The Practice of Death

The characteristic of the Church's life is this practice of death. It is a practice which informs its religious worship, controls its secular life, sustains its servant ministry and inspires its Gospel proclamation. It characterizes also its whole temporal history, so delivering it from static institutionalism that it is kept responsive to the descent of the Spirit.

All Christian worship is worship in the name of Christ, and at its heart is thanksgiving for the salvation He has wrought. Remembrance and commemoration of Christ's death and passion belong not only to the service of holy communion but to all the services of the Church. Amnesia, it has been said, is the basic ailment of many Christians. They need anamnesis. There is an illuminating feature about the forms of the various types of building used in worship. The Hindu temple is built in the form of a man. The outer court raised on pillars and open on all sides is the human body, the inner court with its wide spaces is the human mind, the shrine room is the human soul. Man

100

moves within himself into himself and there finds the presence of God. The Muslim mosque too is built in the form of a man. The central dome is man's head and the minarets are his hands upraised in prayer. Man comes to God through an act of adoration and submission. The Buddhist dagoba too is built in the form of a man. Its figure is that of a man in the posture of meditation: legs crossed, the body erect and the head held straight and unmoving. The approach to reality is by way of inner withdrawal from the world. The Christian church too is built in the form of a man, a man stretched out upon a cross. Man's access to God is through one who died for him.

This contrast can be made sharper by reference to the Hindu doctrine of grace. The Hindu witnesses to the truth that it is grace which makes worship possible. "It is by God's grace," the Hindu says, "that man worships God." But this grace is God's normal relation to man. It is grace that is not costly to God. God remains outside the human predicament even when He is gracious. Man's sin does not press upon the life of God. The grace of the Lord Jesus Christ is grace that was costly (Phil. 2: 6-8). Its symbols are a stable, a cross, and a borrowed tomb. To repeat again, a death is at the heart of Christian worship and, without it, worship is no witness to Him who died, a witness borne until He comes. The joy of that coming too is part of Christian worship. It is as when the streaks of early dawn mingle with the shadows as people meet for worship in the dusk of the morning. Christian worship witnesses to the boundary between night and day. Such worship is part of the mission of the Church. To plant it in every community is the goal of its missionary enterprise.

Death also lies athwart the secular life of the Church. Christians are a people sharing a common life in the world, which life finds expression in secular as well as religious forms. There are the Church's institutions set up as means of service—hospitals, schools, orphanages, etc., there are the Church's organs of administration—such as conferences, synods, councils, and parish meetings; there are the Church's expressions of its community life—áshrams, convents, monasteries, community centres and so on; there are the instruments forged for the fulfilment of its mission—theological colleges, lay academies, literature agencies, missionary societies and several more; and finally there is the secular power and influence wielded by the Church through its administrators, men of learning and letters and the very weight of its common life. In and through all these forms the devil is constantly busy suggesting to the Church—Fall down and worship me and the kingdoms of the world will be yours (Matt. 4: 8-9).

None of the forms of life and expression that have been mentioned are for their own sake but for the sake of the spread of the Gospel; and yet the devil constantly suggests that they must themselves be safeguarded for their own importance. The Church is under constant temptation to make its service institutions (Lk. 22: 25) expressions of the Church's patronage of the world rather than of its true servanthood. There is the besetting sin of seeking to administer the Church's affairs without patient listening to the voice of the Spirit which may speak either through a majority or a minority (Acts 15: 12), perhaps even through one lone person. Expressions of community life within the Church are specially exposed to a holier-than-thou infection (Phil. 3: 2), while the very instruments intended to lift up the Christ become means of self-advertisement (Phil. 1: 15). The experience of the Cross ought to mark the secular life of the Church; but how can this happen as long as Christians, as bearers of the Gospel, are not at the mercy of the world but are able to protect themselves against those whom they would win for Christ? Jesus was crucified because those who rejected Him had the power to crucify Him: the Church in many a given situation is too powerful to be crucified.

The servant ministry of the Church is its true vocation. Those who serve are not necessarily servants. Jesus called them benefactors. Men in authority can serve most efficiently, but no one can reject their service or reject them. Those who represent the Master must not expect to enjoy this advantage. The servant is not greater than his Lord (John 15: 20). Jesus who was Son became servant by emptying Himself (Phil. 2: 7). So must it be with His disciples whom God must empty and make His servants.

What can we, who belong to Christ and bear His name, expect? We must expect to be taken by Him and mixed by Him in that aspect of the world's life in which He wants us to be leaven (Lk. 13: 21). Once the leaven is mixed with the dough it has no other function except to lose its identity. We must expect to be taken by Him and scattered into earth's remotest places, there to grow along with the tares until the harvest is reaped (Matt. 13: 24-38). The seed that is scattered means the children of the Kingdom. Too often the seed remains too long growing in seed-plots. Of how many Christians in the West is it not true that the clubs and societies of which they are members are exclusively for Christians and often under the aegis of the Church! Of how many Christians in the East is it not true that their secular life is lived within Christian institutions or walled within mission compounds! We must expect also to be taken by our Lord and set upon lampstands from which we can radiate the most light (Matt. 5: 15). When men light lamps they do not hide them. God does not do otherwise. He too will set the lamps He lights where they can be set to most advantage. But these places of advantage are also the places where the winds blow. A sudden gust of wind and the lamp may go out; but that is part of the lamp's adventure. Always facing death in order that it may communicate life—that is the Church's unavoidable role.

So also is death a characteristic of the Church's proclamation of the Gospel. Somehow we Christians often give the impression to others that the Gospel is a bludgeon in our hands with which to beat them into acceptance of our faith, or that it is a kind of badge which not only distinguishes us from others but confers on us a distinction. Somehow we find it difficult to communicate the fact that we ourselves are captives of the Gospel, and that our evangelism is a showing forth of our captor-Lord. Many reject the Gospel because the challenge which the preacher presents seems to them to say: Come and stand where I stand, come and belong to what I belong to, come and believe what I believe. The preacher has to find a way of leaving the hearer with his Lord, without obtruding himself between them. If the preacher remains in the picture then the situation is not one of evangelism but of proselytism.

I have found that for me the most effective safeguard against this obtrusion of the preacher is to keep always in the foreground of my thought the fact that all those to whom I am privileged to speak about my Lord are already one with me within His saving ministry. I believe Him and confess Him, they do not: and yet the essential facts of the Gospel remain true for them as for me.

God made us.
God loves us.
Jesus died for us.
Our trespasses are not counted.
When we die we shall go to Him who will be our Judge.

These affirmations are true of all men and for all men whether they know them or not, like them or not, accept them or not. I am able to speak with men who do not yet bear the name of Christ, as those with whom I am one because the wall of partition between us has already been removed (Eph. 2: 14). Faith in Christ they have yet to find; but already they belong with me within the saving facts of the Gospel. Allow this conviction to dominate one's thought, and one will find oneself delivered from standing in front of one's hearers. One learns thereby to stand alongside them and point them to their Saviour. This "standing-alongside", where the hearer does not need to look at the speaker, is the practice of death which every preacher must learn.

And finally, as we have said, this practice of death belongs to the nature of the Church in its temporal history. God's ark must eternally dwell in a tent because God is a God who moves. To build for the ark a house of cedar (2 Sam. 7: 2f.) is to turn the historical moment after the moment is past into a mummy; it is to attempt to turn the place of revelation into an idol when the living God Himself has moved on and now beckons from afar. Dr George MacLeod in his John Knox lecture (1959) vividly illustrates what this means in terms of Church history.

> A right reading of history [he says] is not an accumulation of differing strands. The everlasting Spirit seems to descend with the same message on a differing key to attune with the differing environments of the changing epochs. Regrettably, it appears never to have been true in history that the Church has grasped some new insight, directly communicated from above. Rather has the secular order so pressured the laziness of God's elect that they have been forced to come to terms with it and so most painfully have found again the Living God.
>
> Pressured by the tragedy of the decaying environment, St Martin of Tours was wearied of an Empire that had grown old and institutional. Martin's fellowship houses were the chrysalis of the priesthood of all believers emergent in its ancient colours. Five centuries later the Church became institutional in its turn. The Gothic revival was the next organism: in the superb words of Chesterton "Up shot the Gothic like a flight of arrows"— only, towards some five hundred years later again, to become the static scandal that was the Roman Church before its counter-reformation. Pressured again by the evils of its time, God's lazy elect once more were stirred by a new descent of the Spirit which issued in the Reformation. Of our own day it is true to say that the elaborate design of the reformers has simply faded out. Our key, once more, will emerge by coming level with our environment. Once more it is our environment that pressures us.[1]

A moment dies, the Church has moved from organism to institutionalism: the practice of death means awaiting again a new descent of the Spirit, ready to leave behind and to move on.

An Indivisible Inheritance

"The Lord's death"—that is the first determinant of the life and mission of the Church. But in the text quoted, at the beginning of this chapter, three determinants are mentioned: the Lord's death, the Lord's coming again, the time until. What is the meaning of the second determinant for the life of the Church?

[1] *John Knox and Today*, John Knox Press, pp. 8-10.

When the Lord comes in glory it will be finally to fulfil the Father's plan for His whole creation. This plan comprehends all that God has made. So that the Church in its task in the world has but one way open to it and that is to teach all men how they may inherit together that which is their indivisible heritage. The rightful insistence on the necessity of personal conversion and commitment to Jesus Christ has in large measure given rise to the impression that salvation is an individual matter. "I believe and am saved." In terms of the New Testament perspective this is a distortion. The truth is that when I believe, I find myself involved in God's work of salvation. My own salvation is part of that work. Grace and apostleship (Rom. 1: 5) are received together, grace becoming more fully one's experience as the apostolic privilege is exercised and its responsibility discharged. To put the matter crudely but simply: salvation in Christ, which is God's will for all mankind, cannot be given to me as a separate and separable portion. Rather, salvation can be for me only a call to follow Jesus in His saving ministry. "Follow me" was what He Himself said to everyone whom He called and those who sought Him. This experience of following Him is the experience of salvation.

The phrase that Paul uses, to describe the Christian experience, is the phrase "in Christ". Christ is not a person in the past tense only. He is present Lord, and the Lord who is to come. To be "in Christ", therefore, is to live by all that He has done, to be involved in all that He is doing, and to prepare for all that He will do. In John's epistle this truth is stated quite vividly. "You know," he says, "that the Spirit teaches you in everything. Remember that his teaching urges you to live 'in Christ'. So that if he were suddenly to reveal himself we should still know exactly where we stand, and should not have to shrink away from his Presence." (1 John 2: 27; J. B. Phillips).

To repeat again, salvation is mankind's indivisible inheritance in Christ, this quality of indivisibility determining in every way both each man's experience of salvation and his mode of obtaining it. "Let us give thanks to the Father," says Paul (Col. 1: 12-14), "who has qualified us to share in the inheri-

tance of the saints in light. He has delivered us from the dominion of darkness and transferred us to the kingdom of his beloved
Son, in whom we have redemption, the forgiveness of sins."
Redemption is in Christ. It is an abiding experience. This Christ
is the King of a Kingdom, a Kingdom which has been established and which is being accomplished. In this work of Christ
the King those who are redeemed share their inheritance with
the saints in light. It is this light which enlightens every man.
He is the light of the world (John 1 : 9; 8 : 1).

What are the consequences of this indivisibility of man's
inheritance in Christ? First of all, it means that the Gospel is
not truly proclaimed where the proclamation does not make the
Kingdom of God the explicit context within which an individual is invited to accept the Gospel. Since there is no other
name given by which men can be saved except the name of
Jesus Christ (Acts 4 : 12), no man should be invited to accept
Jesus Christ without, at the same time and in the same act,
accepting the world for which Jesus died and to which Jesus
belongs as its Lord and Saviour. If there were many ways of
obtaining salvation, it would be possible for a man to choose a
way on which he can go alone or only with those whom he
chooses. But, since there is only one way, all humanity is bound
together by this circumstance. They belong together on the
road of salvation. There are many Christians for whom the
natural way of speaking about the issue of salvation is to say
that one is saved by accepting Jesus Christ as personal Saviour
and that thereafter one lives responsibly in the world. It does
not seem to me to be a mere quibble to insist that the primary
act must involve the awareness that one does not really accept
Jesus as personal Saviour unless that acceptance is informed
from the beginning as to who He is. He is Lord of the world and
Lord of the Church and any one who accepts Him accepts Him
only to the extent that he accepts to be implicated in the exercise of Christ's double Lordship. The issue is always what the
acceptance of Jesus Christ as one's personal Saviour means.

A second consequence of the indivisible nature of the salvation which God offers to men in Christ is that such a salvation

is truly proclaimed only when its indivisibility is effectively demonstrated. Where it is not manifest that Christians share an indivisible gift in Christ, their proclamation of the Gospel is already mutilated. The basic issue here is not only that of the unity of the Church. It is even more pointedly the issue of the unity of each congregation. Sunday worship in most churches to-day, in East and West, is not the activity of a family. Discrete individuals gather together in one place to worship God. This has its own validity, but a worshipping congregation must possess a community life which is both secular as well as religious. It is this need that is driving Christians to create what have come to be called "para-parishes" where the secular sharing of common life, whether in terms of a common occupation or a common neighbourhood, provides the basis for congregational unity.

The Evangelism Department of the World Council of Churches, in one of its monthly letters, puts the matter thus:

> This question of the witness to the Gospel of the corporate life of a congregation becomes acute when it faces the prospect of opening its doors to the outsider. The outsider is already frequently a sharer in group life in the secular world—a labour union or a work group or a teen-age gang, or a neighbourhood athletic club. There he finds the reward of fellowship; he is known by name, is accorded the dignity of being permitted to speak and to be listened to. Ultimately, to be sure, none of these fellowships may satisfy his deepest needs. Rootlessness, and the fate of the wanderer, and suffering the loss of personal freedom in subjection to the power structure of a technological society, hover in the background. But every congregation is called upon to become a fellowship so clearly witnessing to Christian brotherhood that it can witness as *from community to community*. Surveys of evangelism in area after area report the despair of many an evangelizing effort directed to the outsider as this confronts the problem of introducing the convert to life within a local congregation ...

The consideration of this need to place the corporate life and structures of the churches under the judgment of the call to proclaim the Gospel can give rise to many questionings. Can renewal of the fellowship life within church walls take place unless a congregation becomes an agency of witness to the world outside church walls? What has the fellowship of Christians in a congregation to offer by way of witness that can differentiate it from community life in the secular world? Is it true that the Church will rediscover itself only in small groups? Have the churches in our time, overwhelmed by the complexities of our era of social change, lost the sense of expectancy and the courage to endure the pain of renewal? Are we building walls of protection against the world within which we can indulge in nostalgia for a vanishing "Christian culture"?[1]

The issue is plain (is it not?) and can be put directly by asking whether there is not but one way of entering into an indivisible inheritance—the way of love. The full impact of the New Testament insistence upon love is lost when love is looked upon primarily as a virtue to be cultivated, a commandment to be obeyed. Love is the very method of inheritance. It is the way by which one enters into and abides in the world-embracing love of God. "The man who loves his brother lives and moves in the light." "We know that we have crossed the frontier from death to life because we do love our brothers" (1 John 2: 10; 3: 14; J. B. Phillips). In these verses John is saying: Love is the way by which one enters into and lives in the light. It is the way by which one passes from the sphere of death into the sphere of life. It is the way by which one comes to the knowledge that this transition from darkness to light, from death to life, has taken place in one's life.

In his first letter to the Corinthians (8: 1-13) Paul writes at length on a comparatively trivial problem—can a Christian eat food offered to idols? In his letter to the Romans (14: 2f.) he deals equally at length with the question of eating meat. There are similar questions dealt with in all the letters in the New Testament. Why? Because trivial differences become major irritations when people have to live closely together. As long as Christians can erect effective barriers between themselves so that the area of their common life, their life in fellowship, is reduced to controllable proportions, so long the differences will not matter. But differences, even on small things, do

[1] Monthly letter, June-Nov. 1960.

109

matter where people have to live together. The writers of the New Testament accepted this living-together as one household as their major premise, and so dealt with the problems which this living-together raised: we, in our day, in our several churches, denominations and congregations have made our differences sufficient reason for not-living-together. And then we are caught in the situation that these differences cease to matter. Those who have participated in Church Union negotiations know the meaning of this as far as organic union between Churches is concerned. They know that several of the questions raised by persistent differences cannot be answered until the differences are within a united Church.

Again and again in all discussion about the Church's renewal, conversation finally comes to the question: what new patterns of life, new structures of fellowship and witness, are necessary for the Church as it faces its task in the world to-day? It is a question posed by the inescapable fact that the Church and the Churches cannot live their life or fulfil their mission without effectively expressing the Church's solidarity with the world as well as the fellowship within which fellow Christians are bound. In both these spheres there is necessity for common action and also for common life; for programmes of work that involve co-operation and collaboration, as well as for social structures within which there can be real belonging to one another.

In this area there arises too the need to re-formulate for practical purposes the relation between Law and Gospel. Christian solidarity demands a common Christian way of behaviour, those standardized Christian reactions to the recurrent situations of life which put a stamp of conduct on the community and set it free for its special tasks. There must be those habits of the Christian life on which the freedom and individuality of the Christian can rest. The danger of legalism is avoided not by avoiding Law but by offering one's obedience to it as one's grateful response to grace. The danger of uniformity is avoided not by individualism but by accepting the discipline of a common life as rightly belonging to the calling of a Christian soldier. The theological issue concerning Law and

Gospel is met when Law is recognized as preceding the Gospel in the matter of Christian nurture, as contradicted by the Gospel in the matter of Christian conversion, and as flowing from the Gospel in the matter of Christian witness.

Church and World

Man's inheritance in God is indivisible. This throws light on the nature of the Christian life as it is lived within the Church, but it also has its consequence for the relation between the Church and the world. While the Church is the instrument of God's mercy and judgment with respect to the world; the world, in its turn, is the instrument of God's mercy and judgment with respect to the Church. An illustration of this is seen in what is happening in Ceylon to-day. For nearly twenty years now the schools run by the Churches have been a source of controversy both within the Churches and within the community at large. The Churches failed to make up their minds as to what to do, while all the time clinging to the hope that nothing would happen to change the status quo, a situation in which the schools were a source of secular power and influence for the Church. I was in Europe when the last general elections in Ceylon took place, and I remember being asked which party in Ceylon, I thought, would win. I was out of touch with political trends in the country but still I replied to the question. I said, "In my view the schools have become a source of embarrassment to the Churches and a source of spiritual temptation. The party which has announced that it will take over all schools and make all education state controlled is the Sri Lanka Freedom Party. I have a feeling, therefore, that for the sake of the Church this party will win." My intention in giving this illustration is not to discuss the rightness or wrongness of my view of Ceylon politics or of the schools issue. Rather, it is to give a very concrete illustration of the point which I am making that the Lord does use the world to lead the Church into discerning and doing His will, and that we can expect this to be so.

This double relation of Church and world was one of the most significant insights of the Jewish people, and through them has become an essential element in the Christian understanding of history. Two passages from the prophecies of Micah may be quoted as examples of this teaching. The prophet bewails the sin of Israel and announces to her that the Lord will use the nations to execute His plans against her:

> The Eternal declares,
> I plan something, plan a fate
> from which you cannot shake you free,
> nor rid you of its crushing weight:
> so evil is the time.
> Then shall you be taunted,
> as this dirge is chanted:
> Undone! we are undone!
> the soil of our folk is parcelled out,
> past all restoring;
> our captors are dividing up our fields.
> (Micah 2: 3-4; Moffatt.)

And then turning to the Church, the prophet cries:

> Arise and thresh
> O daughter of Zion,
> For I will make you horns of iron,
> hoofs as hard as bronze,
> to trample many a people down,
> consecrating their spoils to the Eternal,
> their wealth to the Lord of all the earth.
> (Micah 4: 13.)

In both these prophecies, the Church and the world are set out as instruments of God's judgment with respect to each other: the teaching in the Bible is equally clear that they are also instruments each to the other of God's mercy. Cyrus of Persia was God's instrument of mercy to Israel (Is. 44: 28), Jonah was God's herald of mercy to Nineveh. To quote Micah again, it is by this double movement that God's will shall finally be accomplished and the nations come to share in the glory of Zion.

It shall come to pass
that the mountain of the house of the Lord
shall be established ...
and peoples shall flow to it.
Many nations shall come, and say:
Come, let us go up to the mountain of the Lord,
to the house of the God of Jacob;
that he may teach us his ways
and we may walk in his paths ...
And they shall beat their swords into plowshares,
and their spears into pruning hooks;
nation shall not lift up sword against nation,
neither shall they learn war any more.

(Micah 4: 1-3.)

The Church and the World—when the Lord comes in glory He will bring to its fulness His dealing with both of them. Perhaps one should also add, not only both of them but of all His creation. The Bible reference is to God's salvation of His whole creation (Col. 1: 15-20), and even if this reference up to now lacked any warmth of meaning, it should be so no more. Outer space has become part of man's world and man has taken his first step into space. Our expectation of the great consummation must, therefore, necessarily make us wonder whether God, who was made flesh for us and amongst us, would not also have devised for all parts of His creation their own appropriate visitation.

Nor, in our little day,
May His devices with the heavens be guessed;
His pilgrimage to thread the Milky Way,
Or His bestowals there, be manifest.

But in the eternities
Doubtless we shall compare together, hear
A million alien Gospels, in what guise
He trod the Pleiades, the Lyre, the Bear.

O be prepared, my soul,
To read the inconceivable, to scan
The infinite forms of God those stars unroll
When, in our turn, we show to them a MAN.[1]

[1] From *Christ in the Universe*, by Alice Meynell; Burns and Oates Ltd.

The Time Between

The Church lives by making public "the Lord's death", the Church's faith and mission are conditioned by what the Lord will accomplish when He comes again, the realm which the Church is to occupy is the realm between His death and His coming. It is here that the peculiarity and uniqueness of the Church and the Gospel which it proclaims become most evident. The life and mission of the Church are within "time", and the events of time are primarily what that life and mission are about. Time is time-between. It is between the now and the not yet. Christ has come, He will come again. God's Kingdom has been established, it will be consummated. The Son has begun to reign, He will hand His realm over to the Father. The Holy Spirit has been poured out, He will come upon all flesh. The Church has been gathered, it must gather the nations. We have become the children of God, we have yet to become like Him.

This time-between is the sphere of the Church's task. Its concern is to see that during this time God's will is done on earth as it is done in heaven. The perspective of the Old Testament was limited by death. After death there was Sheol, a state of shadowy existence of the soul. In Sheol the praise of God was silent (Ps. 30: 9). Therefore, this life on earth was seen to be real life. It was here that God's will was done, that God's name was praised, that God wrought out His purposes, that God and man lived together. The history of the world, its nations and its peoples: the history of men, their life in family and community—that was the very stuff of Jewish faith. But since Jesus overcame death, the way was open to two alternative developments. There was the possibility of glimpsing the truth that human history would be gathered up into the accomplished reign of God, there was also the possibility of denying any but instrumental meaning to historical development and of thinking that salvation was the salvation of individuals, so that man's life on earth simply constituted the opportunity for obtaining that salvation.

New Testament faith fixed itself firmly on the first alternative. It was able to do this because its Scriptures were the books of the Old Testament. It saw and knew Jesus as the Messiah. But right from New Testament times has come the choice of the second alternative. Among its many elements the Gnostic heresy also contained this element of making salvation an individual matter, of treating this world as unreal because it was temporal. This Gnostic tendency against which the early Church so consistently strove has, however, become the chief climate of opinion in large sections of the Christian Church to-day. In them the individual soul and its salvation has become the matrix of thought, the life on earth is the process within which personal sanctification has to be obtained, and heaven, after death, is the goal of religious striving.

In the ecumenical document published by the Evangelism Department of the World Council of Churches, entitled *A theological reflection on the work of Evangelism*, there occurs the following paragraph:

> When it describes the mighty deeds of God, the New Testament uses political, juridical, sociological and other secular terms. Kingdom of God, Son of David, King of the Jews; Redemption, Faith, Forgiveness; Healing, Freedom, Service—all such words by which the person and work of Jesus Christ are described are secular words. This secular terminology of the New Testament is not only a form of speech. For the coming of Jesus Christ in the flesh and in the power of the Spirit is a "secular" event. It is an event in the world and for the world. For many, however, the language and message of the Bible have become merely "religious". It is the task of evangelism to discover and to proclaim the Gospel in its specific, concrete, unique and secular sense.[1]

"Christianity is a secular movement and not a religion," were the words with which Dr Hoekendijk opened his speech at the Strasbourg Conference of the World Student Christian Federation. "We must," he said, "de-sacralize Christianity and the Church." What did he mean? He meant that Christianity was becoming too exclusively concerned with the private

[1] P. 13.

solaces of personal religion, it was losing its momentum as a movement launched by the visit to the world of its Messiah-King. At a recent consultation held in India between Hindu and Christian scholars, one of the Hindus remarked that if ever he felt compelled to take history seriously, he would then have to become a Christian. How easily many Christians manage to empty history of its meaning except as the stage for the drama of their own lives!

There is in one of the Psalms a rather quaint reference to the birds.

> Even the sparrow finds a home,
> and the swallow a nest for herself,
> where she may lay her young,
> at thy altars, O Lord of hosts.
>
> (Ps. 84: 3.)

One can almost hear the birds, as they discussed the temple, its altars, and its eaves, saying to one another, "What kind people these human beings are! How well they have built for us places to live in and to bear our young!" Can it be that our conversations about the great deeds of God are not very different? It is true that for our wounded spirits the temple of our God does afford a home, but the temple itself was not built for this purpose.

The third determinant, then, of the life and mission of the Church which is "the time-until" must be taken so completely seriously that this life and mission are not subverted into anything less than the working out of God's election of His Church within His total purpose for the world. The Scriptures make plain that the time until the end is the time during which God's election of Jesus Christ, as the new man, explodes in power and fills the very crevices of human history with His wrath and grace. The Church is the agent of this explosion.

When Jesus was baptized (Matt. 3: 17) the declaration was made, "This is my beloved Son"; a fulfilment of the prophecy which declares, "Behold mine elect, in whom my soul delights" (Is. 42: 1). But in His death this chosen one was rejected. The bystanders at the Cross (Lk. 23: 35) cried out, "If you are the chosen one, come down." If there was any reply from the Cross, it was the cry: "My God, my God, why have you forsaken me?" (Matt. 27: 46). Yes—here is the new man in whom all men find their destiny. He is before them all; He is the "pre" of their destination. In Christ's experience of being forsaken, men are elected for rejection, just as in His covenanted love which took Him to the Cross they are elected for salvation. "God has consigned all men to disobedience, that he may have mercy upon all" (Rom. 11: 32).

The Church's task, therefore, is to declare this mercy and to make it operative by entering fully into the life of the world and there experiencing the mercy of God as God brings men to repentance and faith; or as God works out His purpose with an Esau, a Pharaoh or a Judas (Rom. 9: 13, 17, 18; Acts 1: 16). Just as the Scriptures reveal, whether in the Old Testament or in the New, a chosen people implicated in the life of the nations around them and by that very implication becoming God's signature in the world, so it must be always. To be the Church-until is to be the Church in the world and for it. To be severed from Christ is to have fallen from grace (Gal. 5: 4); but the time-until is the time in Christ, the time to announce that God does not will that any should perish but that all should come to repentance (2 Pet. 3: 9). It is true that the Church has consistently made this announcement, but it has often gone unheeded because Christians have behaved towards others as if those others had already perished. To preserve the patience and hope, that belong to the time-until, together with the sense of urgency that belongs to the nature of the Gospel: that is the crux of the matter.

Faith and Obedience

In bringing this chapter to a close, let us tie together two truths which in the course of the argument may have seemed to stray apart. These are, on the one hand, the intrinsic importance of personal faith in Jesus Christ, and, on the other hand, the equally important acknowledgment that obedience to Jesus

Christ finds its substance in the relation of His Gospel to the world. Three passages from Scripture must suffice for this purpose.

In the Acts of the Apostles, Peter, speaking to the Jews after the healing of the lame man at the temple gate, says to them (3: 19): "Repent, and turn again, that your sins may be blotted out, that times of refreshing may come from the presence of the Lord, and that He may send the Christ appointed for you." The challenge to repentance is a challenge to personal decision, but the consequence of such decision is announced to be the gift of the Holy Spirit and their involvement in the coming of the Messiah.

In his first epistle, Peter writes (2: 9), "You are a chosen race, a royal priesthood, a holy nation, God's own people, that you may declare the wonderful deeds of him who called you out of darkness into his marvellous light." The words used here— race, priesthood, nation, people—stress the corporate existence of those who bear the name of Christ. Their life and function is a life and function together, to declare the deeds of God by which "light" has become man's inheritance. But before such declaration can be made, one must be able to say: "He called me out of darkness into his marvellous light." The personal situation is decisive. Howard Thurman, commenting on this use of "light" to describe the Christian experience and vocation, alludes to a common practice among desert dwellers. "It is the custom of the desert dweller," he says, "to leave a lighted lantern by the road side at night to cheer the weary traveller. Beside the lantern there is a note which gives detailed directions as to where his cottage may be found so that, if there is distress or need, the stranger may find help."[1] Each lamp must be lit, each called out of darkness into light; and all along the way many lamps must be set singly and together fulfilling the Christian mission.

In his letter to the Romans (8: 38-39), Paul concludes his magnificent statement about man's heritage in Christ with almost a hymn of confidence. "I am sure," he says, "that

[1] Howard Thurman, *Meditations of the Heart*, Harper and Brothers, p. 90.

nothing will be able to separate us from the love of God in Christ Jesus our Lord." That is faith's true standing ground. But his experience is wrought in a contest that faith must wage on every battle front. "Death and life—man's existential alternatives; angels and principalities—his cosmic neighbourhood; things present and things to come—the march of temporal events; powers—those who hold and wield authority; star ascending or descending—whatever providence has decreed; nor anything else in all creation."

The battle that is being fought is a tremendous and all-inclusive one, and man is both the fighter as well as the cause of the fight. He is the ultimate object of God's concern and the central hope of God's design. No wonder Scripture exclaims in thankful surprise, "What is man?", and to this question raised in the Old Testament the New Testament gives answer in the confident faith of the Gospel.

> What is man, that God is mindful of him?
> or the son of man, that God cares for him?
> For a little while he has been put lower than the angels,
> and yet God has crowned him with glory and honour,
> putting all things under his feet.
>
> But, as it is,
> we do not yet see all things controlled by man.
> What we do see is Jesus (Heb. 2: 6-9).

5

THE OBEDIENCE OF THE DISCIPLE

These men who have turned the world upside down
have come here also (Acts 17: 6).

SOME years ago a Christian lady, a Protestant, came to
me with this problem. She was married and for many
years had had no children. She said that she had gone on
pilgrimage to Madhu, to the Roman Catholic shrine there, and
had besought Mary for a child, but to no avail. Then she went
to Kataragama, to which shrine Hindus go, and made vows
there and received a child. She wanted to know what to do.
Should she not now change her faith and become a Hindu?
I said to her, "Ammah, if having or not having children is to
decide the issue, it does not really matter what you do. You can
choose to belong to any religion you like."

A member of my church recently bought a new car. He himself was just learning to drive. As he left his house to go and take
delivery of the car he broke a coconut (a Hindu practice supposed to ensure a good augury); having taken delivery of the
car he went and lit two candles in St Antony's Church, and
when he got home he asked his mother to pray that God would
guard him from all accidents. It is immaterial to this illustration that his car met with an accident within the week. What is
material is the fact that, in terms of his over-ruling anxiety, this
person found no difficulty in mixing up the various religions.

Syncretism is a denial of the Kingship of Christ (Phil. 3: 19),
but His Kingship is easily denied when His Kingdom ceases to
be the goal of one's search, the object of one's devotion (Matt.
6: 33). Whether one is going to be a syncretist or not simply
depends on what one is looking for. This driving desire, of
course, need not always be some form of material wealth or

security. Dr Visser 't Hooft has said that "syncretism is the secret religion of many intellectuals in the West."[1] This is because their over-ruling concern is for a synopsis of intellectual systems, for a way of holding together various philosophies of life and truth. A quality of a true thinker is his intellectual humility, but in the realm of religion this humility can prevent one from committing one's life to personal discipleship to Jesus Christ. A syncretist can be committed to great causes but, within the inner citadel, the God he worships is a God he has chosen and not a God who has chosen him. Professor Toynbee has this to say about Christianity:

> We ought to purge our Christianity of the traditional Christian belief that Christianity is unique. This is not just a Western belief; it is intrinsic to Christianity itself. ... It is a congenial feature which is part of Christianity's and also part of Islam's heritage from Judaism. Just as the vision of God as being love is a heritage from Judaism, so is the other vision of God as being a jealous god, the god of my tribe as against the Gentiles outside my tribe or my church or whatever my community may be.[2]

To know that one is possessed is to be aware of the jealousy of the possessor (Deut. 4: 24); where this jealousy can be purged the relationship has been made different also. The question is not one about God's relation to others but about God's relation to oneself.

The Christian Commitment

Paul and Silas were in trouble in Thessalonica because they proclaimed that Jesus was the Christ. It is a proclamation whose climate of thought is as far removed as can be from desire for babies, or anxiety about security, or humility in thought. It is concerned with a truth that leads to its own consequences for the person who believes it. It refuses to be compromised with any other truth. It in itself and not the believer decides the

[1] From a speech reported in *E.P.S.* of Nov. 4, 1960.
[2] Arnold Toynbee, *Christianity among the Religions of the World*, Scribners, pp. 95-97. (For a discussion of this position of Toynbee see the article by Charles W. Forman in *Religion in Life*, Vol. xxvi, no. 3, 1958; also Hendrik Kraemer, *Why Christianity of All Religions?* Lutterworth and Westminster Press.)

issues. No form of syncretism ever turned the world upside down, nor will it serve if one's mission is to overturn the world (Jer. 1: 10). Jesus is King—that will do it; that alone will do it (Acts 4: 9). For, as in the day of Paul and Silas, Jesus immediately challenges every other rule. The cry of the Jews to the city authorities in Thessalonica was: These men are acting against the decrees of Caesar, saying that there is another king, Jesus. The cry of the Jews in the courtyard of Pilate was: We have no king but Caesar (John 19: 15). That is the issue. It is true that the Jews, whether in Jerusalem or Thessalonica, were not men who felt any loyalty to Caesar: but their protest was nevertheless profound because they recognized the exclusiveness of the claims which Jesus made. To accept His Kingship would threaten so many things that they valued as primary. If Dagon was to be protected, the ark of God must not be taken into his temple (1 Sam. 5: 1-4).

The contrary truth, however, is also of equal significance— the truth that Dagon was overthrown because the people of God had been defeated and their ark captured. The obedience of the Christian disciple is rendered under two possibilities (Rev. 11: 10). It may be crowned with success so marked that the world protests at its violence. Ahab could not bear Elijah, the troubler of Israel (1 Kings 18: 17): the men of Thessalonica could not bear Paul and Silas, turning the world upside down. But the Christian disciple may never forget the other possibility: that his obedience may be crowned with failure, and that the world may seek to make his faith captive. Through the centuries, as much has been wrought by the Church from its prisons (Phil. 1: 12) as has been wrought from its positions of power and influence. The essential need is that at no time must the Christian seek to protect himself from the possibility of defeat, the experience of capture, the price of the Cross. At all times and in all circumstances the Christian is a witness to the servant-presence of his Lord. Just as preoccupation with one's personal anxieties can blunt the distinctive relation between the Christian Gospel and the world, so also can a preoccupation with the success of causes that one espouses. Christian obedience is rooted in commitment to a person, a commitment which must be kept exposed to the possibilities of success as well as failure in the causes which that obedience serves.

The Rev. R. K. Orchard, speaking to a group of would-be missionaries, had this to say:

> Our commitment is basically to a person, not to "causes". It is not e.g. to the cause of spreading Christianity throughout the world. It is commitment to Jesus Christ so that he may be known by men everywhere; and that is not the same thing. I think the promotion experts amongst us need to take heed of this danger of commitment to causes. You know how it is; I am exhorted on all hands that, as a Christian, I am required to be concerned with foreign missions, the population explosion and the world's food problem, the refugees, the victims of rapid social change, the race problem, the young delinquents, the slaughter on the roads, the sufferers from typhoons and drought. I can't deny it—theoretically: yet it is not really surprising if I treat this welter of exhortation as I treat advertisements which tell me that I must buy this, that I'm beyond the pale if I don't use that, that I can't sustain the pace of modern life if I don't use somebody's night cap; namely, by saying to advertisers and promoters of Christian causes alike—Clear off, all of you, I don't believe any of you. May it not be that the promotion boys should ask themselves, Are we in fact evoking commitment, or are we in fact producing the spectator attitude?[1]

The spectator attitude to which Mr Orchard refers is simply the reverse side of the coin of which the one side is syncretism. It can be avoided only if it is clearly recognized that Christian commitment involves both a choice of causes that one seeks to serve as well as an acknowledgment all the time that there can be no direct identification of any man's causes with God's cause.

The Life of the World

If, then, the obedience of the Christian disciple is primarily an expression of his personal commitment to Jesus Christ within

[1] From an address delivered in Nov. 1959 at the Annual Meeting of Carey Hall, Birmingham.

the impact of the Gospel on the world, what would its determining marks be? They would be—would they not?—those caused
by the marks of the life of the world itself.

A first mark of the life of the world is the way in which the
processes of life create the marginal person. The broken
hearted, the captive, the blind, the bruised, the indebted
(Is. 61: 1-2): these find themselves increasingly denied their
dignity as persons and treated as of no account in the world.
Was it mere chance that our Lord announced the purpose of
His coming in His sermon at Nazareth (Lk. 4: 18-19) in the
words of the prophet who saw and proclaimed God's act of
deliverance in terms of what it would mean to precisely these
persons? Good news to the poor, release to the captives, sight
to the blind, liberty to the oppressed, the year of jubilee to all.
In His parable of judgment (Matt. 25: 31f.) the Master makes
everything turn on service rendered to the marginal person.
The true test of Christian discipleship is the presence of that
love which gives itself in consideration for those who are not
protected by others nor are able to protect themselves (Matt. 5:
47). The extra which Jesus demanded He defined as those acts
of kindness which its recipients could not repay. No wonder the
main New Testament emphasis falls on the need of men for the
Gospel rather than on the obligation of the disciple to evangelize. An evangelism uninformed by specific knowledge of men's
needs may result, and often does, in converting men to Jesus
Christ but leaving them still captive in society. Christian
discipleship is marked by warfare against the sin of the
world.

The sin of the world is lodged in social structures. The issue
of Good Friday was not the issue of Jesus against certain
persons, but the issue of Jesus against the principalities and
powers as they were represented in the Roman Governor, the
temple priests, the people's Sanhedrin, the orthodoxy of religion, the passion of nationalism, the insecurity of power. The
various religions teach the way to forgiveness of sins. The
Incarnation and the Cross were not necessary if private and
personal sin were all that had to be dealt with. The Cross was

necessary because sin itself had to be overthrown (John 1: 29). Christian discipleship must demonstrate this difference.

A second mark of the life of the world is that it is furrowed. Life is not simply an undifferentiated expanse; it is cut up by many ploughs—family, class, tribe, race, community, occupation, language, government—these and many varieties of these qualify life. The seed of the Christian Gospel needs to be sown into these furrows (Matt. 13: 38). The sons of the Kingdom must belong to all these areas of life. Hence the missionary mark of Christian discipleship. The disciple is concerned that the seed fall into every furrow so that, where in any furrow the seed has not yet been sown, there he feels the missionary calling to be compulsive. The first controversy in the Church was about circumcision (Acts 15: 1). Should they first become like us? The answer was, No. When Paul spoke of himself as a missionary to the Gentiles (Gal. 1: 8), he was announcing that God had called him to cross that frontier between Jew and Gentile so that he might belong to the Gentiles. How well Paul succeeded is evident from the fact that he had to give proof later that he was still a loyal Jew (Acts 21: 17-24).

But the Christian's existence within the furrow is not for its own sake nor is it enough to be the Christian presence there. Ultimately the word of the Gospel has to be spoken in order that there may be gathered around it those who would bear the name of Christ. Witness by word to Jesus Christ is an inescapable part of Christian obedience. The Kingdom of heaven, said Jesus (Matt. 13: 52), is like a householder who brings out of his treasure things new and old. The Christian faith is twenty centuries old but the disciple's witness is new. It comes new-minted from his experience with his Lord. But, it is often asked, why must this witness necessarily be in words? Are not deeds enough? The answer surely is that the word of witness is the climactic deed. It is not enough to make love; one must get to the point of saying, "I love you. Will you marry me?" I once saw a drawing of a boy and a girl sitting on a rock facing the sea. The boy had courted the girl for many months but had been too shy to ask the question. She was determined

THE FAITH

this time to help him out. Suddenly she turned to him and said, "John—I read somewhere that the size of a woman's waist is normally the same as the length of a man's arm. Is it true?" John thought for a moment before he replied, "Mary, you wait here and I will run up and get a string and we will soon find out." He lost his girl. Making love is not enough. One must say, "I love you." Kind deeds are not enough. One must say, "I forgive you." To be a Christian within that particular furrow is not enough; one must perform the duties and obligations of being an ambassador (Eph. 6: 20). One's credentials from his king must be presented, the word on behalf of one's king must be spoken.

The missionary mark of Christian discipleship is that the disciple becomes the means whereby God's word of address reaches persons. If men are to live by the words which proceed from the mouth of God (Matt. 4: 4), those words must first be spoken. Men must be identified and addressed even as the woman, who touched the hem of the garment of Jesus (Mk. 5: 30), was called out by Him and named before the crowd.

> God does not speak to man in the anonymity of categories, whether social, political, or religious. When the Gospel is proclaimed, man is called by his name out of his anonymity and stands before God as the person he truly is. In other words, when the Gospel is addressed, whether to a Muslim or a Christian or a Communist or any other category of man (whatever the furrow be in which he dwells or by which he is known), it cuts through both what he pretends to be and what he imagines. It speaks to his true condition.[1]

A third mark of the life of the world is that it is in constant change and that from all sides claims are made and pressure exercised to control and direct this change. The task of the Christian disciple in this situation is to speak convincingly to men about the truth that the course of human history cannot simply be bent in any direction that man wills. A piece of wood cannot be cut or planed except in conformity with its grain; to

[1] *A Theological Reflection on the Work of Evangelism*, published by the World Council of Churches, p. 7.

do otherwise would only produce splinters (Matt. 12: 30). Life too has an ingrained direction. He who seeks to go against the grain will only cause scattering even if his intention is to gather. Thus, because, on all hands, men and societies of men are seeking to direct life's changes, and because life itself bears its own witness concerning the direction in which it is set, the Christian must find his opportunity to enable men to establish their true relation to Jesus Christ. He is the gatherer without whom men can only scatter. Or, since it is He in whom all things are to be gathered, they, who scatter, scatter Him. A variant rendering of the Gospel text reads as follows: "He who does not gather with me scatters me."

The Christian responsibility, then, in this regard can be put succinctly as follows: All men must be persuaded to say "Yes" to Jesus Christ (Acts 17: 30-31). Those who say "Yes" must be enabled to do "Yes" so that they may be convincing witnesses (1 John 1: 6). But since there will always be those (Matt. 21: 29) who do "Yes" but say "No" (whatever the reasons be for saying "No"), those who bear the name of Christ have a special responsibility towards them to lead them to say "Yes" and to work with them in the "Yes" they do. And, because there are those who neither say "Yes" nor do "Yes" (Jude 23), Christian obedience must be directed towards making Christ inescapable for them. The Church by its witness of word, its service of need, and its fellowship of life must so commend Christ that He is desired.

The crux of the matter is that the Christian faith has a primary reference to man's earthly life. It is not a matter simply of rightly understanding life but of living it, so that the missionary task goes beyond the task of teaching truths. "The crucial claims of the Gospel have to do with matter, not with ideas."[1] It is a question of so burying the seed in the soil that it dies and grows and bears fruit.

And yet, when men ask for Jesus, how often is the Jesus who is presented not the living grain but polished rice. He has been

[1] Charles W. Forman, in an address delivered at a consultation of the Canadian Council of Churches, Feb. 18-20, 1959.

husked and cleaned and made ready for the table, but He will not grow. His multiple reference to all of earthly life has been removed and He has been reduced to the dimensions of man's religious needs.

Meeting Jesus

Let us put the question this way: men must meet the living Jesus—how will they meet Him? When, at the end of an evangelistic mission, the plea is made calling on men to accept Jesus Christ, what precisely are they expected to do? Christ has been offered to them in the preached word. Are they now to say, "We accept what has been preached"?

When the Greeks came to Philip and said, "Sir, we would see Jesus" (John 12: 21)—the disciples took the Greeks into the Master's presence. What is the answer to-day to that question? Does not everything hinge on this, that when men ask to see Jesus, the Christian disciple must be able to say, Here He is.

There are six ways in which Jesus guaranteed His presence in the world, so that those who seek to declare the Gospel must be able to lead men to any one of these six. The foundation fact, on which the experience of the presence of Christ is based, is the fact of His resurrection. He is alive on earth and comes to meet those who would meet Him (John 20: 16), and when He comes He makes Himself known. He made Himself known to Mary by the love in His voice, to the two disciples at Emmaus by His gesture of blessing (Lk. 24: 31), to Simon Peter at the lakeside by the grace of His providence (John 21: 12), to Thomas amidst his doubts by the proof of His body (John 20: 27). To those who would see Jesus, therefore, we can always say, "Wait for Him and He will come to you," except that no one will be persuaded by what we say unless they recognize us as those who have met Jesus.

Consequent on the fact of the resurrection is the promise of Jesus that where two or three are gathered in His name there He would be in the midst of them (Matt. 18: 20). So that it ought to be possible, when men ask to see Jesus, to invite them to join with us in some doing of His will. It is not necessary that someone should bear the name of Christ before he can meet with others in that name. How often men have found Jesus precisely because they were engaged in doing His will, and because among those with whom they worked were men and women who knew His presence. In the private room of Mahatma Gandhi there was only one picture on the wall. It was the picture of Christ with the inscription "He is our peace". Within a week of Gandhiji's death that picture was removed, but it had told its story. It had witnessed to the fulfilment of the promise that Christ is where His servants are. Of course, the primary activity in which men can engage together in Christ's name is the activity of prayer, and it must be always remembered that many a person who does not bear that name will nevertheless be found to be willing to join in Christian prayer when invited to do so. In one way or another, an answer to the quest for the presence of Jesus is to find a means of gathering round His name.

The presence of Christ is guaranteed also in the experience of membership of His body—the Church (Rom. 12: 5)—and especially in participation in its sacraments. To be baptized is to be baptized into His death and to be raised with Him into new life (1 Cor. 12: 13). To receive the bread and wine in the Holy Communion is to feed on Him in one's soul. No answer to the request "We want to see Jesus" is complete until that answer includes the demand, "Repent, and be baptized" (Acts 2: 38). To belong to the Church and to share in its life is itself a way of meeting Jesus and living with Him. Within the Church there are no permissible barriers between man and man, so that love of the brethren becomes an inescapable situation. In finding and exercising that love is the presence of Jesus known. The deepest tragedy for the world is that Christians themselves have erected barriers against one another in the Church, thereby reducing the necessity of loving one another, of living by the love of Christ. God made the world, man erected the fences. How the soul yearns to affirm the faith which can sing:

Love, like death, hath all destroyed,
Rendered all distinctions void;
Names and sects and parties fall:
Thou, O Christ, art all in all.[1]

A missionary friend of mine coming to Ceylon from the U.S.A. told a story of how in one of the ports of call she had to fill up a form in which she was asked what her religion was. She put down "Christian". The Japanese officer to whom she handed her card looked at it and exclaimed, "Yes, Madam, Christian—but what damnation?"

There is a fifth way in which Christ has promised to mediate His presence to men. He said, "When the Holy Spirit comes He will take what is mine and declare it to you" (John 16: 14). This promise is true both within the Church and without. All truth comes from Christ and belongs to Christ. So that with every advance in true knowledge men become more exposed to the truth as it is in Christ. Often the first answer to be given to anyone who wants to meet Jesus is to ask him to face the implications of the truth which he already knows (Acts 8: 30). A tried way of doing this in the realm of religious encounter is in a fellowship of conversation where Christians not only speak of Him whom they know but also, and more resolutely, listen to others as they bear witness to the truth as they know it. Dr Stanley Jones, who practised this method in India with great effect, used to say: "In these conversations, when others sought to express their judgment of Christianity, they often began by contending that Christianity was not true; soon they said Christianity was not new; but ultimately the challenge lay in their exclamation—Christianity is not you." By all means let us talk about the truth but let us always remember that, in the last analysis, the talk will veer round to a conversation about us. It is not when we are talking to people about Jesus but when people come to us to talk about Him that there comes to fulfilment for them the experience of the presence of Christ. But how tardily they come to us! We have spoken to them about Jesus Christ, but we have not convinced them that we know Him and

[1] Charles Wesley, *Methodist Hymn Book*, 720.

can introduce them into His presence. There was a man going around disposing of his collection of pearls (Matt. 13: 46). Everybody talked about him and so gave him the opportunity to speak to them about the pearl of great price.

Lastly, Jesus promised His presence in the marginal person. "I was hungry. I was thirsty. I was a stranger. I was in prison" (Matt. 25: 40). Many have met Jesus in the person in need. They had not known, but they had received Him and served Him. The task of Christian witness is to name Him whom they have served. It was not only the Athenians who worshipped an Unknown god (Acts 17: 23), nor would it be only to men like them that Jesus would say, "It was I."

The presence of Christ needs to be known in all these six ways, though different persons may begin or progress differently. The mark of Christian discipleship is to be able to accompany the seeker to that place where he will find, and then so continue to help him that he may find Jesus in all those ways in which Jesus gives Himself.

The Religious Life

The burden of this chapter has been the obedience of the Christian disciple, and the drive of its argument has been to show that this obedience is truly itself only as it meets the world in those ways by which the life of the world is characterized. Let me conclude the argument by showing what a different thing Christian obedience would be should it consider religious satisfaction as such to be its goal. Indeed there are many, both within the Christian Church and without, for whom the concerns of the Church's mission and of evangelism appear only to have a tangential relation to the real concerns of the religious life. They would hold that the intrinsic nature of the religious life was something apart, something so *sui generis* that it must be sharply distinguished from concerns and activities which may be associated with it but neither qualify it nor necessarily belong to it.

What is the religious life and what does it signify?

There are three aspects of the religious life which can be distinguished. First of all, there is that aspect of religion which is concerned with a person's earthly life, his material and physical needs, his joys and sorrows, his ambitions and disappointments, his hopes and desires for himself and his family and his friends. In this area religion can mean either those practices of prayer and religious discipline by which the divine aid is sought and received, or those practices of renunciation and asceticism by which the pressure of the earthly is reduced and destroyed, or those practices which lie in the realm of the magical and the occult by which the power of the person over his surroundings and circumstances is increased. With respect to all these there is real similarity between the practices and prescriptions found in all religions, and all religions possess testimony about their efficacy. The Christian should not find this situation hard to understand because he knows that God sends His rain both on the just and the unjust, and makes His sun to shine both on the good and the evil (Matt. 5: 45). God's care for all His children in their real need is a real care, and it is exercised independently of men's so-called religious practices. The criterion of truth as regards religious practice, which is concerned with man's earthly life and its need, is not the criterion of so-called success but rather what that form of practice does to the human spirit in its relation to God. Does it enable a person to use the gifts of God for God's glory? Does it enable a person to keep faith in God when the gift asked for is not given? Does it teach a person to value God more than His gifts? Does it train a person to grow in discernment about the gifts that he must ask?

Secondly, there is that aspect of religion which is at the other end of the scale, where it is the very transitoriness of life that has become oppressive, and where transcendence over this earthly life is the main concern. In forms of religion where this is the climate, the main drive is to overcome the manifoldness of life. The One has become the many, and the religious urge is for the many to know themselves as the One. When the self transcends itself and overcomes all separation, then the religious goal has been attained. "Meditation" is the key word in this area of religion, and the transcendental mystic experience is the highest good. Once this experience is obtained, one may either withdraw from the life of the world into a life of contemplation, or live out one's earthly life displaying in one's work and relationships the graces that belong to the saints. In this form of religion too, all religions possess equally effective witnesses. When Paul speaks of being caught up to the third heaven and there witnessing what no words can describe (2. Cor. 12: 2), he is speaking of an experience which is similar to that of transcendental mystics in all religions. No Christian should find it hard to believe that God who made man in His own image presents Himself to man's inner vision when He is sought after with persistence and diligence. Blessed are the pure in heart, for they shall see God (Matt. 5: 8). "Ask," said Jesus. "Ask, and it will be given you. Seek, and you will find. Knock, and it will be opened to you. If you who are evil know how to give good gifts to your children, how much more will the heavenly Father give the Holy Spirit to those who ask Him?" (Lk. 11: 9, 13.)

There is a third aspect of religion in which the focus of attention is not this earthly life at all, neither its needs and problems nor its manifoldness. Neither the world nor the soul occupy the centre of the stage. Rather, the stage is occupied by God, and one feels intensely one's separation from Him. It is in this area that the problem of sin becomes acute. The religious life, therefore, becomes the quest for fellowship with God or for union with Him. This involves the removal of every barrier between man and God. Man must cease from his preoccupations with this life, and this is best done by practising habits of religion which will make God one's preoccupation. Man must overcome his divided interests between God and the world; this is achieved by practices of religious devotion which will fill the mind with thoughts of God and awaken in the soul an exclusive love of Him. Man must turn away from his sin and be forgiven; this is attained by casting oneself upon God's gracious mercy and by living the good life in the strength which He provides. And when every barrier is removed, the religious quest comes to its consummation in the enjoyment of the Divine. Here again in all religions there is similar evidence about man's wrestling with sin. There are indeed tremendous differences between the religions as to what constitutes sin: but all of them know the meaning of guilt and all of them carry evidence of men who found release from this sense of guilt each in his own way and according to his own faith.

All these three aspects of religion have religious validity and there is witness for this from men in every religion. At their base, the institutional forms of all religions are directed towards the same concerns; and the mystics among them, in the last analysis, speak the same language. In other words, simply and purely as a religion, Christianity is just one religion among many.

The Christian Difference

A difference arises, however, when the total life of man is seen to be the centre of the divine concern. Should God Himself become man, then that Man's life will necessarily become determinative for all men. That is why the three aspects of religion, which we have already mentioned, cannot possess a validity in themselves within Christian faith and life. Their truth and rightness become questions not of whether they meet the religious needs of men but of what their place is in the life that the God-man, Jesus Christ, has lived on earth and the life He continues to live to-day. The mission of the Church, in proclaiming and demonstrating the Gospel, is the sign and sacrament of Christ's continuing life in the world. Within that sign and sacrament is the guarantee that God, through the Holy Spirit, will finally accomplish His purpose in creation and bring to its consummation the total history of man. This means that the Christian must bring into subjection to Christ all expressions and experiences even of his religious life.

When the disciples asked our Lord to teach them to pray, the first thing He taught them was to replace the religious "I" with the secular "we". "Our Father"—it is the cry of man in association with fellow-man seeking to share together their indivisible inheritance as children. The prayer then goes on to ask for those things that belong to the heart of discipleship—"Thy name be hallowed, Thy Kingdom come, Thy will be done, On earth." Whence does this prayer arise? It arises from the fact of the Christ. The name of God has been revealed, the Kingdom of God has arrived, the Messiah doing God's will is abroad upon the earth: it is the pressure of this Messianic event on the lives of men which gives to Christianity its specific quality. So there follow the petitions for those needs of body and soul without which discipleship cannot be sustained: food, forgiveness, shelter and deliverance. These last four petitions are Christianly made only when they are made after praying for the first three: that is where the heart of the matter is. To be a Christian is to be in Christ, and this means to be involved in Christ's continuing work and presence upon the earth.

It was not Paul's idiosyncrasy which made him a missionary. When he tells us that he prayed that the thorn in his flesh be removed (2 Cor. 12: 8), he is telling us of an experience of his in the problems of earthly life. "I know," he says, "how to be abased and how to abound" (Phil. 4: 12). He has also an experience to speak about in the realm of mystic achievement. "I know a man in Christ" (2 Cor. 12: 2f.), he says speaking humbly in the third person, "who was caught up to the third heaven—whether in the body or out of the body I do not know —and he heard things that cannot be told, which man may not utter." As for the soul's inner wrestling with sin, Paul knew its poignancy. "Wretched man that I am," he cries, "who will deliver me from this body of death?" (Rom. 7: 24). But all these meant nothing to Paul, except that they were part of a life lived in obedience to the Gospel, a Gospel which demanded that it be proclaimed, that it be shared, that it be demonstrated. The satisfactions of the religious man belong also to the Christian life, but in the Christian life they are not religious satisfactions. They are signs of Christ's presence with His disciples, tokens of His grace, encouragements on the way, instruments for the doing of His will. The only Christian satisfaction is to have Jesus proclaimed, loved and obeyed. Christian obedience has only one set of co-ordinates: Christ and the world; once this obedience is moved out of this reference it may retain its religious quality but it ceases to be specifically Christian. In the realm of religion, syncretism is the reasonable relation between the religions; it is in the realm of the Kingship of Christ and the Kingdom of God that Christian obedience receives its distinctive quality.

Not the mystic but the missionary is the symbol of Christian discipleship, while the burden of Christian religious living is so to live within this area of common existence with men of all religions that in it may become luminous the true Christian differentia—the presence in the world of the Risen Christ, the ministry through the Church of the Holy Spirit, the proof in the lives of Christian men and women that they represent that event which will mark the consummation of God's redemptive purpose for the world because it has already happened to them.

"I do not consider myself to have 'arrived' spiritually," says Paul. "But I keep going on, grasping ever more firmly that purpose for which Christ grasped me" (Phil. 3: 12f.; J. B. Phillips). That finally is the foundation of Christian obedience: the faith that each man's life with all its achievements, religious and otherwise, will be subject to judgment; the knowledge that in the life of the community of believers the acknowledged reign of God has already begun; the certain hope that Christ at the end will return as Judge and Saviour and the promise proved in the experience of the Holy Spirit that God's Kingdom will perfectly come.

> You are God's "chosen generation", his "royal priesthood", his "peculiar people". It is for you now to demonstrate the goodness of him who has called you out of darkness into his amazing Light. Be ready at any time to give a quiet and reverent answer to any man who wants a reason for the hope that you have within you. If you are reproached for being Christ's followers, that is a great privilege, for you can be sure that God's Spirit of glory, unseen by you, is resting upon you. All power is his for ever and ever, Amen (1 Pet. 2: 9; 3: 15; 4: 14; 5: 11; J. B. Phillips).

Part II
THE ENTERPRISE

1. THE SELF-HOOD OF A CHURCH

2. THE INTEGRITY OF THE MISSION

3. THE WESTERNITY OF THE BASE

The mission of the Church is to prepare for the coming of the Kingdom. The objective of the missionary enterprise is to plant and strengthen churches in all lands and all areas of life. The Christian task includes the necessity of ensuring and increasing the momentum of the enterprise itself.

The world in which the mission of the Church is set and the "nations" among whom the Church is to be and to witness are themselves objects of God's governance and design. Missionary policy and procedures, therefore, must take serious account of the tides and movements of secular history.

No less binding is the action of God within and among the Churches. The ecumenical movement is God's call to the Churches to rediscover their essential togetherness and to seek nourishment from one another as they enter into their several tasks.

The Christian mission to-day demands also that the Churches give heed to the significance of the "No" which has been scrawled across their denominational separateness by the plea of men and of nations to be shown the way of reconciliation and of peace.

Indeed, the summons of the hour is for all Churches to ask their Lord to teach them a humbler way of maintaining their loyalty to truth as they see it—a way which will neither obscure the sufficiency of the reconciliation wrought on Calvary nor exempt Christians from those consequences which must follow the love of the brethren.

I

THE SELF-HOOD OF A CHURCH

THE two realities which, in a consideration of the missionary enterprise, determine the nature of its problems and the ways in which we must seek their solutions are the realities of "church" and "mission". The consequence of mission is the establishing and upbuilding of churches. The purpose of churches is the prosecution and expansion of the mission. To look, therefore, at the questions which need to be dealt with first from the point of view of the Church and then from the point of view of the mission would be what would best serve the purpose of this inquiry. The crucial question from the point of view of the Church is that concerning its self-hood, and from the point of view of the mission that concerning its integrity.

The Discovery of Self

"What is being done to promote self-support, self-government and self-propagation?" This question is central in the order and form of business of every "overseas" Synod of the Methodist Church. The mission had founded the church, and now the church had to become itself. The theological assumptions and practical procedures that lie behind this way of thinking are straightforward enough, but they hardly touch the core of the problem.

Some years ago the Ceylon Government launched a big colonization and irrigation scheme in the eastern part of the country. The question was soon raised about a Christian church in the new living area. Many hoped that the Churches would be able to devise some way of maintaining the congregational unity of the worshipping community in this place, without prejudice to the convictions of the Churches regarding communion and intercommunion. Negotiations had hardly begun towards this end, when a wealthy layman in one Church offered money for a separate church building of his denomination in this place, and a separate congregational life for the members of that denomination. The wish of this layman became fact, and now there are two denominational churches in this place with the Y.M.C.A. as the symbol of their unity. The point of this illustration is not that the decision that was made was right or wrong but that the self-hood of a church does not depend so much on any of its qualifications as on its own awareness of what its self-hood really is.

A church or a Christian community does not make decisions in a theological vacuum. Church decisions are concrete, and their body is of the stuff of this world: so that the self-hood of a church cannot be defined by simply speaking of the freedom of that church to order its own life. It is a mistake to think of a church's self-hood as consisting in being self-governing, self-supporting and self-propagating. These are qualities that belong to the self, but the real need is for a church first of all to find itself, exactly as individuals do, by living face to face with its Creator. God said, "Let us make man in our own image" (Gen. 1: 26). That image-relation is finally fulfilled in the new creation. The image of the divine "we" is in the human "we" created and gathered together in Jesus Christ. "For those whom he foreknew he predestined to be conformed to the image of his Son, in order that he might be the firstborn among many brethren" (Rom. 8: 29).

Thinking about the discovery of the self, my mind went back to my two boys when they were babies. They would say: "Baby wants ball," or I would say, "Does baby want milk?" Baby was an object that could be pointed out. On behalf of this object a request could be made. I would say, "Show Baby", and my son would point to himself. Then suddenly, because it was sudden, Baby spoke and he said, "I want sweets," and my wife said, "You must eat your rice now." The self was the same but it had ceased to be an object to itself. It was no more the self to which relationships were established, rather it established its own relationships. "Baby" had become "I", "It" had become "You". Most of the churches founded by missionary societies found their self-hood in very much the same way. For many decades they were objects. They spoke about themselves and were spoken to in the third person. They were dots on a map of the mission field. Then suddenly church spoke to church. The forms of address became "I" and "You". The churches became themselves.

We are speaking about a church and its self-hood, and we are saying that the self-hood of a church is rooted in its experience of address. The essence of this experience will naturally lie in the way in which a church hears itself addressed by its Lord and knows itself as speaking to Him.

But what do we mean by "a" church? In the New Testament we read of "a" church in three senses. There is first of all a church that gathers in a place for worship. "The church in the house of Prisca and Aquila" (Rom. 16: 5) is simply a worshipping congregation that habitually meets for worship in that house. Secondly, there is a church in a place. There is a church in Corinth (1 Cor. 1: 2), in Jerusalem, in Rome. Here the church is defined by its location. Corinth, Jerusalem and Rome are the result of geography and history, and the Christian community in each of them is a church for them. Thirdly, there is a church where its members share a common life. The church in Caesar's household (Phil. 4: 22) is a church defined by the common occupation of its members. In each of these three modes of being a church must be itself.

Worshipping Community

A church gathered together in worship, speaking to its Lord and being spoken to by Him; that is the basis of a church's self-hood. In the experience of a church this is never absent from the beginning, and on it all growth in self-hood depends. But growth there must be: for increasingly each worshipping group must learn to offer its worship in forms most natural to itself.

Out of the stuff of common life must be fashioned the instruments of worship—whether music or architecture, whether themes of prayer or modes of instruction. This is an area of thought and experiment in which there has been a great deal of clarifying discussion. Worship must be Christian—it must be worship of the Triune God: worship must be indigenous—it must be the natural expression in worship of the culture and common life of the group concerned; worship must be catholic —it must be worship with all the saints and all the company of heaven; worship must be missionary—it must proclaim the Lord's death until He come. In such worship each church must find and be itself.

A Mission to a Place

More controversial questions are involved in the subject of a church and its self-hood when we think of a church not as defined by its worshipping activity but as defined by its location. In his speech at Galyeteto in Hungary, at the meeting of the Central Committee of the World Council of Churches, Bishop Ting spoke of the church in China as having found itself.[1] His point was that China had found itself and that the church in China had discovered that it was the church for China. In what many Chinese call "the Colonial stage of the church," the church's evangelistic attitude was that of Noah's Ark. Individuals had to be converted and brought in. Now the church saw that its task was vastly more; that it was to be a city on a hill that had been raised (Matt. 5: 14), to be the leaven in the meal that had been mixed (Lk. 13: 21). The currents of geography and history give character and name to the location: but by that character and name the church there also is defined. That is its self.

Indeed, it should be part of a church's concern that the nation which it is set to serve should live in freedom. The self-hood of a nation is witnessed to by the authenticity of its

[1] K. H. Ting is a bishop of the Chung Hua Sheng Kung Hui (the Anglican Church in China).

culture, its sense of self-conscious destiny, and the freedom with which it is able to share in the concert of the nations. That a nation attains this self-hood is part of the requirement for a church's full discharge of its mission in and to that nation. According to the teaching of Scripture it is the nations that will be gathered unto Zion (Is. 2: 2; Rev. 21: 26). Unto Israel will come the people of the earth (Is. 54: 1-3). It is also the teaching of Scripture that this gathering of the nations will be through a body of messengers drawn from them (Is. 66: 18-21; Matt. 28: 19; Rom. 1: 5). Whereas, in the Old Covenant the people of God were Israel and the others were the nations, in the New Covenant the people of God are to be found in every nation and for them. That is how the Church's mission is established and prosecuted.

God pursues mankind, the whole of mankind [says Dr Stauffer] with the Gospel of Christ. But the peoples of the world take offence at the Gospel, all the peoples without exception! and even more than this: each people takes offence in its own peculiar way, and has its own grounds for rejecting the word of the Cross, its own reasons for holding back. So each people must find its own specific way through its peculiar hindrance. Every people says its own peculiar "no" to Jesus Christ, crucifies him afresh in its own way—and so comes by its own road to that point of extinction where all self-glory is at an end, and Jesus Christ is the *ultima ratio*. But it is along this road that the inexhaustibility of the Gospel comes to light. For the universality of the Gospel finds its historical expression in the fact that it has something specific to say to each particular people and to its particular questions. So we can say about the operation of the Gospel among the various peoples of the world just what had to be said about its operation in the various epochs of history. It serves the same final purpose: the unfolding of the mystery of Christ to the glory of God the Father.[1]

Dr Freytag, who was Professor of Missions in the University of Hamburg, during his last visit to China warned the Church there about the ambivalent nature of all human history and the forces that go to make it. Commenting on this warning a

[1] E. Stauffer, *New Testament Theology*, Eng. trans. S.C.M. Press, 1955, p. 195.

Chinese Christian leader says, "The members of the Chinese church, after facing many problems and difficulties, are full of faith. They realize that in this new stage in history, in this new social environment, the Chinese church has a special mission, and a special opportunity and a special message. We are like a poet, whose spirit has been deeply moved, and who is searching for suitable words and rhythms to express his musical idea. We are right in the middle of the fierce fires of creation."[1]

A church must first find itself as the church for the nation before it can warn itself of the dangers of its task. A church must become a missionary church, its mission addressed to that locus in the world where it has been set before it can rightly understand the complexity of its missionary vocation. All over East Asia and Africa that is the experience through which the churches are passing now. They have been worshipping communities from the beginning. They have been evangelizing centres for many decades. It is now that they are discovering the true dimension of their missionary task. We often say, "The Church is mission," but we do not always recognize that when we speak in this way we are also at the same time talking of the church in its location.

Let me cite two examples to illustrate the dynamic of this discovery by a church of its self-hood. The nations of the West expanded their empires and their influence all over Africa and Asia in the last two hundred years. The churches of these nations matched this expansion with tremendous missionary endeavour. The inner significance of this congruence is not that the missionary enterprise was an instrument of imperialism, but that even in their imperial outposts the nations of the West were the locus of their churches. The mission of a church to the world is primarily and in the first instance its mission to its world. The task of mission is to possess the promised land, to extend the boundaries of the church to the boundaries of its location.

A first consequence of the attainment of self-hood in the

[1] From "Chinese Christian papers", edited by David Paton (cyclostyled for limited distribution).

churches of Asia is the Church Union movement. The Church in Ceylon cannot be many selves, neither can the evangelistic task in Ceylon any longer side-step the main historical currents and geographical pressures which give to Ceylon its peculiar character. As we seek to fashion a united Church in Ceylon we find ourselves in a strange way wrestling also with the realities of its missionary task. These realities are the realities of the country to whom the mission is.

Let me take these two examples a little further. The missionary movement has its own peculiar function at this time in the history of Western empires. It was a true expression of missionary concern when churches of the United States asked that China be admitted into the United Nations, or when the Student Christian Movement of France condemned the Algerian war, or when Christian voices were raised in Britain for a closer scrutiny of what was happening in Africa and why. On the other hand, it is also a denial of the missionary perspective, when world denominationalism enters into competition with the movement for church unity. Confessions and denominations are the outcome of the Church's struggle for renewal throughout its long history. They provide the context within which the churches, as worshipping communities, must find increasing growth in their apprehension of the Gospel, their expression of worship, and their ordering of church life. But the true context for the Church Union movement is not denominations but nations, not the Church as such but the Church for the world. Denominations and confessions have only a tangential relation to the missionary nature of the church.

Christians in Secular Engagement

We said that "a" church is either a worshipping community, or a church in a place or a group of Christians engaged in a common secular occupation. A church must find its self-hood also in this third form in which it exists. Is there not here a true parallel between the nature of the self when we are talking about persons and the nature of the self when we are talking about churches? There is the self in its essence—the self face to face with God: there is the self in its situation—located and entrusted with mission: there is also the self in its penetration—growing according to the multiplicity of its interests and the variety and depth of its friendships. In this third expression of a church's growth we are speaking, to use a phrase of Bishop Wickham's, about the "secular engagement" of the Church. This is a task which is distinguishable from the missionary task. Leaven leavens the meal, but salt simply flavours or preserves from decay. It does not change anything into salt. The task of mission is the task of leaven, the task of secular engagement is the task of salt (Matt. 5: 13). In the doing of this task the churches have still a long way to go and for the doing of it the churches have still many lessons to learn. Speaking of this aspect of the Church's self and task, and how it is being discharged to-day, Bishop Wickham says: "There is a failure to understand the signs of the times, a failure of vision and perception, stemming from theological error that narrows the claims of God and the concern of the Church from the dimension of the Kingdom to the dimension of 'religion'." He pleads for a method and machinery whereby "awakened Christians can be nurtured and held together in a new order of serious-minded laymen, for a creation of a web of personal relationships the continuity of which is maintained by personal contact over a large area and within large institutions."[1]

As is readily evident this aspect of the self-hood of a church is directly related to the church's life as the life of a people rather than of an institution or organization. A church lives its life as the *laos*—the people of God—within the world in all its various occupations: and its secular engagement must be illuminated by a true concern for the secular. The essential liturgy of the Church is the normal day-to-day work of the people of God. A Christian lawyer must live out his profession within the Christian perspective of justice, a Christian agriculturist must be concerned with obedience to the command of God that man

---

[1] E. R. Wickham, *Church and People in an Industrial City*, Lutterworth Press, 1957, p. 245.

cultivate and conserve the earth, a Christian politician needs to remember that all principality and power is under the sovereign rule of Christ and that human history is history until He come. However, these are not individual tasks, they are the tasks of the Church, of the churches as they exist within the various occupations and professions. How significant, therefore, it also is that in God's providence, when the churches are waking to their responsibility in secular engagement, there should also be present in every country Christian men and women from other countries engaged in so many walks of life. The togetherness of the churches in all their tasks has always been God's great gift to His Church.

A further possibility is also indicated by this task of secular engagement. It is the possibility of voluntary service institutions organized and staffed by Christians and adherents of other religions together. In Ceylon, for instance, as the result of the communal riots in May 1958, there came into existence in a place called Dharmapuram a new colony of families displaced from their original homes. These people needed immediately a dispensary, a school, and a community centre. Practically all of them were Hindus. The churches wanted to serve in this situation. Would it not have been the wisest way for Christians and Hindus to join together to provide a dispensary, a school, and a community centre? Do we not mean by the Church's secular engagement not only the task of Christians in the secular world but also the necessity of Christians fully participating in the creation and maintenance of secular organs of community life? At least speaking of Ceylon, I can say that not syncretism but ghettoism is our chief temptation. It seems normal to remain disengaged and to seek the security that comes from such disengagement.

As Dr Kraemer has said, laymen are to-day the "frozen credits" of the Church; they must become "liquid cash" to spend and to be spent.

> In 1940 [he says] when we had to undertake the task of the renewal of the Church in Holland, how did we set about it? We told them that the renewal of the Church revolved around one

fundamental thing—you have to become what you are and, because you do not know what you are, you do not become anything. So we presented a picture of what the Church is in Jesus Christ, and at every meeting various people would say, "Now I understand. Tell us what we are to do and we will do it." The result is a church to-day in which the spiritual membership is really alive to what the Church has to be, this new life being expressed in an enormous amount of approaches and activities and penetrations into the de-Christianized world about which nobody dreamed in 1940.[1]

"Penetration"—that is the key word, and by it Christian strategy must be determined.

This task of secular engagement has also another implication. It means that the service institutions of the Church should be a true expression of the Church's life as the life of a *laos*—a people. Let me explain. During the pioneer stage of missions, a church on the so-called "mission field" together with all the diverse operations of school, hospital, press and orphanage is administratively an integral part of the total mission. Then comes devolution. The younger church assumes control over its own life in all its parts; and soon the discovery is made that the service institutions of the church which at the "mission" stage were part of the mission have now become buttresses of the church.

Let me again illustrate from the life of the church in Ceylon. A developed school system was a feature of church life here. During the "mission" stage, schools and pastorates were equally parts of and dependent on the "mission". Then the pastorates became largely dependent on the schools for their finance, their leadership, their influence in the general community, and their evangelistic outreach. What was disturbing was not this dependence but the way in which this dependence was made the foundation of the Church's organized life. (In the case of Christian hospitals, the anomaly of their position is even more disturbing. They do not have the financial means to serve the poor; but by serving the not-so-poor they are able to

[1] From an address at a meeting of the National Council of Churches of the U.S.A. held at Buck Hill Falls in 1957.

be buttresses of the local church.) What is needed is for these service institutions to be untwined from the central ecclesiastical organs of the church so that they may have their own independent life, so that they may become expressions of the lay-life of the Church, of the life of the Church as it exists not only for the world but as part of it. (In Ceylon, government action in taking control of most of the schools can prove to be a way to this opportunity.) The younger churches can see what this means by looking at the churches in the West and noticing how plural in administrative structure these churches are. The several expressions of the life of these churches are governed by independent trusts, self-governing societies, communities each with its own constitution and order of life and so on. What a contrast to the situation in most of the younger churches where all activities and forms of life—schools, colleges, hospitals, churches, missions are all organized under one hierarchy of power. Just as the freedom of a nation depends on there being a plurality of centres of power and authority, so also it is for a church. A pyramidal administrative structure covering all forms of the church's life with final authority resident at the apex of the pyramid will in reality soon become a mausoleum.

It is a matter for gratitude that the developments of the welfare state and the socialist state in many of the lands of the "younger" churches are increasingly demanding that the service institutions of the churches should express also in their method of administration the autonomy of Christian service. But it is at the same time a matter for grief that on the whole the churches accept this development with great hesitation and only under governmental pressure. It is time, it is past time, for the "younger" churches to work out the full consequence of their having become churches, of their having ceased to be part of a "foreign mission". It is time, it is past time also, for these churches to realize that institutional buttresses do not rightfully belong to the life of a church. Dr Hogg asks, "Can we not expect the miraculous powers of the Kingdom to be available for the King's messengers?"[1] The answer is, "Certainly we

[1] A. G. Hogg, *The Christian Message to the Hindu*, S.C.M. Press, 1947, p. 65.

can." But we can expect this only as we recognize that we cannot live by faith except in the situation of faith. Peter said to his Lord, "Bid me jump from the boat into the sea" (Matt. 14: 28). Our churches must seek the same command and, when it is given, obey. Once in the sea, amidst the swirling waters, the churches, with Peter, will be saved by their Lord.

Hitherto our discussion has had for its starting point the nature of a church as it is defined by its worshipping life, by its call to mission, and by its task of secular engagement. It is necessary now to broaden this discussion and seek to understand what it means for a church to be itself in relation to other churches. Paul prayed "that with all the saints we might apprehend the love of God" (Eph. 3: 18). This relationship "with all the saints" is not an option that a church can exercise if and when it will: it is an obligation which every church must accept and by God's grace discharge. Some years ago I went to the Roman Catholic Bishop of Jaffna to ask for his participation in a theological conference. "Why don't you leave us alone?" he said. "You know that we shall not arrive at any agreement." My answer was, "Bishop, we cannot leave you alone. We are fellow Christians." He came.

What are the Basic Relationships between the Churches?

The Relationship of "Conversation"

"When we were children of disobedience," says Paul, "we had our conversation therein. But now God has raised us up together and made us sit together in heavenly places in Christ Jesus" (Eph. 2: 3-6). "There is one body and one Spirit, one Lord, one faith, one baptism, one God and Father of us all, who is above all and through all and in all" (Eph. 4: 4-6). This means that the reality which we see in one another as churches is the reality of God's operation in each, and the reality of each church's response to that operation. Hence arises the need to understand another as part of one's understanding of oneself. One of the tasks that the Churches were summoned to by the Faith and Order Conference at Lund was the task of understanding their separate histories as part of one history. To arrive at this understanding conversation is our main instrument. To know ourselves as belonging to and engaged in the same realm of discourse, to speak remembering that when one church speaks to another it is but entering into a conversation already going on between that other and its Lord, to listen realizing that in listening to another church one is but listening to one's own Lord as He speaks through that church—that is the relationship of conversation into which we are called. No church may stand outside this conversation or be allowed for long to stand out. Speaking as from within the fellowship of the World Council of Churches, for instance, it is of paramount importance for our conversation within the Council that our conversation should also be with the Church of Rome, the Orthodox Church of Russia, the Church in China, the Pentecostal Churches throughout the world and so on. Not every part of this conversation is on the same level of intimacy or understanding, but no partner to this conversation may relapse or be allowed to relapse into silence.

Also, a new feature of this relationship in conversation is the creation of fellowships such as the East Asia Christian Conference and the All Africa Church Conference. For decades we in Asia or in Africa have known one another as cousins, children of brothers in the West: but it is only now that we have grown up that we are finding one another attractive. Whatever the sociological or physiological judgment may be on the wisdom of cousins marrying one another, it is theologically the right way for churches. We are witnesses together.

The Relationship of "Belonging"

A second relationship that exists between churches is one beyond the relationship of "conversation". It is the relationship of "belonging". There are two primary forms of this belonging that we must notice. There is the form in which churches of the same denomination or confession belong together in one family with a growing family life, and there is the form in which, in the missionary movement, churches belong to one another in a permanent relationship of help sought and help given. Of special importance for churches in Asia, Africa and Latin America is this relationship within the missionary movement. After all, the very concept of a church's self-hood has been articulated as expressing a qualification of the missionary connection.

When a church in the West sends out missionaries to work in so-called "mission lands" their work develops through three stages. There is the pioneer stage in which the missionary-sending church or society is in full control. Then, with the establishing of the Church on the "mission-field", there takes place little by little a devolution of authority whereby the church that has been established assumes control over its own life. And then comes the stage of expansion: when the church that has been established accepts responsibility for being the church in the land and among the people where it has been established. The pioneer stage, with the "mission" in full control, is over practically everywhere or ought to be, and almost everywhere the churches are at the end of the second stage too. The question is, what should now characterize the continuing relation between the younger churches and the various missionary-sending churches or societies with which these churches have had their missionary connection?

It is futile to answer this question with broad generalizations. It is necessary to deal with specific details if the answer is to be at all helpful. Let me divide these detailed matters into three groups. First, there are the questions which belong to the passing phase of the missionary connection. Secondly, there are the questions which belong to the new phase that is emerging. Thirdly, there are the questions which are implicit in the redefinition that must be given of missions to-day.

The Passing Phase

The questions that arise under this heading are primarily questions concerning personal relationships.

There are the personal questions affecting missionaries. Here, ways must be found of fully trusting a younger church to look after the missionaries sent to it. So-called "Field secretaries" appointed by mission boards should not be needed to perform this function. Of course, this means also that the younger church must learn to accept all the responsibilities that go with asking for and receiving missionaries.

A special problem will be the difficulty caused by the reduction of the number of missionaries which is a necessary aspect of the stage of devolution. Here the need is to see that there are in any case a sufficient number of missionaries so that their point of view on all questions is effectually heard and they themselves have a feeling of social and emotional security.

It is my own conviction that in fact more than half the problems in this area lie in the inadequate concern which we in the younger churches show about the personal problems of the missionaries among us. In an earlier day missionaries when they came were looked after by their older brethren. To-day they must be looked after by us. Let me quote from a letter of a missionary friend to me which puts this question in its real seriousness. He writes:

Where do we missionaries belong? Is ..., London, supposed to be our first loyalty? We are often told that it is and that it must take precedence over every other type of belonging. Surely, if Christ is Lord, and Lord everywhere, the Missionary Society which sent me must be prepared to let me go. Then, there is the other side to this problem that even my Indian friends expect me to belong outside this country. If I need a holiday, if I get cancer, now it is the Missionary Society which compels me to have a holiday, or flies me to England to be cured or die there. My Indian friends are not responsible for me. Is it not time that Bishop Azariah's request at the Edinburgh conference of 1910 "Give us Love" was made again and this time by us foreign missionaries to Indians? You cannot separate love from responsibility, and responsibility is in London.

In a report on the place of the missionary in the African Church, issued by a commission appointed by the Copperbelt

District Church Council, an incident is mentioned in which the first African President of the Synod of the United Church of Central Africa in Rhodesia was evicted from a mission house in order to make room for a missionary's wife and children. This is an excellent example of the double point—the separateness which the missionaries maintain and the lack of responsibility for the missionary which is the attitude of the local church.

Another need which must be met which belongs to the present missionary situation is the need to give to the younger churches an inside knowledge of the missionary operation. The point is that there are so few of us who belong to the younger churches who have an inside and understanding knowledge of the problems that belong to the life and activities of a mission board as it seeks to recruit missionaries, as it seeks to interpret missions to its home constituency, and as it seeks to administer its funds with a sense of full responsibility. If a "relationship of knowledge", to use a phrase of Count van Randwijck's, is to be the relationship between missionary society and the younger church, then younger church participation in the missionary operation is essential at the two ends of that operation. Acknowledgment must be made here of the fact that, already on some mission boards in the West, representatives of the younger churches are being employed and put in positions of executive responsibility.

It should be possible too at this stage of missions to follow in general the block-grant system with respect to financial support.[1] The block-grant (i.e. financial help given with the receiving church having the right to use it at its discretion) represents a relationship of mutual trust between churches that have had a long association together. In Inter-Church Aid, the needs of one church which are presented to another are presented in detail and that other church decides whether it will meet these needs or not. The procedure is all right as an expression of simple helpfulness to designated projects, but where it is a question of a permanent relationship between

[1] A qualification of this position with respect to Institutions will be found in the next chapter.

church and church financial policies must be fully adult. When my boys were children they got some pocket money, for the rest they had to make their pink list and submit it to me.[1] But my wife got a block-grant on which the home was run. Her pink list simply contained extras.

Another very simple point that needs to be observed is that money sent to a younger church should not be distributed through missionaries. Financial support should be a direct church to church operation.

The final point I would make as a point to be remembered in this passing phase of the missionary connection concerns the ways of life of the missionaries themselves. Missionaries are of three kinds. There are those like C. F. Andrews or Murray Rogers in India who learn to live like the people they have come to serve. Such people are naturally few, but they are immensely important. Then, there are those who are the large majority, who live in their adopted lands very much as they would live in their own countries. And then there are those who adopt the ways of life of the people among whom they have come to live, but who are constantly conscious of having done so. It is this third group who are a real botheration. But my plea here is with regard to the second group. It is essential that there should not exist between them and their national colleagues too obtrusive a difference in standards of life.[2] Two things are necessary: that missionaries belonging to different churches and different countries, but who work in the same land, should learn to adopt more or less the same standards of living; and that where for any reason a missionary society needs to give higher pay than the standard adopted demands, then it should be stipulated that only a part of that pay should be spent in the country to which the missionary has come.

An important question, in this connection, which has emerged in the last few years because of the increasing number

[1] The Department of Inter-Church Aid of the World Council of Churches types out the lists of needs of the churches in the various regions on different coloured paper. The colour used for Asia is pink. Hence the use of the term "pink list".

[2] A discussion of experiments along this line made by several missionaries will be found in the book *Adventures in Simpler Living*, by Daniel Fleming, I.M.C.

of representatives of "younger" churches who are going out as missionaries to other lands is the question of the standard of their financial support. Since most of these missionaries are being sent through the established mission boards of the West, and also since in the churches to which they go they have to work alongside missionaries from the West, they are on an equal footing with their western colleagues with respect to their scales of pay. It is inevitable that this situation should give rise to a profound concern. Equalitarianism is a doubtful method of maintaining equality. It is essential to devise a method by which the missionary calling and career make the same demands, both in terms of spiritual commitment and material adjustment, to whosoever from wheresoever decides to be a missionary.

The Emerging Phase

Here the issues are issues of inter-church relationships.

It should increasingly become true that the missionary connection is a connection between churches and not simply a connection between a mission board and a church. Such a change would mean not only a change in relation between a mission board or missionary society and the church or churches in its homeland to which it is related; it would also mean a growing area of life and decision in which two churches missionarily connected increasingly belong together.

Let us take as an example the Methodist Church in Ceylon and the Methodist Church in Britain. The Ceylon Church Union proposals are considered by the Church in Britain, but the Report on conversations between the Church of England and the Methodist Church in Britain are not considered by the Methodist Church in Ceylon. The Methodist Church in Britain appoints a commission to study and draft a statement on "the Missionary Obligation of the Church", but in this study the churches which have a missionary connection with the Methodist Church in Britain are not partners. Or, where rules are being framed as the basis of church discipline is there not need for a much closer consultation between those who have been declared to be partners in obedience? (May I, in an aside, comment here that one of the subjects which is an obvious omission among the concerns of the W.C.C. is this subject of the nature and standards of church discipline.) The inherent weakness of the Whitby formulation about "partnership in obedience" was that this partnership was conceived as finding expression only at one end of the missionary connection. It is not enough to say that partnership at the other end of this connection is ensured by an increasing family life among the churches of the same denomination. World denominationalisms are concerned with getting all the eggs of the same kind into one basket. What is here being pleaded for is for poaching two eggs in the same pan at the same time, so that at least the white of the eggs may mix together. The making of omelettes only the church union movement can achieve.

If partnership is to mean not simply a relation of mutual helpfulness between two partners, but an actual growth into interdependence, then a qualification is immediately necessary of the concept of independent self-hood of the younger churches themselves. It will not do simply to say that on all matters affecting them the younger churches must have complete autonomy of decision, the missionary-sending churches or societies being free either to support the younger churches in carrying out these decisions or to leave them to carry out these decisions on their own as far as they can. True inter-dependence must rule out both the assertion of and the withdrawal into independence. The maturing of the missionary connection must mean that there is a true belonging-together for the sake of the mission. Independent self-hood for the younger church is Dead Sea fruit where that self-hood is attained by a neglect or even a relative neglect of their missionary obligation.

To put into concrete terms what such inter-dependence within the missionary connection would mean, it will be necessary to fashion organs and procedures of partnership whereby there is achieved not simply joint consultation but joint decision on all matters concerning the mission of the church, i.e., on the discharge of the church's obligation to be the church for the people among whom it is set. It will also be necessary for missionaries to be prepared to serve on the frontier of the mission without possessing the freedom or the authority which their missionary forebears working on the frontier had and exercised. And it will be necessary for the younger churches to realize that even now in so many ways it is true that the "foreigner" is one who has the greater chance of success at the "frontier". His very presence is a witness to why he is there.

This accent on partnership points the way also to a solution of the much discussed question—what term shall we use? It is suggested that the term "fraternal worker" be substituted for the term "missionary", because to speak of missionaries recalls to many minds outworn methods of administration and questionable connections with empires. Others find in the word "fraternal worker" an idea "rooted not in the Gospel but in the wrestling of men on the political plane to find ways of mutual help between nations, while assuming the final reality of political frontiers."[1] The essential fact is that when a missionary is given he is given, so that in the church to which he goes he is just a member. He does not need a distinctive label, be it "missionary" or "fraternal worker". As Bishop Stephen Neill argues in his book *Creative Tension*, what is needed is to use the word missionary generally to point to a missionary's distinctive vocation but, in the church, simply to know him by the work it has been given him to do, whether as pastor or evangelist, teacher or doctor.

Are missionaries from the West wanted in Asia or Africa? In an article by Professor Schultz which appeared in the Review of the National Christian Council of India three things are said in answer to this question:—"That missionaries are needed; that missionaries are invited; that, even though invited, missionaries are on the whole not wanted."[2] A different light is thrown on this complex situation by the comment of a missionary who worked in Indonesia who said that there missionaries

[1] From an article on "The Missionary and the Church", by William Stewart, in Indian *N.C.C. Review*, Feb. 1961.
[2] Vol. LXXVI No. 5 (May 1956).

were both needed and wanted but not invited. The Copperbelt Report, already quoted, pleads that "an agreeable way of requesting for missionaries must be found because there seems to be quite a clear understanding by the overseas sending missionary societies that missionaries are invited by the Church." The plea here, according to the evidence summarized in the Report, is for ensuring that an invitation given should in honesty express the mind of the inviting church and not simply the mind of the missionaries who dominate the councils of that church.

This present position is one between a passing and an emerging phase in the history of missions. A truer situation can arise only when attention has been paid to the specific questions which have been mentioned as questions belonging to these two phases. In the meanwhile it is enough that missionaries are needed. As for their not being wanted, or not invited, it is inevitable that this should mean for the present generation of missionaries some sense of disappointment and even unreality; but it is inescapable that part of the cost of the mistakes made in the past should be borne by the present. It is not possible to inherit the glory of the past without also paying for its mistakes. That many of these mistakes had a relative justification in their time is of relevance for a historical understanding of the course of missions, but it has no moral relevance. Mistakes always produce consequences, and there is only one way out of them, the way of repentance and amendment of life.

But this having been said, it is also necessary to say that one main reason why there is a sense of disappointment, and even unreality, felt by missionaries is the absence in a general way of a conviction about "mission". This is true first of all in the younger churches. There is in these churches a conviction about the necessity of preaching the Gospel across the boundary between belief and unbelief, but there is very little passion or expectancy about seeing that boundary crossed. "We need to evangelize but we do not believe that they need to be evangelized." This loss of conviction about mission is present, however, not only in the younger churches. It is present also in the older churches and even among missionaries. Dr Max Warren speaks about the embarrassment to missionary societies caused by the unwillingness of the younger churches to set missionaries free to work on the missionary frontier. It is equally true that large numbers of missionaries are much more anxious to work in established church institutions. (The frustration of a missionary with a research degree teaching in a high school is not a missionary frustration but a human one.) Both in the lands of the younger and the older churches the missionary conviction needs new power before it can sustain the strains involved in the missionary connection. It is a matter for gratitude that the Division of World Mission and Evangelism of the W.C.C. is putting so much thought and consultation into providing a theological underpinning for the missionary conviction which is adequate for to-day. Why must we evangelize? and why must they be evangelized? are two questions demanding an immediate and convincing answer in terms relevant both to the world of religions and the world of nations.

The emerging phase of missions needs also a new financial policy. As immediately as possible the essential structure of church and congregational life in the younger churches must become financially fully self-supporting. A block-grant made towards the financial maintenance of this structure must be so applied as to strengthen this structure rather than support it. Then only can the block-grant cease, whenever and for whatever reason it has to cease, without causing damage. This policy of self-support has also to be followed in the case of ecumenical agencies. There may be some justification for pleading that organizations like the National Christian Council or the East Asia Christian Conference or the All Africa Church Conference should not be allowed to become burdensome on struggling churches, but it is equally true that they must be made fully dependent for their continuance on the faithfulness of the churches in their support. Self-support may not be possible, but when there is not even faithful support it is arguable whether the organization concerned should be carried on with money from outside. In this whole area missionary societies and other agencies must pursue a rigorous policy even when short-sighted self-interest prompts requests for support which those who ask must learn to do without. Speaking as an Asian I would risk the comment that we are not averse to riding in rickshaws when we may just as well walk; but it is still true that we want to be rid of rickshaws.

Already on theological and ecclesiological grounds we have pleaded for the administrative independence of the service institutions of the churches. This independence is also financially sound policy. Grants can be made to these institutions according to their need, but the institutions themselves will depend for their continuity and efficiency not on subsidies received but on having become an organic part of the life of the total community which they serve. It is this organic relation with the community, so necessary for their life, which they are unable to establish without administrative independence. To put it baldly, the service institutions of the church must be parts of the world and not of the church.

Missions Redefined

It is already clear that in talking about missions to-day we are talking about a missionary connection which has now become an inter-church connection. The task of missionary policy is to strengthen and make adult this inter-church connection, to make it a partnership at both ends and to keep it true to its task in mission. This, however, cannot be done unless there is real conviction about the importance and significance of preserving the missionary connection. At the Oxford Consultation of the I.M.C. held in 1958 three qualities were mentioned as belonging to and constituting the missionary essence of this connection:—

  (i) the relation between the partners must be a permanent relationship of knowledge,

 (ii) the financial commitments of the one partner to the other are, in the main, long term commitments,

(iii) while the missionary differentia lies in crossing the

boundary between belief and unbelief, something that is characteristic of missions is lost where the crossing of a geographical boundary is held to be of no qualifying significance.

It seems to me that all these three points are of real and crucial importance. First of all, what are some of the things that are involved in a permanent relationship of knowledge? The main implication surely is that not only are two partners comitted to one another; but also the missionary call itself is heard, at least by most of the missionaries concerned, as a call to become part of another people. A generation ago when a missionary offered to come to one of the mission lands, his offer was to live in it for a substantial part of his working life, to accept its people as his people in Christ, to serve them in His name and to belong to them. To-day, this form of the missionary calling is under question. Indeed, the very use of the term "fraternal worker", intended as it was to avoid difficulties arising from the use of the word "missionary", has distracted attention from the nature of the missionary calling and centred it upon the conditions of partnership. That this shift has taken place no less in those churches where the word "missionary" is still in use is a sign of the acuteness of the issue. What is needed is the clear recognition that behind and beyond all questions of partnership is the given fact that the Lord is calling and sending missionaries from one land to another. The problems which arise are the result of a *fait accompli*. God poses the problem as to what we shall do with the missionaries He sends.

Some years ago I was talking to a missionary lady in Ceylon about this problem. She listened to me for some time and replied, "All that you are saying is that some of us missionaries are queer people. Don't you see that if we were not queer we would not have been missionaries at all?" There is a fundamental sense in which the challenge to the younger churches to-day is to welcome and use the missionaries whom the Lord sends. It was true that when the younger churches were in the process of growing up they had to talk a great deal about the kind of missionaries they wanted; but now they have grown up and ought to be able to use all kinds, befriend all kinds and deal with all kinds. The only thing we in the younger churches ask from our missionary brethren is that we be treated as adults. If you think differently from us on any question, speak and make your point; if you feel that we need rebuke, rebuke and don't pull your punches; we are not children. Let us agree on an adult relationship. The reverse of this is equally true. Nothing is more disconcerting for us in the younger churches than to have around us missionaries whom we must treat tenderly because they get emotionally upset so easily, or find the weather too trying, or get "frustrated"—that blessed word which is now used to describe the mental condition in which a missionary is either because his wife insists on a "fridge" for the house, or because his national colleague does not have a sense of humour. Certainly there are cases where the sources of frustration lie deeper, where a missionary asks to be used missionarily and is not, or where a missionary finds himself out of sympathy with decisions which he has to carry out. But the issue is still that mutual understanding is lacking and that not only do missionaries need to be understood but also to understand.

Count van Randwijck pleads for the creation of a group in the younger churches who will be to the younger churches whatever missionary societies are to the older. He says:

> The creation in the younger churches of specialist agencies and specialists for missions might be a normal development analogous to the history of the missionary movement in the churches of the West. There was no reason why a re-adjustment of this kind should necessarily entail a loss of mission-mindedness among younger church leaders. But by creating special missionary agencies the younger churches might perhaps further mutual understanding between those who, both in younger and in older churches, are under instructions first of all to be responsible for the missionary cause.[1]

This suggestion is worth pursuing. But a more radical need is to find a way of overcoming the main difficulty which long term

[1] I.M.C. Oxford Consultation, 1958: Report, p. 44.

missionaries have to face, that of the education of their children. Is it unthinkable that there would be a response to a call for celibate missionaries? In any case it is absolutely certain that as long as the discussion about "missions" is dominated by discussions about the usefulness or otherwise of short term missionaries so long "missions" cannot recover their true dignity. At the heart of "missions" is the call of God saying, "Go from your country to the land that I will show you" (Gen. 12: 1). It is not simply a missionary society but the missionary himself or herself who is called to a permanent relationship. There can be no other way by which identification is achieved. The sacrifice involved in such identification has been and will always be the glory of "missions".

Speaking of parish priests in industrial areas, Bishop Wickham pleads: "No missionary policy in the parishes would have any chance of success without a halt to the present rapid movement of the clergy." I too can speak about this from my own experience and observation as a Methodist minister. We are proud to be an itinerant ministry but the result is that we have become a professional class who are rarely called upon to pay the price of identification. Here is our call and the measure of our obedience, whether missionary or local pastor, that unless we are identified with the people we serve—and identification takes time—we shall be able to render only professional service.

The second quality of the missionary connection is that of long term financial commitments. Here the contrast is with the Inter-Church Aid pattern of giving which is year by year. But more is involved in this contrast than just this difference. The financial commitments of missionary societies are based on long term policies which are related to missionary strategy.

A word at this point about these policies will not be out of place. There are two things which missionary societies are doing increasingly as part of their financial policy but which need a greater thoroughness of execution. There is their support of union ventures where several denominations working in the same place come together to run a theological college or some similar institution. But not all missionary societies or denominational agencies accept the priority of these ventures. In a paper to a Student Christian Movement Conference in New Zealand, the Rev. Alan Brash gave two examples of such contrary policy. "Recently," he writes, "a mission of a very respectable Church in the West offered an equivalent of $75,000 to a poverty-stricken Church in an Asian land to build a Theological College, provided the Western Church still retained the ownership, and provided every teacher in the College signed a profession of faith dictated from the West every year." Again, "In one Asian country a western group came out to build a Christian Radio Station. They found a good one already in existence and as a group they approved it. But the folk back home wanted one with their label on it, so now there is a competing station in opposition to the first, all in the name of Christ!"

Through various conferences of missionary societies common policies are agreed upon; but again and again it becomes clear that this common consultation among mission boards is not geared to a common consultation among their related younger churches. Student work is a notorious example of this lack of co-ordination. Sometimes missionary societies are willing to support a unified strategy in student work in a particular country but the churches in that country desire to go separately, and sometimes it is the other way round. There is need everywhere and at all levels to insist that the making-more-visible of the Church's unity should control missionary financial policy.

With regard to the Inter-Church Aid pattern of financial support, it has seemed to me that the real potential of this operation for the future, as far as the lands of the younger churches are concerned, lies in the help that it can bring to the lay-life of the Church. As Christian laymen engage in forms of Christian service and witness which are organized independently of ecclesiastical control, i.e. control by the official courts of the churches, such forms will need support and strengthening particularly in their initial stages. At present, in large measure, the Inter-Church Aid operation is not dissimilar to the missionary operation. Both run through official channels.

Hence the necessity of clearing the lines lest these trains running on the same rails collide. Inter-Church Aid must look forward to laying down new rails to new stations and the names of these stations will often have to be not the names of Churches or of Christian Councils or of projects run by them. The fact will also have to be faced that not all forms of Christian witness which can be helped financially from outside to great advantage will ask for that help. The Ashram in Ceylon is a case in point.[1] In other words the Inter-Church Aid operation will have to develop its own relationship of knowledge. It must also take greater initiative in helping experiments that are both unofficial and have not yet even proved themselves.

The third quality of the missionary connection is concerned with the boundary to be crossed. As we have already said, missions of an earlier time did cross geographical boundaries but most of them operated within the area of political influence of their countries of origin. Now, however, with conscious and aggressive nationhood everywhere missions face the real challenge of "foreignness". Yes, with churches everywhere, "the home base" of the missionary enterprise is everywhere in the world. But what is of equal significance is that to-day, when churches cross their geographical boundaries, they not only meet with sister-churches with whom they will engage in mission, but they also find themselves in an alien land and an alien culture which is defiantly free and consciously itself. A missionary from another country working in China to-day will be truly engaged in a foreign mission: nor will this be less true should a missionary go from Indonesia to Holland.

In fact, the necessity of the foreign missionary is a universal necessity. As Dr James Matthews said at the I.M.C. consultation, Oxford 1958, "Because we have come to terms with our own society, the total word of God has to be declared to us by another." "A missionary," said the Rev. R. K. Orchard at the same consultation, "may reach the world outside through

[1] The Christa Seva Ashram in Jaffna, Ceylon, was founded twenty years ago. It is an attempt at a Protestant adaptation of the monastic life within a Hindu environment.

another church or be sent to the 'non-church' but he is not sent to another church. A church must be involved beyond its own culture; there should be witness to the 'foreignness' of the people of God as a whole in the world." To be foreign—that is part of the nature of every church, and by no other function does a church so fully realize or exhibit this foreignness as by being missionary beyond its borders. The missionary enterprise is an enterprise of the churches but it constitutes the ambassadorial service of the Kingdom.

The Relationship of Oneness

We have spoken about churches in their relationship of "conversation". We have spoken about them in their relationship of "belonging". We must speak about them now in their relationship of "oneness". The Church is one and it is within this oneness that the churches have their life and being. The missionary movement realized and expressed this oneness of the Church in mission. The missionary movement was the result of the conviction that all churches had as their common and primary responsibility the task of taking the Gospel wherever it was not known or believed. And in this common task the churches sought and found one another. To-day we speak about the ecumenical era and by that we mean that the churches have come to recognize that their oneness is the basis of their whole being. They do not just come together to perform a common task; in their togetherness is the very dynamic for this task.

The discipline of love and understanding involved in the search to make the Church's unity more visible is the very discipline which will imbue the churches with power to prosecute their mission. The evangelizing community is the fellowship of the Holy Spirit; and by this fellowship of the Holy Spirit we mean nothing else and nothing less than the churches in their oneness. An equal truth is that the Holy Spirit at work in the world is what makes the very mission of the Church possible. Were not the Holy Spirit besieging every soul, were not the Holy Spirit controlling the currents of history, were not the Holy Spirit gathering the nations—nothing which the churches can do would make any difference. All history, that of the Church and that of the world, is set towards this end. A world in travail to find its peace, a church in travail to find its unity: these are the two explosive realities whose dynamic produces and supports the ecumenical movement and gives meaning and direction to its missionary concern.

It has been said that "missions" have as their double perspective the "ends of the earth" and "the end of time". We have seen what it can mean to speak of the "ends of the earth" as a quality of missions. What does it mean to speak of the "end of time"?

First, that we do not know when that end is and that therefore missions are charged with urgency. To-day is the day of salvation (2 Cor. 6: 2). It is morning now. The night comes when no man can work (John 9: 4). Secondly, this experience of the significance of the "now" as the *arrabon* of the "not yet" sets for the mission of the Church its double goal (Eph. 1: 4). When time is over, the nations will be gathered into Zion; therefore must the Gospel be first preached as a witness among the nations before the end comes. When time is over the Church will be ready as a bride for her bridegroom (Matt. 24: 14), therefore even now must the bride be engaged in her wedding preparations (Rev. 21: 2). To speak of the "end of time" as part of the perspective of mission is to be committed to a strategy of mission that accepts the visible unity of churches as one of its goals, and the penetration of every nation in its national and cultural life by the Gospel as its main endeavour.

The World Council of Churches

The self-hood of a church is its self-hood as a worshipping community. It is its self-hood as the church in and for a place. It is its self-hood in the width of its secular engagement. This self-hood grows in relationship with other selves: in the relationship of "conversation", in the relationship of "belonging", and in the relationship of "oneness".

The World Council of Churches integrated with the International Missionary Council is the most significant expression of this growth of the churches together into self-hood. It is the instrument of the resolve to be churches together in the World. It is to be the means by which the churches enter into a meaningful participation in the missionary task of the Church. Here must be devised the procedures by which the churches shall ensure that they listen to one another, here must be devised the organs through which the churches shall help one another. And what is true for the World Council of Churches is true in their own measure for the various regional developments within the ecumenical movement. The way forward is certainly beset with many difficulties. But whatever the temptations and the trials on the way, they are truly blessed whose temptations are where the Holy Spirit has led them. It is written of our Master that "He was led by the Spirit into the wilderness to be tempted by the devil" (Matt. 4: 1).

THE INTEGRITY OF THE MISSION

WHENEVER and wherever I see a missionary I am aware that I am seeing a person who is away from home because of the Gospel of Jesus Christ. The missionary reminds me that I too, in my own homeland, am a sojourner (Ps. 39: 12), and that the Gospel which took him away from his country is a Gospel which can never become domesticated in my own. The Christian faith will always remain a faith which must arrive from outside because it is pegged down in history to one place and one time, and even there it was rejected and cast out. "Born of the Virgin Mary, crucified under Pontius Pilate"—there is no escape from the geographical and historical particularity which belongs to the Gospel of Jesus Christ.

The missionary is also evidence that the event in which God visited the world at a particular time and place is an increasing event. As with a rocket thrown into the sky at a fireworks display, the first burst only signals a beginning; there will be many bursts to follow, and at every burst the night will be sprayed with stars. The missionary is the result of the continuing explosion of the Gospel. Often the missionary is spoken of as a person who takes Jesus Christ to other lands and peoples; in reality he is someone whom Jesus takes and gives as His gift of love to those to whom He goes.

Jesus called God's vast enterprise "the Kingdom of God". Of this Kingdom He spoke to His disciples during the forty days between His resurrection and ascension (Acts 1: 3), and to this Kingdom He consecrated their purpose and endeavour. The missionary movement is the on-going result of this consecration: it prepares the visit of the King, it announces His arrival, it becomes the chariot in which He arrives.

Many have said that the unresolved question which characterized the thinking of the Willingen assembly of the I.M.C. was concerning the relation between salvation-history and secular-history and how this relation determined the nature of the Church's mission to the world. A practical illustration of the importance of this question is that a missionary society secretary explaining how missionary policy should be made uses it as his determining consideration. "The method to apply," he writes, "is to take the history of our time seriously, to have in some fashion a prophetic interpretation of history, and to plan accordingly."[1] In other words, the Church's obedience in mission is to be conceived in terms of what the Lord is doing in history, and both have to be seen in relation to the coming of that Kingdom which is what history is about.

The significance of the current word "ecumenical" is that it points to this truth. When at the Ghana assembly of the I.M.C. the study was projected of which this book is one result, the question for study was formulated as follows: "What does it mean in theological terms and in practice in this ecumenical era for the Church to discharge its mission to the world?" The use of the phrase "ecumenical era" testifies to the fact that the whole world is now one world; and that the Church's task is directed towards it. This is the accepted use of the word *oikoumene*. It designates the whole and that part of the whole which gives it distinction. The Greeks used the word to mean the whole inhabited world, and also the civilized and civilizing world of the Hellenes. In the New Testament the *oikoumene* is the whole world and the kingdoms therein (Lk. 4: 5). God made it and rules over it (1 Cor. 10: 26), and to it the Gospel of His Kingdom is proclaimed (Matt. 24: 14). In the words of Gregory of Nyssa, "The foundation of the Church is as it were the foundation of an *oikoumene*." The Gospel is proclaimed by it and, by that proclamation, the whole *oikoumene* receives its significance. In the Roman empire the unity of the *oikoumene* was said to be in the emperor, in the one world of to-day there can be no unity apart from its Lord, Jesus Christ.

[1] M. A. C. Warren; from a paper presented at a Conference held in Toronto, Oct. 17-18, 1958.

To speak, then, of the Church's mission in this ecumenical era is to affirm the faith that this mission is addressed to this world, and that this world with its history affords the context within which questions about the mission should be considered.

In the ensuing discussion on the integrity of the mission, therefore, it is necessary constantly to be aware of the temptation to treat the many questions concerning the missionary enterprise as a set of problems to be solved; and to think that, when they are solved to the satisfaction of those concerned, that in itself is enough. Nothing would have been gained if answers which were allowed to satisfy those engaged in the discussion did not meet the requirements of the mission itself. Indeed, the Gospel being what it is, it is to be expected that we shall find it impossible to maintain the integrity of the mission without the mission remaining a problem all the time. This is all the more clear now that secular history has destroyed the original expectation which lay behind modern missions that by them the world would become progressively Christian.

It will be found that a number of the issues raised here have been raised also in the previous chapter, but this overlapping is deliberate. It is when a problem is looked at from the point of view of the Church as well as from the point of view of the mission that it becomes possible to see the true way forward.

There are five facets to this total discussion which may be distinguished and treated separately. They are:—

(1) the place and role of Christian people,
(2) the place and role of Christian institutions,
(3) the place and role of financial assistance,
(4) the place and role of the ecumenical relation,
(5) the place and role of the missionary involvement.

The Place and Role of Christian People

The Rev. Douglas Thompson, General Secretary of the Methodist Missionary Society, writing on the expansion of Methodist missions, sets forward two facts as explaining this expansion.

One key to the riddle of expansion [he says] is the word "spontaneity". Our ancestors knew this and there is a wealth of meaning in their watch-word, "What hath God wrought". They were constantly awe-struck and amazed by the expansion of the movement and never quite caught their breath—except perhaps when they sang, "See how great a flame aspires, kindled by a spark of grace", which they probably did to keep their courage up when frightened by grace. Indeed the fire was out of human control, and never was in ecclesiastical control at any time. The second principle of expansion appears to be that the Believer opened the door, the Preachers then entered it and both expanded and consolidated the gains. A correspondence between Dr Coke and a gentleman in Moldai, Bengal, is typical. The gentleman urged Coke to establish a Mission in the hill country of Bengal. Coke in his answer wrote: "Somebody informed me that you have a little company or Society of Christians consisting of sixteen or eighteen at Moldai. The full confirmation of this would give me great pleasure. Who knows but you may be a little leaven to leaven a great lump; the little hand rising out of the sea, that will in time water the whole land" (Arminian Magazine, 1792). The astute mind of Coke saw that were it the case that a lay-founded group already existed under "the Gentleman of Bengal", his own condition for testing whether the work was of God would have been fulfilled.[1]

What is true of Methodism has been true everywhere. Many a Church in Africa began with the work and witness of a lay believer. The Tamil Christian plantation-coolie has taken the Gospel with him into all the lands where he has gone. After the last war, when the Japanese occupation was ended, in so many of the lands of East Asia the returning missionaries found strengthened and spreading Churches which were the result of the faithfulness of ordinary Christians. Whatever missionary work may be going on in any place, the integrity of the mission is lost where the Christian community in that place is itself not missionary. To use a phrase of Christoph Blumhardt—"the sheep is for the wool".

One of the directions in which one must look for a strengthening of the missionary cause is that of a renewed dedication

[1] *Friends of Reunion* Bulletin, January 1961, pp. 20-22.

among the laity to the apostolic privilege of Christian witness. There are many things happening which are part of this renewal. There is first of all the quest to understand the significance of the secular. This includes an understanding not only of the secular nature of the Church but of the secular nature of the World. A layman is a person for whom in the world as well as in the Church things exist as things. They have their own validity and do not need to be justified by their relation to the religious. Then, there is the theological concern to discover the full implications of being a layman, a member of the people of God. Together with this goes the determination to understand the nature and function of the ordained ministry as something provided to maintain the lay character of the Christian community. From this arises the hope of so de-professionalizing the ordained ministry by disentangling the threefold functions of prophet, priest and pastor, that these functions will not necessarily be bound up together in one person, but will be seen as the functions of the Church which the Church fulfils through different persons and in several ways.

A second direction in which one must look for the strengthening of the missionary cause is that of a development in unofficial initiative in forwarding the Christian mission. One of the weaknesses, particularly among the younger churches, is to be too dependent on action by the official courts of the Church. In this connection, such organizations as the Y.M.C.A., Y.W.C.A., and the W.S.C.F. have an important part to play. A sign that this development is well on its way can be seen in the increasing number of Christian community houses or ashrams which are springing up in all parts of the world; the several ways in which Christian students are participating in the work of Christian witness—as for instance in the sit-in demonstration in the southern states of the U.S.A., or the strong participation of Christian students in the recent student demonstrations both in Korea and Japan; and, what perhaps is most significant, the impatient desire of so many Christian students in universities to give at least the first years of their young manhood and womanhood to manifesting the Christian presence on some frontiers of the Church's advance. The following quotation from a letter of a young Australian couple written towards the end of a short missionary term is typical:

We are enquiring as to avenues of service as viewed by the Church, as within its world mission strategy—particularly as envisaged by W.C.C. and E.A.C.C. We do not feel inclined to man a dying mission enterprise somewhere where there happens to be a vacancy—pegs to fill a vacant hole. We feel that most of the medical mission enterprises belong to the past and it is better that they be handed over to governments. This means that the Church's role will be more and more to advise where Christian laymen (doctors and others) should seek employment—by governments or other agencies—in order to be strategically placed to undergird needy churches. This applies to foreigners and to indigenous Christian lay leaders alike on all frontiers—and there are frontiers everywhere in Africa, Asia and the Pacific to-day. The frustrations of work here are such that one always wonders whether it is worth while. In the end the only answer is that it is worth while because we have done it for Christ's sake. For the government's sake, and even for the sake of the people around us whom we seek to serve, the question is only answerable with a hesitant query at best. But we are willing to do for Christ and for the Church things which for government's sake or even for the sake of fellow men we would perhaps not undertake.

Arising from discussion at Student Christian Conferences held in 1960, both in Europe and in the U.S.A., a plan for "frontier internships" in mission was presented both to the Administrative Committee of the I.M.C. at St Andrews and to the General Committee of the World Student Christian Federation meeting at Salonika, and was accepted by them.

The proposal called for small ecumenical teams of carefully selected people to engage in Christian witness of study and action in a particular frontier for two to three years. Sharing a common discipline and a subsistence standard of living, the team would seek to reach out and witness to their total local environment. The interns would try to share their understanding of the Mission of the Church with church members by participating in the life of local congregations. An experienced person in each situation would counsel the team and help them relate their work to the on-going work of the Church. The initiative to begin such a project would be, however, the responsibility of the churches or National Christian Councils. Pilot projects and interns would be sought in Africa, Asia and Latin America as well as in North America and Europe so that the internship program will be genuinely ecumenical, international, and reciprocal among the churches.[1]

There is a third direction in which one must look for a strengthening of the missionary cause, and that is through the programmes of stewardship and evangelism which are seeking to renew the congregational life of Christian people. We think we are owners of all that we possess; we find that when we are converted to God in Christ we have also been changed from owners into tenants. The inevitability and significance of this change of status must be driven home as part of every evangelistic message. It is futile to speak about being saved by the Cross, when at no point of one's life has the Cross been allowed to fall athwart natural ambitions and desires. The Cross that saves must be planted within the life of the person to be saved. The evangelistic message must crash home with specific obligations.

A popular measure that is being adopted everywhere in order to renew the life of the churches is to invite a missioner to conduct a mission. Useful and effective as this may be, there is one fact which must be remembered. A Christian community that seeks to conduct a campaign of mass evangelism needs to be already involved in service to the world in the situation in which it is set. Where a Christian community is an ingrown one then a programme of mass evangelism will only distort the Gospel in the eyes of those outside. Mass evangelism rarely turns an ingrown Christian community into an outgoing one.

I have a feeling that there will be many who will read these paragraphs and say, "What a perfect grasp of the obvious!" Why not? for however obvious it may be, still the root of much missionary weakness lies in the life of Christian congregations. These congregations go on and increase in their several activi-

[1] Quoted from *World Mission*—the I.M.C. newsletter—October 1960.

ties. They are prosperous churches—only this proves nothing. Sodom and Gomorrah would have gone on in peace and prosperity had there been only ten righteous men among them.

The Place and Role of Christian Institutions

Christian institutions as an integral part of a Church structure is a phenomenon peculiar to the younger churches in Asia, Africa and Latin America. These schools, colleges, hospitals, agricultural institutes and the like were conceived as part of the Church's mission and had three objectives: the nurture of the Christian community, the service of the world, and the commendation of the Gospel. But the problem to-day is that two developments have taken place which have created an ambiguity as to what a Christian institution really is and what it is meant to do.

The first development is what has been variously called devolution or integration. When action was taken to recognize the fact that "the mission" had become "the Church", most missionary societies followed one of two policies. There were those who separated the congregations and everything that belonged to congregational life from the institutions. The former were called "the Church" and the latter "the mission". This meant that a doubtful apologia had to be put forward to justify the institutions as mission, and there was evolved the category of what came to be called "indirect evangelism". This became a source of perplexity to colleagues who were not Christians who worked in these institutions, to mission supporters in the sending churches, to the skilled workers who had to vindicate their work in terms other than their skills, and to missionary evangelists who were made to feel that it was not enough to be evangelists unless they were also engaged in some form of service. In a trenchant article on this subject, William Stewart, the principal of Serampore College, has this to say:

> May it not be that it is the very hand of God which is forcing us to re-think a policy which held a fallacy in the very heart of it? He is telling us by our sheer failure that we have been confusing

the fruit of the Gospel with the means of proclaiming it. Service in Christ's name is the fruit of the Spirit. We have been offering men "all these things" in the faith that somehow or other the Kingdom would be added to them. So the hand of God is laid upon it all to overturn this unreal structure, to warn us that not by this means will men be brought to salvation. This service is altogether not the Gospel of God and was never meant to be used as a means to an end. There is indeed something intolerably arrogant about the very thought that we can plan or execute a piece of work which by its own quality will demonstrate the Gospel. It is a thought from which we recoil with dismay when we realize the implications of it, and this all the more so when we remember the pitiful failures of our work, spoilt so often by selfishness, pettiness and jealousies, which sometimes men of other faiths must come and help us mend.[1]

But why did it happen that institutions came to be called "the mission"? Because they were dependent on funds and trained personnel from abroad. The churches had to be self-supporting. But just here arose the problem that inasmuch as the institutions were the channels for funds, the missionaries were felt by the local churches to have retired upwards rather than sideways—to use the colourful phrase of John Taylor—remaining still in the position of power. It also produced the unfortunate consequence that young missionaries with excellent academic qualifications but of spiritual and personal immaturity had to be put into positions of authority in these institutions. "The worst thing about this practice is that it is bad for the missionaries themselves," was the comment of a young African in a consultation on this subject. "A young missionary," says Charles West, "coming out at the age of twenty-five or twenty-six, having been trained in one of the Western seminaries, had a body of knowledge which gave him a theological authority which did not correspond to his insights into the situation, to his wisdom or to anything else about him. Here was a false relationship already in the realm of expounding Christian doctrine."[2]

---

[1] Quoted from an article in the *Scottish Journal of Theology*, March 1953, pp. 47-48.

[2] Quoted from a speech delivered at a course for missionaries and pastors held at Bossey, July 1-15, 1959.

But this policy of splitting up the Christian work into "the Church" and "the mission" was not the only policy followed. There was also the policy of devolving the whole work on "the Church" and of supporting "the Church" as such with missionary funds and personnel. (Indeed, even where the original action was to split up "Church" and "mission", this was soon followed by a process of integration where both were brought together.) The mischief caused by this form of devolution or integration was to transfer to the Church the administrative procedures and set of mind which characterized the original mission. The service institutions which were part of the mission became the buttresses of the Church and an expression of its secular power and influence.

Radical action is now needed to deliver the younger churches from this situation. The action must be radical enough both to preserve the usefulness and Christian distinctiveness of these service institutions as well as to lift their burden from the local church. "The national church," writes a Christian leader from Pakistan, "is handicapped financially and otherwise to run these white elephants, and the missions are running them at a very high premium of finances and personnel."[1] The action must be radical enough also to remove every excuse for the missionary to sit loose to the local church. There was no point at which African voices were more unanimous or more persistent than this one: that missionaries were too much "apart" from the church and in many instances were even the centre of exclusive white congregations. "Sunday is 'apartheid' day in Africa" was the comment of a young African Christian in a student group discussing this question. A true solution of this issue about Christian institutions must also point the way to a true integration of "mission" and "church". There must be no need to complain, a complaint still too common in Africa particularly, that so many missionaries, because they work in institutions, do not learn the language of the people and that often they do not even seem interested in the life the people live.

[1] Inayat Masih, from a paper presented at a Conference held at Nasrapur, Oct. 13-20, 1960.

The only kind of radical action adequate to this situation is action that will deal directly with the institutions themselves—their place, their support and their control: and, within this new framework, find solutions for the other consequential problems. Missionary administrators have recently proposed what have been called "area consultations for joint action in mission", in which consultations full account will be taken of the nature and forms of the total Christian enterprise in an area in order to map out for that area future lines of Christian advance.

This approach will mean a series of strategy consultations, held area by area, in which all denominations working in the area collaborate—both the leaders of the churches as well as leaders of mission boards related to these churches being present—so that common decisions might be arrived at as to which were the institutions that need to be strengthened to serve as training institutions; which were the institutions, and what was the programme needed, for the nurture of the Christian Church and the life of its community; and which were the institutions and what were the programmes that were expressions of the service of the Church to the world.

Agreement must then be arrived at with respect to the support of these institutions. (i) With regard to the support of training institutions—theological, medical, teacher training and so on—arrangements must be made for increasing co-operation among the various denominations. (ii) With regard to those institutions and programmes that are concerned with Christian nurture such as centrally located schools, colleges, hostels, and all activities in the realm of religious education—these must be farmed out for support among the various denominations. (iii) With regard to all service institutions, these must become the care of Christian groups who are willing to support and engage in that service. These groups can seek support from mission boards and foundations following procedures similar to those at present employed in the Department of Inter-Church Aid of the World Council of Churches.

The thought behind the suggestion made above with respect

to service institutions is that these institutions should now be devolved completely on the Christian community and not wedged into the administrative machinery of the Church. If the Christian community concerned is not willing to undertake to run a particular service institution, let that institution be closed down; and let every Christian group which puts its shoulder behind any project be free to develop that project in the way it wants. Centralized control and direction cannot be the method of healthy growth for the life of Christians in society.

If this pluralism in the life of the Church is to be achieved, this sprouting here and there of Christian community life in the service of the world, it is essential to maintain certain principles. First of all, Christian service institutions must be guarded against becoming means of secular power for the Church. Secondly, an institution may be useful without being an expression of Christian diakonia. Such an institution must be turned over to the general community and not carry the distinctive label—Christian. Thirdly, the role of Christian service and the forms it must take must be thought through in relation to the social goals of government policy and the provisions of the Welfare State.

The essential consideration always must be that the mission of the Church is not obscured. There must be no doubt in anybody's mind, even the mind of the outside observer, as to what the Church is for. All occasion for people to think that the value of the Church is instrumental to the realization of human hopes and needs must be removed. The instrumental functions of the Church must somehow point to its real nature as the sign and guarantee of God's presence among men.

The Place and Role of Financial Assistance

Not only is it true that the mode of financial assistance given to Christian institutions must not destroy their integrity as expressions of the Church's mission, but it is also true that the whole scheme of financial assistance from abroad as it is given to the younger churches must be subject to certain common principles and policies which are relevant to the present situation.

It has already been argued that service institutions conducted by the Christian community must by nature and execution remain autonomous and dependent directly on the faithfulness of the Christian community concerned. Help from outside can then be solicited on a project basis. It may be contended that this is a backward step from the present practice of block-grants where the receiving Church itself decides how to spend the money it receives. But such an argument would be based on a determination to maintain the present relationship between the Church and Christian service institutions. It is against the maintenance of this relationship that we are pleading. What is necessary is so to set free these institutions that there is also restored to missionary societies their freedom with respect to them. It is unthinkable that missionary societies and mission boards should become passive agencies recruiting personnel and raising funds at the behest of the receiving churches. The project method of asking and receiving will ensure partnership in decision-making.

But, on the other hand, if this project method of asking and receiving is to be fruitful, the operation must have about it a very great deal of decision by discretion. When individuals and groups are engaged in all kinds of Christian activity all over the place, it is neither possible nor desirable to set up official channels through which all requests must go or be granted. A major part of this operation of help must take place through official channels, but there must be an increasing possibility for the exercise of individual discretion. A small gift here and a small gift there may make all the difference. Decision by discretion may have to be restricted to small gifts, but provision must be made for such decision. Already the Division of World Mission and Evangelism of the W.C.C. has provided for the operation of a discretionary fund by its Divisional Secretary, and there is a similar discretionary fund at the disposal of the Department of Inter-Church Aid of the W.C.C.

There are two other factors which are relevant to this discussion which are crucial enough to be listed here. The first factor concerns the autonomy of the Church, and the second concerns its dividedness.

It must always be remembered that a church is a church from the very beginning and that, therefore, from the very beginning it must be itself. There should be no question of a church being granted autonomy. What is possible and necessary will be for churches to agree among themselves as to how they may help one another. If this be so, will it not then be true that the one way for a church to grow in autonomy will be by complete self-support with respect to the financial cost of its workers?

There is no plea here for self-support as a principle. The plea is that a church must make financial provision for its workers out of its own life. To-day, in South India, there is a great deal of discussion about an unpaid ordained ministry and a permanent diaconate. This discussion would have taken place a hundred years ago if mission funds had not then been available to pay church workers. It may be objected that even if this were so it is impossible for a church to retrace its steps. That is only partially true. Indeed, the continuation of the present arrangements for the ordained ministry in so many of the younger churches is the result of the cushioning effect of mission grants. Let every church devise its own leadership and pastoral structure. Theological and liturgical truth can be enshrined within different financial arrangements. So will there be ensured true growth and organic increase. At present, in so many ways, the availability of funds from outside is making possible the erection of pandals[1] which have no relation to the main house; but where the ordained ministry itself is such a pandal, the integrity of the mission is seriously compromised.

It may be that the point is here made in too sweeping a fashion, and that there is a case for some subsidies towards workers' salaries in order to ensure for the churches concerned workers with higher professional training. But, true as this may be, the general effect of past financial policy has been to

[1] An *ad hoc* structure of wooden poles and thatch.

superimpose on the younger churches a professional class of church workers cut to a pattern that has become the accepted pattern in the West. Pentecostal Churches in Asia, Africa and Latin America have shown that this is not at all necessary.

The second factor, which is that of the Church's dividedness, has many consequences. There is a disparity of resources between various countries, and the effect of this disparity is heightened by denominational differences. The result is the need for agreed policies, pooled resources and common action. Already, in this chapter, the plea has been made for area-by-area strategy consultations. The present practice of supporting training institutions on an inter-denominational basis has been also recognized. To these must be added the possibility of increasing the number of specified areas in which financial support is given through centralized funds. Theological education is one area in which this method of working is being used. Christian literature is a second such area. Student work in the universities is a third area in which centralized funds can make a big difference. More and more of such areas can and ought to be defined.

The advantages of this method of support are that resources are available on a scale large enough to produce significant effects within a defined area of action and to stimulate related action by other bodies; that there is freedom to apply resources irrespective of the sources from which they come; that it provides for action on the basis of thorough investigation and competent judgment; that resources are available in advance of commitment, so that prompt and decisive action is possible; and that centralized funds will themselves create on the local and national levels greater co-ordination and collaboration.

The important thing to remember is that effectiveness would be jeopardized if the funds were disproportionately large or small in relation to the task, if the objectives were either not clearly defined or defined too narrowly, if provision was not made for qualified staff and competent planning, if support was uncertain or subject to restrictive conditions, if the governing body was inadequate, or if rate of action was not controlled. It must also be remembered that while hitherto the objectives of centralized funds have been defined in functional terms, a purpose could also be defined in terms of an area. A fund for Church-related purposes within an area will be a useful means of equalizing resources.

In this connection specific mention should be made of the various studies undertaken by the World Council of Churches on situations of rapid social change, especially in Africa, Asia and Latin America. These studies have shown that there are in these three continents Christian tasks clamouring to be performed for which the Christian communities in those continents are hardly prepared. On the one hand these Christian communities over the years have had to struggle for their own existence with the result that their own vision has been narrowed. Henry Makulu, writing from Bossey after a few months' experience there, lists what he has learnt at Bossey and then comments: "Perhaps these things are not new. They have been said over and over again. But for Christians from young countries these are discoveries of some importance, for then we can begin to see why, as Christians, we have not been so effective in our witness in our various communities—namely that we have tried to maintain insular positions while living in a dynamic world."[1] On the other hand, granted the vision, these Christian communities still remain weak in numbers and resources. In other words, the tasks to be performed call for the resources of the whole Church. But just here is the problem. As an African leader remarked at one of the consultations, "The tasks are introducing on the missionary scene methods of operation through Inter-Church Aid, centralized missionary funds, World Confessional Organizations, all of which emphasize the Western Churches in their strength. The missionary need is for the service of the Western Churches in their weakness." Can a way be found whereby the strength of the Western Churches is made available without that strength becoming an embarrassment?

[1] Quoted from *Bossey News*, Dec. 1960.

The Place and Role of the Ecumenical Relation

The underlying concern in re-thinking the patterns of financial assistance between Churches was that this assistance should be controlled by policies which are consciously intended to strengthen the Church in mission. Another area where patterns of action and administration need to be re-thought is that of the relationship between Churches in the ecumenical movement.

The World Council of Churches. In the next chapter will be found a strong plea that the World Council of Churches should not allow itself to become either in name or substance a confederation of confessions. It must remain a Council of Churches. This must naturally mean a Council of Churches in mission. If this is to find effective expression, the next stage of advance, now that the World Council of Churches and the International Missionary Council have been integrated, would seem to require an answer—at least in stages—to the following question: How can the World Council of Churches help its member churches, in the fullness of their programmes, to find natural and effective places in a truly ecumenical pattern of relationships at this time of mutual inter-dependence of all Christians around the world?

The fact to be remembered is that a member church is not only that church in its ecclesiastical structure but also in its constituent agencies: its mission board, its evangelism department, its committee for social action and so on. It is too easy and too schematic an answer to say that the departments of the World Council must be the points of relation of similar departments and divisions in the Churches. What is needed is for the divisions and departments of the World Council to express the World Council and not simply its constituent churches, but for this expression to be in effective relations with the relevant constituent agencies of the churches. The World Council is more than a forum of the churches. It is more than a reflection of the churches and their concerns. It is in itself a form of their realized unity. This form must become discernible above the programmes and activities of its various divisions.

In connection with this mention of the World Council, attention must be drawn also to another issue. We have already spoken about the many questions raised by the relation of financial assistance between churches. There is a popular fallacy that these questions can be circumvented by shooting money through the World Council. It will be a major problem for the World Council in the coming years to deal with this misunderstanding. There is no simple answer to the problems of money-pressure where money is given or received.

Regional Developments. The East Asia Christian Conference (E.A.C.C.) is not a regional Council of the World Council of Churches. It is the association in a region of the Churches and National Christian Councils in that region. This regional independence is essential if the World Council of Churches is to remain truly a World Council of Churches and not become even covertly a Council of Councils. It is important also for the regional development itself because not only is it unnecessary to apply on the regional level the conditions for membership concerning the autonomy of churches which are imposed by the World Council, but also the churches in the region will be able to establish their relations to one another without having to contend with the problems incident on the world nature of the World Council. Thus, for instance, in the E.A.C.C., even in spite of the fact that its secretaries are also the East Asia Secretariat of the W.C.C., there is a growing cordiality between the churches which are conservative-evangelical and those which are not. Developments similar to the E.A.C.C. are taking place in Latin America, the Caribbean Area, Africa, the Near East and in the islands of the Pacific.

These developments can help the churches in mission in different ways. They can be used to stimulate missionary relationship between the churches in the region and between the regions. They can initiate the strategy consultations which are needed, whether on functional or regional lines, in order to correlate to maximum advantage the strength of the churches and all agencies of those churches which are ready to participate in a total Christian thrust. They can build up a programme of their own for their several regions, which programme can then be supported by churches in other regions. In the E.A.C.C. there is an accepted principle that it must raise from within its own area a quarter of the finance needed for its programme and the whole finance needed for its statutory meetings. A quarter is a small proportion, but at least it represents a controlling principle. Regional developments offer also the possibility of bringing together in a region those subsidiary agencies of churches or National Councils which are concerned with the same things. Mass communication, Christian literature, industrial evangelism, Christian home and family life, are cases in point.

The Bilateral Relation. The missionary movement during the last century adopted the principle of comity as the best working arrangement to overcome the handicaps set up by the fact of divided churches. Children of divorced parents were thus saved undue hardship. But now the parents are in process of reconciliation, while the children are seeking ways of living a common life. Besides, comity arrangements themselves are breaking down as members of established congregations move across comity lines. It is also absurd, with the growing strength of the missionary movement, to hold up missionary advance in any area on the grounds of comity. It is meaningless for a church or a missionary society to talk of "my pagans" whom someone else cannot approach with the Gospel. In this situation there is need for greater flexibility in inter-church relations. While the principles of comity ought still to be maintained in order to prevent rivalries, procedures of co-operation must be worked out to increase effectiveness.

A significant change will be to modify the old bilateral relationship between a church in the West and a younger church. It is wasteful to seek to replace these bilateral relationships with multilateral ones. What would be more useful would be to contain these bilateral relationships within multilateral ones. Experience in the Church of South India (C.S.I.) can point the way as to how this can be done. Let the American Congregationalists support the work in Madurai, for instance, but let that support go hand in hand with two other developments. By arrangement with the C.S.I. as a whole, more than one missionary society can be related to the Madurai diocese, while by similar arrangement the American Congregationalists support work in another part of the C.S.I. to which they were not originally related. It is too neat a solution to say, let all support go to the C.S.I. as such and let the C.S.I. distribute this support in its own way. A way forward is necessary which will not betray past responsibilities or sever past connections of affectionate concern. There are not united churches everywhere, but everywhere ways must be found of acting as if the churches were united.

The establishment of multilateral relationships will also have another consequence. It will mean that when a younger church is able more adequately to raise its own resources, the natural result will not always be to reduce "mission grant". To put it concretely, when the Methodist Church in Ceylon is able to raise more money, why not send part of that money to support Christian work in Burma rather than have the Methodist Missionary Society in London reduce its grant to Ceylon and increase its grant to Burma? A multiplication of the channels of help between all churches everywhere is what is needed. Otherwise, the tendency will be to create three types of churches—those which only receive, those which only give, and those which are able to look after themselves.

Outside the Church Relation. The strengthening of the Christian task through mutual support takes place also in the work of such bodies as the Y.M.C.A., Y.W.C.A., and the W.S.C.F. In these organizations, help given and received is seen directly as a sharing within a world community. It is true enough that in the Y.M.C.A., for instance, the International Committee in America still hesitates to accept the procedural implications of this fact: but all in all the programmes of mutual assistance in these world lay organizations strengthen the pattern of missionary endeavour by pointing to the centre rather than to the discrete units on the circumference.

Another form of missionary outreach is the increasing

number of Christian men and women going from one country to another employed by private or governmental agencies. These Christians go from one world to another, but as in the normal missionary operation they are not sent by the church here to the church there. It would be of immense benefit were ways found to support this world-to-world movement with a church-to-church relation.

The Place and Role of the Missionary Involvement

There is only one issue which I want to discuss under this heading—the necessity of preparing plans for a full participation in the future of the younger churches in the missionary movement. The theological and ecclesiological necessity for this participation have been stressed elsewhere. What is here intended is to discuss procedures. Already there are four types of action which can be used to point the way.

(i) The United Church of the Philippines has set up its own mission board whose function is both to send and to receive missionaries. This mission board receives support from mission boards of the churches of the West whose historic relations are with the churches that form the United Church of the Philippines. There are missionaries from this Church in the Philippines working in several Asian countries. (ii) The Methodist Church in Ceylon has sent three missionaries to Africa. They were sent through the Methodist Missionary Society in London. The Methodist Church in Ceylon sends an annual gift to the Society in London towards the support of these missionaries. (iii) The Mar Thoma Syrian Church (this is not a younger church) has developed its own missionary arm, and more than a hundred Mar Thoma missionaries are working outside the milieu of this church. This work is fully supported by the Mar Thoma Church itself. (iv) The East Asia Christian Conference is helping to find missionaries who can be sent to meet known needs. When the missionary sending and receiving churches have made all the arrangements, the Conference helps with finance to meet the expenses of travel and other small incidentals.

All these four ways of action can be brought together into a single pattern. The primary need is to encourage every church to set up its own mission board which will be responsible both for the sending and the receiving of missionaries. On the receiving side two points should be stressed. First of all, greater attention must be paid to missionary training in the countries to which the missionaries come. Missionaries need to learn not only the language of the country but also its customs and manners, its political and religious history and the social and economic goals towards which it is set. Secondly, the time has come to change the policy whereby missionaries were employed only in tangential tasks. In every church, workers are needed to shepherd congregations, to direct departments, to man institutions and to pioneer across new frontiers. In all these four areas missionaries and nationals from the countries concerned must work together. The policy under which missionaries, for instance, were not put as pastors in charge of congregations is an invidious policy. In a healthy relationship the missionary community will be spread out over the whole church in all its life. It should not be their tasks which define them as missionaries but their vocation. On the sending side the existence of a mission board in every church will give that church a permanent sense of responsibility towards the task of missions. It will also give that church freedom to decide about the conditions of service of the missionaries it sends. Where a Central Board is responsible for sending missionaries recruited from different countries, problems of relative right and wrong arise which can be very troublesome.

But, if all that has been said in this book about the importance and implication of the Unity of the Church has even some truth in it; and if the claim which has been made that the location of a church is of intrinsic significance for its life has even a partial justification; then it will not do for the younger churches to reproduce the simple denominational pattern of the older churches in their missionary outreach. Two things can be done. First, the various mission boards in a country can so help one another and work together that every missionary who goes can go as from the church in that country. Secondly, while each mission board receives primary support from a mission board in the West to which it is historically related, it should also be helped according to the measure of its missionary operation through such an organization as, for instance, the E.A.C.C. In specified areas of co-operative work, the National Christian Council of the country can act either as a missionary sending or receiving organ as the case may be.

As the younger churches increasingly take seriously their missionary involvement, it is essential that they should also recognize the importance of linking their missionary publicity with their own spiritual needs. Indeed, this will be true for all missionary-sending churches. Too much missionary publicity is pitched at a level where the slogans are—this is an on-going enterprise, we are responsible for it, it must go on, it must maintain its own identifiability out there, we have to keep faith with what we have begun. Missionary advocacy must be aimed directly at the revival and renewal of the sending church.

Is this the time?

One last word, and that must be to refer to all the problems and upheavals which are now so characteristic of the lands in which the younger churches are. Is this the time for missionary advance?

Dr Kenneth Latourette, calling for a modern missionary advance on the part of the churches of the West, makes this plea:

> In the Thirty Years' War, from 1618 to 1648, Germany and Bohemia and Moravia (what we now call Czecho-Slovakia) were the battle field of a general European struggle. At the end of the war they were prostrate. Protestantism was all but stamped out in Bohemia and Moravia. Only a few hidden remnants had survived. The Protestant Churches of Germany were formal and appeared to be dying of dry rot. Yet within the German Protestant Churches a few faithful souls formed themselves into inner circles for self-dedication, prayer and evangelism. A small band of persecuted refugees from Moravia took refuge on the estates of Count Zinzendorf, one of the leaders of that German movement.

Led by Zinzendorf the little group sent out missionaries to every continent and from the Arctic to the Tropics. It was through contact with them that John Wesley had the profound experience of Christ which gave birth to Methodism.

Moreover, it was in a period of revolution and world war that many of the strongest missionary societies came into being. From 1789 to 1815 Europe and with it much of the world were upset by the French Revolution and the wars which came out of it. Yet, undismayed by these world-shaking events, inconspicuous groups of Christians led by obscure men laid plans for giving the Gospel to all the earth. In 1792 the French Revolution was approaching its acme of violence. Yet in that very year, just across the English Channel, the cobbler-preacher, William Carey, induced a few of his fellow ministers to form the Baptist Missionary Society. The following year, the year of the Reign of Terror in France, Carey went to India. In 1799, when Napoleon was returning to France from his effort to break Britain's communications with India, the Evangelicals of the Church of England organized the Church Missionary Society for Africa and the East. In 1804, not far from the time when Napoleon was giving to England its greatest threat of invasion between the Spanish Armada and Hitler, men of faith formed the British and Foreign Bible Society. In 1812, while American ports were being blockaded by the British, Adoniram Judson sailed for India. At the time all these movements were small. They attracted almost no public attention. Yet they and the others associated with them have grown to world-wide proportions.[1]

We live in comparable times and face a comparable challenge. We know, however, that the times by themselves will not produce the advance or the impetus to it. It is written of the disciples in the garden of Gethsemane that they were "asleep because of sorrow" (Lk. 22: 45). How strong that temptation always is during times of stress. And yet, how near the disciples were to the hour of victory.

[1] Leaflet issued by the Foreign Missions Conference of North America.

3

THE WESTERNITY OF THE BASE

A CONSIDERATION of the nature, procedures and practices of the missionary enterprise has to take account of the movement towards self-hood in the churches of its founding. It has to take account too of the necessity to ensure and increase the momentum of the enterprise itself. But, in addition to these two factors, it must reckon also with the situation that, while the great missionary era of the last one hundred and fifty years has seen the Church planted in every continent and country, in terms of present realities Christianity is still a Western religion.

Speaking at the 1961 Kirchentag held in Berlin, Professor C. G. Baeta of Ghana, President of the International Missionary Council, declared:

> The idea of one part of the world evangelizing another will not bear scrutiny. Missions are not a movement from the haves to the have-nots, from the educated to the illiterate. They are a movement from the fellowship of faith all over the world to all who stand outside this fellowship, whoever and wherever they may be.

That is well said, but another voice from Africa spoke truly also when it laid emphasis on tasks to be performed in the West as strategic to the performance of the total task. Dr John Karefa-Smart, minister of foreign affairs of Sierra Leone, speaking to the 1961 General Assembly of the United Presbyterian Church in the U.S.A., put it thus:

> To-day, with a single exception (the new nation of Somalia) the Christian Church is to be found, sometimes firmly established and sometimes with a mere foothold, in every one of the thirty

194

nations on the African continent. At the recent Monrovia Conference of the Heads of States and governments, in Africa and Malagasy, ten out of twenty national leaders were Christians. But were I to stop here, I would not be doing my duty. I must ask further: What is your continuing Christian responsibility for the direction of the Revolution in Africa?

Our African nations, singly and collectively, are called to play a more positive role contributing to the realization of world peace. But we can fulfil such a positive purpose only if we can influence you, our Christian brothers in Europe and America, to make effective in your own national policies the same revolutionary ideas which your missionaries so freely shared with us.

The challenging word here is the word "only". The task is one, the base for the task is one also; but unless in the West, both in the life of the Churches and the nations, the Christian Gospel becomes more compelling the whole task will be immeasurably weakened. The next crucial struggle in the mission of the Church is not in Africa or Asia but in Europe and North America, and derivatively wherever the white man is in a position of dominance in Africa.

Wherever there is a Church, there is a home base for mission; wherever there is the world in its unbelief or other belief, there is the need for missionaries; and yet in terms of the over-all picture to-morrow's tasks demand that we take seriously the present Westernity of the missionary base.

First of all, *Christianity is a Western religion because the large majority of those in the world who bear the name of Christ live in Western lands.* (I am not including in this statement any reference to the great Christian Church in Russia.) It may be contended that this is not of much importance, since such a large number of those who do bear the name of Christ in the West attach so little significance to it. But that is precisely what spells the task for to-morrow.

Let me explain what I mean by using three illustrations. Some years ago a young American, going to teach English in one of the high schools in Ceylon, met me in Europe on his way to Ceylon and asked me whether there was anything I could tell him which would help him in his stay and work in Ceylon.

I said to him, "There is one thing you must remember—that you will always be judged as a Christian missionary." He looked startled. "But, I am not a missionary," he said. "I am simply going to teach English." I said to him, "That makes no difference. You will be judged as a missionary. You in the West who bear the name of Christ can discount responsibility for it in your own countries, but abroad that is the Name by which you will be judged."

I was reading the speech made in 1959 in the political committee of the U.N.O. by Dr G. P. Malalasekera, one of the Ceylon representatives in the U.N.O., a leading Buddhist, when he spoke on the racial policies of South Africa. There is more than a hint in his speech that, judged by its history, Christianity has bred more racial intolerance than any other religion. He calls attention to the fact that the white South Africans are Christians and that the policy of their government is based "on the doctrine that the white races, as heirs to Western Christian civilization, are in duty bound to maintain that civilization inviolate." With scarcely concealed irony he remarks, "In the belief that it is a Christian duty to preserve the categories of God's creation and to prevent its diversity from degenerating into a mongrel chaos, the government follows a policy of apartheid." The Negro, the Bantu, the Jew, the peoples of colonial lands, all bear witness to the way in which Christian nations have behaved. There is little point in arguing that there are no Christian nations. Theologically that is true: but in terms of the task of Christian witness it is not true. It is not only a fact that the Westerner abroad, if he bears the name of Christ, will be judged as a Christian; it is also true that those who are not Christians will judge Christianity by those who bear that Name anywhere.

About two years ago I shared in a consultation of Y.M.C.A. secretaries in New York in which earnest consideration was given to the Christian witness of the Y.M.C.A. in all countries where it was at work. At the close of the meeting one of the secretaries present offered to drive me back home. On the way he said to me, "I offered to drive you back because I wanted to talk to you. It is true that I am a Y.M.C.A. secretary, it is also true that I have been baptized, but I do not believe in most of the things you believe as a Christian. Would you say that I am a Christian or not?" My answer was, "What do you say? Do you say, when people ask you what your religion is, that you are a Christian?" He said "Yes". "Then," I said, "that settles the matter for me. If you say you are a Christian then you are a Christian. I think your belief about what it means to be a Christian is wrong. But you are a Christian nevertheless." To be a Christian in name, to be willing to be known as a Christian, that is in itself a solemn decision. There is too much glib talk about "nominal" Christians as if there could be any other kind, and there is too much easy rejection of one's fellow Christians because their beliefs are heretical or their lives sinful. Sin and heresy must be held within the controversies and discipline of the Christian fellowship, for where the fellowship itself is denied, the controversies and discipline are futile.

Jesus Christ is the light of the world (John 8: 12). But every time a Christian bears testimony to this fact, he is aware of Jesus pointing to him and saying, "You are the light of the world" (Matt. 5: 14). We must never point to ourselves nor can we escape from the situation that He is constantly pointing to us. It is a common experience in India or Ceylon, when an evangelistic team visits a village, that in the meeting that is organized the small Christian community in the village will be sitting in the middle while the Hindus and Muslims will be standing all around. And, in that situation, the evangelist is aware that whereas he is pointing to Christ, his listeners are looking at that small group sitting in front of them. The message will carry no conviction unless it is being proved in the lives of those who bear the Name that is being declared. This village situation is the world situation too, and for good or ill it is still the Christians of Western lands who are sitting in the middle.

It is one of the tasks of to-morrow to accept this fact and make it good. There is no way for the peoples of the West to contract out of this situation. It is a responsibility they must bear whether they like it or not.

Speaking as a fellow Christian from Asia, one is struck by the many movements in the life of the Churches of the West which bear witness to the concern that Christ be honoured by those who bear His name both by word and life. One is specially struck by the ingenuity and purposefulness with which, in place after place, the attempt is being made to take and plant the Christian presence in areas of life which have for long remained outside the Christian community. The worship of the Churches is being deepened, and there is tremendous intellectual drive to think through to a Christian wisdom that will give direction to human living in the kind of world in which man finds himself to-day.

But there are at least three questions which an Asian Christian is tempted to ask.

(i) Can mass revivalism play any major part in recalling the Christian West to its vocation? It is often forgotten that when people are invited to accept Jesus Christ as their Lord and Saviour, Jesus Christ as such is never available for acceptance. He can be accepted by accepting to belong to the community that bears His name, He can be accepted by dedication to do some particular deed which is His will for the person concerned, He can be accepted by accepting the teaching about Him and His Gospel which is being presented ... Mass revivalism, when it neglects to see this situation in which preacher and hearer stand, can result in producing a merely religious revival with little relation to the actual tasks in which the Lord is engaged to-day and where only He can be met and obeyed.

(ii) What is the consequence of discontinuing so completely the quest for the Jesus of history? Nothing is more striking to a person whose normal habitat is the world of Hindu thought and life, when he visits the West, than the assumption which he finds so pervasive in theological circles in the West that the Jesus of history is unknown and unknowable. That Jesus lived and died and still lives is not doubted: but apart from this nothing is certain except that the early Church preached certain things about Him. As to whether this teaching is true, this can be judged, it is claimed, only in terms of its relevance for life to-day and in terms of its verifiability in personal experience. This attitude is so completely Hindu that one is staggered by its consequence for Christians living amidst Hindus, if Christians there should come to hold this position.

(iii) Why is "topical" preaching such a feature of the Christian pulpit in the West and particularly in the U.S.A.? My reason for raising this question is not to argue about the relative rightness of "topical" preaching, or to discuss the different ways in which "topical" preaching can be done. I want rather to ask this kind of question—suppose someone in a congregation kept a record of the sermons preached to that congregation Sunday by Sunday, and then at the end of a whole year wrote a summary of the Christian faith on the basis of those sermons alone, what would that summary be like? Most Christians, among those who attend public worship, live on the basis of the faith they learn on Sunday mornings. The preacher has no right to waste a Sunday morning talking "tit-bits".

There is a second reason for saying that Christianity is a Western religion. *It is a Western religion because Western culture and civilization have their roots in the Christian faith.* Let me list just three examples of the kind of climate of thought and conviction which is so pervasive in the West but which has no meaning apart from the Christian faith from which it has flowered.

(i) There are many varieties of opinion about the nature and procedures of "democracy", but underlying all these there is a common conviction which can be articulated. "Government must be by the free consent of the governed." This conviction has no foundation except that free consent is what God awaits from man. Democracy is an attempt on the part of men to deal with one another in a way that is consonant with the way in which God deals with them. This way of God with men is the way of God in Jesus Christ.

(ii) Since the practice of democracy usually is that of government by the majority it is essential for the health of the whole to keep inviolate the absolute importance of the individual. But this belief in the absolute importance of the individual has no basis in fact apart from the Christian proclamation that each man is God's immediate creation. Biological and historical processes belong to the realm of secondary causation. God is "final" cause—His purpose determines you and me.

(iii) But we are not simply units in a heap, we are members of a race or a nation with a common life and sense of common mission and destiny. The history of the nineteenth century is simply the result of the working out of the sense of "nationhood" of the peoples of the West. But has "nationhood" any validity except that God recognizes nations and peoples? Where men bind themselves together God does deal with them together. It is the "peoples", the "nations", the human "groupings", which must be brought into subjection to the Gospel.

Now, let me ask, can these convictions be sustained in the West apart from the Christian faith? One can already discern how these convictions are being emptied of content and consequence simply because they are held as political convictions and not as religious ones. Is government by consent for Portugal only or also for Angola? Is it for the U.S.A. only or also for Taiwan (Formosa)? In South Africa, is the absolute importance of the individual an unqualified truth or is it qualified by colour? A competitive society with minimum government control may be the best guarantee of individual freedom, but how are the weak to be protected in a competitive society? Is "nationhood" of equal legitimacy in the Rhodesias as in Britain? Can civil rights in a nation be defended if they belong to white citizens alone? This kind of question can be multiplied. Political questions must be answered in terms of political realities. But once the religious roots of political convictions are cut there is lost the religious compulsion which must control political thought. An Australian steward on a boat once said to me, when he discovered that I was going to Australia to conduct missions, "Oh, I don't believe in Christianity but I believe in our civilization and for that Christianity is important."

The churches of the West face a tremendous task for tomorrow. They must find ways of recalling their several nations and the communities among them to allegiance to the faith which so far has shaped their destiny. This has to mean two things—the revival of Christian belief itself, and witness to that belief in the ways in which the nation behaves as a whole. When the Church of Scotland in its Assembly discussed Nyasaland, it was performing an evangelistic task of the greatest significance. When Bishop Bell of Chichester protested in the House of Lords against obliteration bombing, he was witnessing to his Lord. When the Student Christian Movement of France protests against the war in Algeria it is pointing to the one humanity in Christ. A great deal in the future depends on the churches of the West discovering the political dimension of their evangelistic witness. In fact, a great deal depends on the nations of the West discovering the Christian dimension of their political tasks. What is the lesson to be learnt from the tenderness of the British Government towards Portugal during the recent events in Angola, or from the emergence of the John Birch society in the U.S.A.? In purely political terms, the West is simply engaged in a holding operation; it can play a decisive role in shaping future events only if it dares to be Christian. The governments and nations of the West must some time be brought to listen to the witness of the churches in their midst. Paul speaks of "bringing about obedience to the faith among the nations" (Rom. 1: 5): that obedience depends on so being "under" the word that one "hears".[1]

Another factor which calls for serious attention in any consideration of the relation between Western culture and the Christian faith is the rapid spread to all parts of the world of elements of this culture in a disintegrated form. The basis of all old cultures is the family unit, whether it be the immediate or the extended family; and this family unit has been preserved by suitable patterns of marriage and property arrangement. Under the pressure of technological developments this type of culture is breaking down all over Asia and Africa. Into this situation are being injected those ideas which spring from the breakdown of a family-based culture in the West.

It has been said that while the churches of the West in the

[1] The New Testament word translated "obedience" literally means "to hear under".

nineteenth century launched the missionary movement to lands overseas they lost the working classes at home. The truth is, however, that they never had the working classes in spite of the successes of the evangelical revival. The characteristic of the churches of the West previous to the Industrial Revolution was that they were home based. But "with the advent of the Industrial Revolution a new group of people entered the social scheme who had no relevance to this pattern of church life. Although the church could adjust its message which was dominated by the virtues of rural life to the family life of merchants and manufacturers, it found that it had little or nothing to say to the city proletariat."[1] Ralph Morton remarks, "The idea that the family is the basic unit of Christian social living has ceased to be true of the middle class, even as it was never true of the working class. And with that change the congregation has lost its root in the common life of men."[2]

The problem then is this: that there is a double need in the West which must be met if a missionary outreach by the churches of the West is to be powerful enough to serve the disintegrating social situation in the lands of Asia and Africa. The churches of the West must, on the one hand, help to restore again the integrity of the family; while, on the other hand, they find new ways of structuring congregational life so that the masses of men who have become "anonymous, identical, replaceable units of society" may find in the family of God a community which is relevant to their way of life and culture. At the moment the situation, by and large, is that the churches of the West do not yet possess the word to speak to the rapidly changing society in the lands of the younger churches and that the word they do speak is Christian in form only and not in power. The polygamy issue in Africa is a case in point. Most Christian churches in Africa insist on divorce as a pre-condition before a polygamist can be baptized, but the issue is not clear as to which is the way of building Christian family life in Africa.

[1] Letty M. Russel in the Union Theological Seminary *Quarterly Review*, Nov. 1960.
[2] Ralph Morton, *Household of Faith*, Iona Community, 1951, p. 75.

Must the Church begin with divorce or with polygamy if those are the two alternatives? and what of the situation in which lack of economic progress and education poses an even more poignant question? During the All-Africa Lutheran Conference held at Marangu in 1955 the Hon. Mrs E. M. Marealle, wife of the paramount chief of the Chagga tribe, put the issue in these words:

> There was one advantage in this system of taking many wives and that was that the girls who reached the right age could always be assured of a husband. These days we think the system of marrying many wives is a bad thing but the towns are now full of young women who have no education with which to help themselves by way of work and not enough young men who are prepared to marry them. Many of our older people are often asking us if we think this is a good thing; we cannot reply easily because it is a choice between many wives or many prostitutes.[1]

The point I am making is not that we need greater discernment on how to handle the polygamy issue in Africa, nor that we must somehow maintain the sanctities of family life. Rather, my plea is that the churches of the West have a radical discovery to make in their homelands, the discovery of how to preserve the family unit within a Christian congregational life which itself is based not on the family but on the social unities of modern men. Until this discovery is made in the West where Christianity is still the dominant religion, the missionary enterprise must remain seriously handicapped.

A third reason why Christianity is a Western religion is *because in money and personnel the resources of the Christian enterprise are still largely in the West.* How to put these resources at the wisdom of the whole Church throughout the world is one of the tasks for to-morrow. In this connection the first and over-riding consideration must be that of evangelism. Dr Donald McGavran in his book *How Churches Grow* has the following paragraph:

> Immediately after the I.M.C. Conference at Willingen in 1952, Dr R. Pierce Beaver penned the following sentence which

[1] Quoted from the C.M.S. *News Letter* of Feb. 1961.

the Division of Foreign Mission published: "The delegates at Willingen say, as they reviewed the situation of the Church around the world to-day, that the missionary enterprise is in great measure a colossal system of inter-church aid, with relatively little pioneer evangelistic advance." This terrific assessment frightened no one. "The colossal system of inter-church aid" passes for good missions—whether the younger churches grow or not. If we are aiding them, that is good mission policy. The "no-growth" situation is accepted without remorse.[1]

The point here must be well taken. "Missions" must primarily be driven by the hope and prayer that God will so use them as to bring into being churches where there are none and an increase in membership of the churches that are. At the moment the largest use of the resources of the churches of the West in many countries is towards maintaining and deepening and broadening the life of the "younger" churches but not towards their expansion. "Expansion" is the primary category with which to define the unfinished evangelistic task. The point is often made, and seems to me convincing, that wherever the churches are expanding they are doing so because evangelism has become a people's movement. Part of the problem of "the established missions" is that their help in terms of personnel and resources is too institutionally channelled so that it does not meet the situation of spontaneous advance. Together with this goes the problem of releasing men and money for new projects which can stimulate and undergird evangelism as a people's movement: the establishment of Christian communities—ashrams, monasteries, institutes, the training of the laity for Christian witness in daily life, frontier groups who will be the Christian presence where at the moment there is none, mobile evangelistic teams, and so on.

Indeed, it may not be an overstatement to say that the execution of the Church's mission as a people's movement will depend in large measure on an immediate investment of men and money into that field of work in which at present it is sought to mobilize and train the laity to be the Church on the frontier.

[1] Donald McGavran, *How Churches Grow*, World Dominion Press, p. 11.

This mode of understanding the nature of the Church's mission is relatively recent and, therefore, needs a concentration of thought and study to bring out its chief implications. Let me use a passage from the writing of Hans Ruedi Weber, who was Director of the Laity department of the World Council of Churches, to set out the main idea. Writing on the Christian witness in Asia he develops his thesis as follows:

> The tiny Christian minority living as a "diaspora", a community scattered, in the midst of Asia is set there in order to make the choice between Christ and anti-Christ inescapable for the new Asian nations. How are these weak churches going to fulfil this mission? They cannot even support and continue all the missionary activities and missionary institutions which were started by Western missionary societies. But many Western missionaries who had the exasperating privilege of working in modern Asia have made a great discovery (and this discovery is now being made by many of the Asian churches themselves): when through outer and inner circumstances they had to cut down or even stop their well-meant missionary activities, they saw that their mere presence (if it was really a Christian presence) had meaning and was perhaps more important than all their activities. They discovered that in the life and mission of the Church the Christian dimension, with its spontaneous "radiation", is equally or perhaps even more important than the Christian intention with all its deliberate Christian activities.
>
> This distinction between the dimension and the intention has been blurred in the Western Christendom situation. To be a Christian came almost exclusively to mean a set of intentional activities: going to church on Sundays, helping in organized evangelistic activities and joining in planned Christian service. The mere existence of a Christian community in the midst of a society lost its power and force of "radiation". The Church was no longer a sign, but an interest and often a pressure-group. Where this happens the specially trained and full-time employed church worker comes into the forefront. He is the specialist and will soon be regarded as the functionary to whom the Church has delegated its ministry and mission. And the laity will at most be the active "hands of such functionaries". This conception of the Church, which is reduced to intentional Christian activities and the work of church functionaries and their helpers, has been

exported to Asia and Africa. Many impressive missionary institutions and the whole variety of centralized missionary activities have been built up—often at the expense of the all-important growth into maturity of individual Christians and local congregations outside the mission station or the church centre.

dimension

As soon as the primary importance of this dimension in the life and mission of the Church is seen, the laity come into the forefront. It is in and through their costly choices and decisions in their daily life and work that the Church grows into maturity and fulfils its essential mission. Those set apart for a special ministry in the Church are now no longer considered as the functionaries of the Church. They are recognized as those who are given to the Church in order to discern the gifts of grace bestowed on each member of God's people, in order to harmonize these gifts of grace and let them flourish so that the whole people is directed towards the work of service[1] (Eph. 4: 11-12).

To draw out the implication of this thesis, let me give one example. One of the crucial areas of life in which the Christian presence is of the utmost importance both for the present and the future is the university in which Christian students are a minority as well as a diaspora. Here, if anywhere, is the need to maintain the diaspora status and use the diaspora strategy of the Christian community. How right Weber is in his main protest can be seen, however, in the calculated development of denominational policies in Christian student work which instead of seeking unitedly to besiege the University world on behalf of Christ, seek rather to fragment the Christian witness in the university on behalf of the Churches. (The climate of a competitive society in the U.S.A. has helped this development of autonomous denominational student movements. But just when, in the U.S.A., the tide is turning in the direction of greater unity in Christian student work, Britain announces the formation of the first British Confessional Student Christian organization. An Anglican Student Federation has been formed. One had hoped that the University world would prove the first area of life where Christians would have found the name of Christ enough and not felt any necessity to add other names

[1] Quoted from the Laity Bulletin of the W.C.C., No. 8.

whether Anglican or Lutheran or Methodist etc. to distinguish them.) The university ceases to be important for its own sake, and so the Christian students become important as members of their several churches. Not the Christian mission but Christian nurture becomes the over-riding category of student work, and the minority and diaspora situation of the Christian community is redressed by gathering together the separate clans and drawing circles around them. Here again the Westernity of the base puts the major responsibility on the churches of the West for strong leadership in the right direction.

To emphasize the idea of the mission as a people's movement, however, is not to forget that it is the Church which is on the move. And yet, here again the implication of emphasizing this churchliness is to emphasize the nature of the Church's mission to the world. The Church is part of the Gospel and a demonstration of it. In it is experienced already as foretaste the climactic fulfilment of God's Kingdom. In this realm, the consequence therefore for missionary policy is the compulsion to demonstrate the nature of the reconciliation which the Church proclaims in mission. To be a people's movement in the true sense, the mission must be the mission of one people. The search to make visible the unity of the Church is not motivated by a desire for evangelistic efficiency. It is the consequence of realizing that the Church deprives the world of living by the reconciliation wrought in Christ where the Church itself does not live by that reconciliation. The Church as "mission" may convert, but where the call to unity is not heeded the Church refuses its mission to be the place where the new humanity is fashioned and the new creation is begun. The cosmic dimension of the Gospel must not be separated from the personal. Obedience must include both.

If the Church's mission is reconciliation, in every sense of the term, it is clear that it must first be reconciled within itself and regain the unity it has lost. It is clear also that the Church will not become reconciled within itself unless it starts by listening and by letting itself be questioned. The world does not question us; it condemns us, or at least scorns us. We must also listen to this message of contempt, for it confirms our own inner certainty that we cannot speak of reconciliation as long as all Christians are not reconciled within the Church itself.[1]

The practical consequence of this demand for reconciliation, with respect to the task of missions, is the need to pay urgent attention to the questions concerning the inter-nationalizing as well as the inter-denominationalizing of missions which are discussed on all sides to-day. The coming together of the International Missionary Council and the World Council of Churches must provide the right context within which to work out the solutions to all these questions.

The importance of the denominational question, however, is not only forced into the foreground by the financial and personnel potential of the churches of the West. It is intrinsic to their very development. This is the fourth reason why Christianity is a Western religion. *The ecclesiastical forms of the Christian faith as found in the world to-day are largely the result of the history of the churches of the West.* A task for to-morrow is to break the entail on this heritage and so to set free the Church in its mission that it can discover what it means to be the Church.

Let me express myself once again as an Asian Christian. As I work with my fellow Christians in the West I am struck by certain attitudes which so many adopt without question. It is assumed that it is right to give organizational expression to theological variations. Great play is made of loyalty to truth, but what is meant is that such loyalty demands separate and separated households of faith. Often, in the West, I have been reminded of one of our late Ceylonese ministers—the Rev. R. C. P. Welch—who told a story of the man who was cured by Jesus with the application of "earth and spittle" (Mk. 8: 23) setting up a faith-healing Church in which he contended that that was the true way of faith healing, and of the other man whom Jesus cured purely by the spoken word (Mk. 10: 52) setting up another Church to witness to the unaided form of faith healing because that was the truth. I have also wondered

[1] Pierre Burgelin, *Unity and Mission of the Church*, John Knox Press, p. 13.

whether truths are true in isolation. Thus, for instance, can the teaching about the historic episcopate as an essential guarantee of the Church's continuity in time be true unless it is also true that only one guarantee is needed for the Church to remain, always and everywhere, the Church—the guarantee of the Lord's presence? If these two truths are held by two different denominations, do they not both become at least distorted? Within the World Council of Churches, all truths are in conversation with one another. That conversation helps to keep each true. Truths can be served loyally only as they are brought together—for truth is one and He is Christ.

> Heresy [says Pierre Burgelin] is firstly a case of spiritual solitude. It is the role of the living community, the role of church tradition which is a dialogue with the Church of the past, to draw us out of that solitude. No single person can claim to be in possession of every aspect of the Truth. That is why the mission of the Church is inseparable from unity. The unity of the Church is no unanimity. Neither the living Church nor its tradition are unanimous. The Church is one in its inner dialogue when every member is prepared to let the others question him, when differences and oppositions are examined together, when its members at least agree to look together for the signs whereby the Truth may be recognized.[1]

Reconciliation is by the Cross. The Cross would not be necessary if the basis of unity were complete agreement and not dialogue.

The importance of stressing this aspect of the Westernity of the Christian base lies in the fact that unless the churches of the West achieve a break-through on this front, the Church Union achievements in the lands of the younger churches cannot by themselves arrest the growth of the sectarian spirit or its manifestations. It is said that the main causes, humanly speaking, which lie behind the separatist and messianic movements in Africa are:—the impression that division does not matter, an impression which the established churches and missions themselves conveyed; the personality cult which the missionaries

[1] *Op. cit.*, pp. 9-10.

seemed to practise; and the lack of opportunity within the established churches and missions for the development of indigenous African leadership. In Asia, the strength of sectarianism lies in the fact that it provides an easy way out of the confessional situation. Daisuke Kitagawa, analysing the causes for the No-Church movement in Japan, expresses the view that confessional differences which inevitably present themselves in a doctrinaire form give an impetus to the belief that Christianity is primarily a matter of intellectual assent to intellectualized propositions. If this were so, it would be an easy step from this misunderstanding to the further position that Christianity can be accepted and practised without the hindrance of confessional organizations, which after all are not in themselves an intellectual necessity. The No-Church movement was an attempt to recover an untrammelled Christianity where the intellect and the spirit were free.

Once Christianity was reduced to one form of an intellectual system or another, confessional difference becomes a factor of crucial importance. Protestantism in Japan has been infected by denominational competition much for this reason. This explains why Japanese Lutherans outdo Lutherans in Europe in their strict adherence to Lutheranism, and Japanese Presbyterians outdo both all types of the Reformed in Europe and all types of Presbyterians in America in their adherence to what they had been taught as the central tenet of Presbyterianism; and one can go down the line from Anglicans and Congregationalists to Baptists and Pentecostals. Even those groups which in the West are regarded as non- or anti-intellectual, present their respective versions of Christianity in intellectualized (though not necessarily intellectual) formulae, either in terms of dogma or in terms of moral law; and the difference between their teaching and those of other denominations is magnified chiefly to justify their own existence. This intellectualization of the Christian Gospel is at the very bottom of the failure of the modern Protestant missionary movements in Japan insofar as they were carried out by the missionary societies and boards of the West and inherited by the mission-supported Japanese churches. It is against this historical background that one must assess the meaning of the Mukyokaishugi Christianity in Japan. Mukyokaishugi, which may best be translated as *No-churchism*, is, therefore, not an "ism" against the Church like a spiritual anarchism or isolationism. It is a revolt against "churchism" and does not advocate "no-churchism". It is neither an organization nor a system, and much less a sect or a denomination. It is a movement to do away with all denominationalism.[1]

The No-Church movement in Japan can be paralleled in the other countries of Asia by the growth of the pentecostal type of churches and societies, of which the best illustration is in Latin America. Here the established churches and missions are making a desperate attempt to maintain confessional distinctions which carry so little conviction to those in the country for whom the reformed faith has brought deliverance from an unreformed Catholicism. When I was in South America, how often did I hear the comment, "If only these missionaries would leave us alone; we could then come together as Christians!" The underlying hope was not in terms of Church Union as normally understood, but in terms of a sectarian denial of the importance of confessional differences.

It seems to me that the strength and direction for meeting this situation must come in the first place from the churches of the West. It would be a tragedy if the theological insights which lie behind and beneath the various confessions were brushed aside as of no account. Un-denominationalism is a blind man's way out of the problem. What is needed is a swifter attempt to hold together in one universe of discourse the various confessional positions and a greater resolve to express at the local level the maximum amount of churchly unity. Ways must be explored of building local congregational unity without prejudging or compromising theological issues. There are already in many places signs of this kind of experimentation—community churches, shared church buildings, ministers ordained both episcopally and non-episcopally, one congregation with more than one community roll, shared communion, etc. There is need to press on with all this because here at least is the

[1] Quoted from a paper on "No-Church Christianity in Japan", by Daisuke Kitagawa, published by the I.M.C. as its *Occasional Paper* No. 8.

dictum true that "we shall not know what we do not do". (A student Christmas letter sent out from East Germany in December 1960 pleading for the maintenance and strengthening of the unity of the Christian student community in the whole of Germany carried this caption: "Here we shall not know what we do not do.")

Defining this goal of churchly unity at the local level, the Faith and Order Commission of the World Council of Churches made the following statement:

> The unity which is both God's will and His gift to His Church is one which brings all in each place who confess Christ Jesus as Lord into a fully committed fellowship with one another through one baptism into Him, holding the one apostolic faith, preaching the one Gospel and breaking the one bread, and having a corporate life reaching out in witness and service to all; which at the same time unites them with the whole Christian fellowship in all places and all ages in such wise that ministry and members are acknowledged by all, and that all can act and speak together as occasion requires for the tasks to which God calls the Church.[1]

The promise in this approach is that while this unity is by its very nature visible, it does not imply a single centralized ecclesiastical institution.

It is a matter for great thanksgiving that all this is not just a matter of wishful dreaming. In the words of Archbishop Fisher:

> Through the centuries the churches have allowed themselves to be drawn overmuch into what St Paul called philosophy and vain deceit, after the tradition of man, after the elemental spirits of the universe, and not according to Christ. But there is blowing through the churches a great wind of fellowship in Christ, a wind of the Holy Spirit. In many parts of the world a resurrection is at work. There is in the ecumenical movement an authentic voice of the Holy Spirit to the churches of the world.[2]

But having said all this, there is need to say also that there is taking place in the churches of the West another development which is a cause of real concern for many in the younger

---

[1] Minutes of the Faith and Order Commission (1960), p. 113.
[2] Quoted from his sermon preached at the Anglican Cathedral in Jerusalem and reported in the *E.P.S.* of Dec 2, 1960.

churches. The problem can be put this way: In the West the organizational defences of separated traditions are themselves objects of loyalty and veneration. With us, in the younger churches, it is largely still not so. It is essential that we find one another before we become like our fellow Christians in the West. But just here where we need most help, we are alarmed by the recrudescence in the West of denominationalism. Confessionalisms, organized in world organizations, are for us in the younger churches not merely an obstacle but a temptation. God in His mercy led us to the point where in our lands both secular and sacred history showed us that denominationalism is not viable. The Church in its dividedness is not the Church but the world. World Confessionalism is an attempt to make denominationalism viable again.

I know that leaders of World Confessional movements deny this vigorously. The issue is not one about their intentions but about the results of what they are doing. In a staff memorandum of the I.M.C. there occurs the following sentence, "While centralized administration of the Lutheran missions in a country (e.g. Tanganyika) fosters the sharing of resources within the confessional group, it intensifies confessional consciousness at possible cost to inter-confessional co-operation."[1] The hard truth is that in spite of their genuine interest and participation in the ecumenical movement, the churches of the West are still uncertain about the implications of the ecumenical summons.

A fifth reason, therefore, must be added to underline the importance of recognizing the Westernity of the base of the Christian enterprise, and that is *the decisive role of the churches of the West in determining the shape of things to come*. Already, in other connections, tentative mention has been made of the development of world confessionalism; but even at the risk of being misunderstood one feels compelled to attempt a concise statement of how the confessional development looks to at least one member of a younger church.

[1] Quoted from memorandum on Disparity of Resources and Related Issues I.M.C., April 1960.

An over-all impression which one carries as a result of continuous contact with the churches of the West is that these churches are being asked to move in two opposite directions. Those within these churches who are related to missionary societies and mission boards and the operations of the missionary movement are seeking to lead their churches into a recognition of the significance of the lands and nations in which the Church exists; while, on the other hand, many of those carrying responsibility for the internal life of these churches seem to be primarily conscious of the world distribution of their particular denomination or confession, and anxious to lead their churches in the direction of strengthening denominational ties. This is naturally an over-simplification and an over-statement, but at least it makes the contrast clear. The reason why this contrast so often remains hidden is that among both groups mentioned there are those who are equally committed to the ecumenical movement and are therefore concerned that denominational participation in the ecumenical movement should be as strong as possible.

A good example of the double direction in which it is sought to lead the churches of the West can be given by quoting a letter from the Rev. G. E. Hickman Johnson, the General Secretary of the Methodist Missionary Society at that time, which appeared in the *Methodist Recorder* of October 7, 1954.

In the account by the Rev. E. Benson Perkins of the meeting of the Methodist World Executive, he said two major concerns came before that Executive. The first of them was, Methodist schemes of Church Union. The Rev. Wilfred Wade raised the question "whether the right way forward is to create national Churches or to consider a unity at international and inter-racial levels. ... It may be that confessional unions provide the way forward, or something along that line." It is on this point that I would venture to comment.

The question raised by Mr Wade, whose preference for "confessional unions" appeared to receive considerable support in the Executive, was raised in the General Committee of the Wesleyan Methodist Missionary Society in the early days of the discussion on Church Union in South India. I remember clearly a forceful speech made somewhere about 1929-30 by the late Dr F. Luke Wiseman whose capacious mind put before the Committee a vital choice—the choice now discussed afresh at the World Executive: are we out to set up united Churches in our overseas areas, he asked, or should we leave any such unions to other Churches and ourselves stand for the spread of world Methodism? He set forth the arguments for each cause.

No one could have made the choice clearer than did the speaker, and yet with its eyes wide open, and with an almost unanimous vote, the W.M.M.S. General Committee declared its belief that it was God's will for His Church in India to become united.

The question, and its attendant argument, were repeated in the following Conference. Finally, after many years of discussion the union was, I think, unanimously blessed by Conference. With both hands Methodism gave all she had to give in South India—people, land, buildings—to the Church of South India, together with a continued supply of missionaries and funds: surely one of the noblest acts our Church has ever performed, and one which the work and experience of the Church of South India have completely justified since its inauguration in 1947.

The point I would raise here is that the issue raised by Mr Wade at the World Methodist Executive at Evanston was faithfully faced a quarter of a century ago—and was settled for British Methodism. It is surely a little late in the day to raise it afresh, seven years after so considerable a union as that in South India has taken place and with schemes for similar unions now nearing completion both in North India and Ceylon, and discussions along such lines also afoot in some West African areas.

On this whole issue the churches of the West must make up their minds as to what they want. Do they want to retain their position of leadership within denominational families—for in such families the younger churches will always remain weaker partners—or do they want to put their strength at the disposal of the younger churches in the common tasks which these younger churches face in the lands in which they are set? As far as the younger churches themselves are concerned the development of such organs as the East Asia Christian Conference and the All Africa Church Conference is an indication of the direction in which they have decided to move.

Almost as an aside it is perhaps necessary to interject a paragraph here to register the fact that the various confessional movements are also not all of one kind. The Presbyterian World Alliance, for instance, seeks to make its contribution by maintaining and expounding the historic presbyterian emphases in Christian theology; while, on the other hand, in a body like the World Lutheran Federation financial and organizational power are at the service of confessional difference. In the Methodist Church both in America and Britain, there are those who would like to construct a world Methodist administrative structure; whilst the Missionary Societies of these churches are committed to policies set in the opposite direction. Anglicanism is committed to the policy of national or regional Church Union, but almost everywhere maintains its confessional character by dragging its feet when it comes to local co-operation and united witness with other churches in immediate tasks. Congregationalism in its many forms is busy in all parts of the world disappearing into various united Churches while the Baptists maintain on the one hand their general aloofness from Church Union movements and on the other remain flexible for co-operation because of their congregational polity. It is rarely an issue of what these confessional organizations intend, it is always a question of what their effects are simply because they are world organizations with administrative power and financial strength.

It is conceivable that the characterizations given in the above paragraph are too superficial to be fair or even helpful, but an attempt had to be made to indicate how crucial it is to discern what the appropriate form should be of witnessing to confessionally-held differences within the ecumenical and church union movements. The tides of history in Asia, Africa and Latin America have changed the situation for the churches of the West. It would be foolish for them to commit themselves to a policy intended to arrest or neutralize this change. A railway guard got so used to having his meals in the train, that even at home his wife had to keep on shaking the table while he was eating his dinner.

The churches of the West must, in the development of organized world confessionalisms, face not only the issues raised by the church union movement but also the issues raised by the increasing programme of Inter-Church Aid. Within the missionary connection churches belonging to the same confessional family help one another, but the department of Inter-Church Aid of the World Council of Churches has raised the question as to the most appropriate form of Christian witness when the need to be met has no denominational or confessional relevance. Suppose there is a famine in Malaya and aid is to be channelled through denominational lines. The Methodists in Malaya related to American Methodism can get substantial help. The Anglicans related to British Anglicanism will not be so advantageously placed. The powerful Lutheran Church in America will have little obligation to do anything ... and so on. To say that all this can be ironed out is futile pleading. The fact is that the problem of need must not be distorted by the denominational imbalance in the resources of the Churches. In other words both the missionary connection and the confessional family connection need to be held within limits where the meeting of need is the point in question.

The same principle applies in other realms. Just as a common need can afford a principle of unity so also can a common life. A student community in a university is one community. The Student Christian Movement was an attempt to bring to this one community the one Gospel of Christ. To-day the various churches in the West are seeking to reverse this situation by fragmenting the student community along denominational lines. The positive gains of confessional student movements could have been achieved without this negative result. Another example can be given in the field of Christian institutions of many kinds. There is no reason why a Christian hospital has to be a Methodist hospital or a Christian High School has to be an Anglican one. Confessional differences must take seriously all forms of secular unity. Otherwise the churches may be in disobedience to the Lord of the world.

I do not want to give the impression that world confessional organizations are in the main an unfortunate development. It is my conviction that, in a suitable form, they are necessary at the present time to ensure that past gains and the treasures of the several churches are conserved in all future developments within the ecumenical movement. They are necessary also to put at the service of the ecumenical movement the acquired experience and strength of the various confessional families. There is too the dependence of churches on their confessional heritage as they grow into mature self-hood. But the protest which is being voiced here is against the kind of con-federalism which these confessional developments envisage as the form which the ecumenical movement must take. The ecumenical movement, including the church union movement, must be a movement out of one centre which is the Church and not out of many centres which are the churches. It must grow from the given forms of unity already experienced in the Church and not from the differences which divide the churches. In the words of Nikos Nissiotis, "To be together as Churches to-day implies an open continuous invitation of the Holy Spirit—to realize both eternally in time and historically in the history of the Church, the event of the one and undivided Church towards which and from which all actions must be re-examined and re-adjusted. We all of us have to re-plant our new roots which are the old ones of our common baptism in the Holy Spirit."[1] The World Council of Churches is only a Council and must remain a Council, being the hedge which gives protection to the tree as it grows. The activities of the Council, however, must concern the tree and not the hedge. The hedge should absorb only minimum time and money.

The one centre, the given forms of unity already experienced in the Church and in the churches, the forms of secular unity provided by the world: these constitute the base for future advance. It is this base, in all its three aspects, which is threatened by world structures of confessional allegiance. In the Lutheran World Federation, a discussion is being conducted on

[1] Nikos Nissiotis is Assistant Director of the Ecumenical Institute. The quotation is from *Bossey News*, Dec. 1960.

the ecclesiological significance of the Federation. The basis of the discussion is an article by Dr Peter Brunner which appeared in the *Lutheran World* of December, 1960. His plea is for the creation of a World Lutheran Church. In urging this plea, he says:

> According to Lutheran doctrine, the only legitimate divisions between churches are those which are caused by the Gospel itself and therefore are based upon a difference between false and true doctrine. There is only one means that has been given to us to overcome such divisions and that is responsible doctrinal discussion. Such doctrinal discussion can be carried on—at any rate in its decisive stage—only between "church" and "church". A commission of theologians appointed by the World Federation could, it is true, prepare such a doctrinal discussion, but it could not carry it out. Is any individual Lutheran church in a position to carry out such a discussion by itself alone? As long as the Evangelical Lutheran Church appears in the form of individual autonomous churches, but as a church has no common organ through which it can speak, it will be able to co-operate in the solution of the ecumenical task only in a very limited way when this task enters its decisive stage.[1]

Here we have the crux of the matter. The issues and experiences both of unity and disunity among Christians must be dehydrated until they become matters of doctrine only, so that theological professors may decide if and when divided Christians should unite! What chance is there that the Batak Church, for instance, will find its unity with the other Churches in Indonesia, if the pressures of God on Indonesian life are treated as secondary? Does the One Gospel become a living power by embodying it in one doctrinal and ecclesiological form? Will not the one centre be replaced by competing world centres if confessions repeat the pattern of Rome?

> Suppose [says Peter Brunner] that the course of the council which the Pope has announced should make it necessary for the Lutheran Church as such to address a message to all Christians in the world and especially to the Roman Catholic Church. Who would do this? The Assembly of the Lutheran World Federation

[1] P. 25.

dare not by any means think of itself as a church synod. An "ecumenical council" of the Evangelical Lutheran Church does not exist. In such a case could the Evangelical Lutheran Church be content with the fact that it can raise its voice only through the agency of individual churches?[1]

This argument is valid only if the message to be issued is to have some legal binding force on Lutherans throughout the world. Has not the World Council of Churches often issued messages to all Christians and to all men?

The confusion which causes all these questions arises because the importance of formulated doctrine is given precedence over Christian obedience to the truth. Truth is always present only in solution, dissolved in the concrete processes of human living. Jesus is the Truth: He cannot be formulated but only obeyed as He makes His will known in the tasks and circumstances of life. The work for increasing the experience and forms of Christian unity is work to mix the solutions in which Truth is found. Truth in oil and Truth in water may not mix, Truth in acid and Truth in alkali may mix, Truth in some other base may only make a colloidal solution: but oil or water, acid or alkali, or any other base—these are the secular unities which the world provides.

The Easternity of the Base

In spite of its title, however, this chapter cannot conclude by merely discussing the questions incident to the dominant role which the churches of the West have to play in the future of the Christian enterprise. The Westernity of the base of this enterprise has to be taken seriously, but it is nevertheless true that the tasks of to-morrow will be determined also by the truth that there is an Easternity to the base as well.

The word "East" has three common usages. There is the geographical east which lies between the Suez Canal and New Zealand, there is the political east which lies to the east of the "curtains" which divide the nations, there is also the ecclesi-

[1] *Ibid.*

astical east represented by the Eastern Orthodox Churches. Christianity is an Eastern religion in all these three senses.

Let us say a word about each of these three in the reverse order. Christianity is an Eastern religion in the ecclesiastical sense. This means that there is an Eastern Church which in its history has withstood the vicissitudes of time. Neither Turkish domination of yesterday nor Communist dominion of to-day has destroyed this Church. Its strength has been in its worshipping life so securely fixed on the "glory" that shall be. A church which constantly celebrates the resurrection of the Lord and ardently longs for His return in triumph has a witness to bear to-morrow as it has borne that witness yesterday.

But if this witness is to bear its richest fruit for all Christians, the Eastern Churches must break away from their isolation. It is a source of great joy that the first steps have been taken for a closer collaboration between the Orthodox Church of Russia and the other churches in the World Council of Churches. It is a necessary task to lay at rest the kind of questionings that still plague the Church of Greece as it seeks to break its isolation. It is important also that the World Council of Churches multiply its contacts with the Church of Rome so that ecumenical conversation can be truly tri-partite. But the problem of isolation for the Eastern Churches is not simply a problem of increasing contacts and conversation. It is essentially the problem of isolating "the glory of God" in worship from the meaning of the cross and resurrection in daily life. Protestantism in all its forms of expression in the countries where the Eastern Orthodox predominate poses the challenge of individual conversion in a form that cannot be side-stepped. Proselytism can and ought to be controlled, but when that is done, the issue still remains—Have you met Jesus Christ? Have you received the Holy Spirit? To these questions each individual must make answer; the Church cannot answer on his behalf.

Christianity is also an Eastern religion in the political sense. In the countries which are politically East, the Christian Church has found weapons of warfare which are blunt in the West. The simple fact of going to church, the act of having one's baby baptized, a Bible text on a bill-board, acceptance of imprisonment and even death—these are potent means of witness. The Church exists in its elemental forms, and when the forces of secular life identify the atom which is the Church and seek to smash it they find a release of energy which is as unexpected as it is alarming.

It is one of the urgent tasks of to-morrow that brotherhood be strengthened between the churches of the politically East and the politically West. The first requirement is that each party ceases to rejoice in the blunders that are made "politically" by the nations on the other side. Where wrong is committed, the temptation must be avoided of saying, "Didn't we say so?" Nothing is gained by proving that we were right in saying that they were bad. More consistent prayer for one another alone will sweeten again the channels of communication and conversation.

And lastly, Christianity is an Eastern religion in the geographical sense. The missions of the West have become the Churches of Asia and Africa. The missionaries from the West have become colleagues in the younger churches. "Your" has become "our". But the task remains. There is the unfinished evangelistic task. There is the task of addressing Eastern cultures with a relevant and a pungent theology. There is the task of making the Church in Eastern lands congruous with its background. There is the task of giving regional expression to the ecumenical idea.

New thrusts have been made with respect to each of these tasks. "Missions" have largely disappeared in Asia as separate administrative structures. Soon this must happen in Africa and in Latin America too. Procedures and policies now make certain that missionaries from one country to another are not only sent but received, not only offered but asked for. Evangelistic advance is everywhere being planned and undertaken. Indigenous theological thinking is receiving great impetus. Indigenization of the Church is an accepted goal everywhere. There are from the churches of Asia more than one hundred missionaries working in lands other than their own. The East

Asia Christian Conference is in being, and similar bodies are in process of formation in Africa and Latin America.

Everywhere, both in East and West, the Church is set amidst revolutionary happenings. This is a period in which through His activity in the world the Lord is speaking to His Church. The Churches are under pressure to assess their past and to prepare for the future. Can we not hear the sound of a going in the tops of the mulberry trees? (2 Sam. 5: 24.)

marching

Part III
THE ENCOUNTER

Jesus Christ is the life of the world and the light of men. All light received by men anywhere is from Him and by Him; so that light wherever it may be found is always set towards Him.

The purpose of the Gospel is to make men free to walk by the light that is in Jesus Christ. It leads them to repentance that they may eschew the works of darkness. It calls them to faith that they may surrender their lives of piety. It bids them live as disciples of Jesus Christ that they may find release from themselves in His service.

The Gospel relates men securely to this world and challenges them to live in it as Christ's fellows.

It is this world in its manifoldness that Jesus loved and came to save. He became part of it in an incarnate life and remains part of it through His risen presence. As ascended Lord He is Lord of its history and when He comes in glory He will bring that history to its culmination.

This world, then, in all its variety of peoples and nations, and men in their several cultures and religions, are the subject and object of the Church's mission. This mission is in order that all things may come to a head in Jesus Christ.

THE WORLD OF RELIGIONS
—THE RELIGIOUS FRONTIER

THERE is a natural home to which each man belongs. Indeed, a man may belong to many such homes—a home being defined in terms of neighbourhood or family, of occupation or social class, of culture or religion, of race, tribe or nation. The Gospel must become present in each home, and everywhere also make its pressure felt against the boundaries which separate home from home, for there is but one household of faith.

The world of religions and the world of nations are two of the insistent realities which condition the homes in which men live. Into these two worlds, interpenetrating one another, the missionary must enter with the Gospel. What happens when he does so?

A Summary of Answers Given

The relation between Christianity and other religions is a question with a long history behind it; and yet, in spite of this subject being so essential to an understanding of the Church's task, the argument concerning it has resulted in many and varied answers. There have been five distinct points of view on this subject which have found vigorous expression in recent theological debate.

1. It has been held that the attitude of Christian mission should be that Christianity must supplant the other religions because they are of purely human origin (John 14: 6). The primary method of those who advocate this attitude is that of polemic.

An important variant of this attitude and consequent method is that the Christian witness does not need to and, indeed, cannot express a judgment on other religions. Christianity and these religions are of two different kinds. So, what is permissible and effective is to set Christianity over against other religions, making the demand that those of other religions give them up and embrace Christianity instead. To challenge those of other faiths with a presentation of the Christian Gospel is the one responsibility of the evangelist.

2. A second point of view which is urged is that Christianity is the fulfilment of other religions (Acts 17: 23). There is in these religions a real yearning for God which is itself a partial response to His approach, and this yearning is truly met by Christ. Indeed, since this yearning for God in these religions is not only something inherent in the religious consciousness but is also the inspiration of the very teachings of these religions, these teachings find their full meaning and significance in and are truly construed as pointers to Jesus Christ.

> Our little systems have their day:
> They have their day and cease to be:
> They are but broken lights of Thee,
> And Thou, O Lord, art more than they.[1]

The method of approach, which this attitude would support, is one grounded in the study of comparative religion. It is a method which seeks to isolate truths from a whole body of belief and show that these truths point to the truth in Jesus Christ.

3. A third attitude of Christian witness which is set forward is that there is in all religions the possibility of "faith" between God and man (Lk. 7: 9)—a possibility which is realized by many persons—yet that in Christianity this possibility has become a free gift to all men. In Jesus, a transformation of man's religious situation has taken place. Let a man meet Jesus, and Jesus becomes indispensable to him.

Those who share this attitude would insist that the primary method which Christian witness must follow is the method of conversation. The man who has "faith" but who is not a Christian has something to say which the Christian must listen to, not only in order to understand that "faith" but also to

[1] Alfred Tennyson, *In Memoriam.*

acknowledge it. The Christian Gospel must then be addressed to that faith in order that that faith may be made secure in the Gospel.

4. A fourth position which is maintained is that in Jesus all religions are brought to judgment, and that He remains the judge of all religions including Christianity. Religion is man's response to God's action on man's behalf. The only way of receiving the Gospel of Jesus Christ, however, is by radical repentance; for there is no theological continuity between the religious life and the life of faith which is rooted in the Gospel (Phil. 3: 7).

The consequence of this attitude in missionary practice and evangelistic preaching is a dialectic approach to other religions. On the one hand, the messenger of the Gospel stands alongside his hearers—Christianity and other religions being set side by side; and, on the other hand, he stands facing his hearers as the emissary of the Gospel to them. The Christian is in the world, the Gospel is over against it.

5. A fifth point of view would hold that the motive of Christian witness should be not one of seeking to make Christians of adherents of other religions, but of so presenting Jesus Christ to them that He Himself will become for them the point of reconception with respect to their own religions (John 1: 9). Thus, it is held, in course of time there will emerge a new religion in which all religions, including Christianity, will be comprehended.

In this process Christianity has to give as well as to receive, so that the true method of approach is that of co-operation. Worshipping and working together, Christians and those who are not Christians will help one another to a fuller understanding and a more comprehensive acceptance of all that it means when one says "I believe in God".

> Each sees one colour of Thy rainbow-light,
> Each looks upon one tint and calls it heaven;
> Thou art the fulness of our partial sight;
> We are not perfect till we find the seven.[1]

[1] George Matheson, *Y.M.C.A. Hymnal* 86.

The wide difference in point of view and conviction, which the above summary must disclose, naturally raises the question as to whether those who partake in this discussion are sufficiently agreed on what the discussion should be about or on the frame of thought within which the debate should take place. It is to this question that we shall address ourselves, in the hope that a reflection on the general terms of the discussion may uncover where some of the inherent difficulties lie, and also shed light on why Christians, who are equally committed to the Church's task of proclaiming the Gospel, find themselves in such sharp disagreement.

As has already been hinted, the conviction which lies behind the argument of this chapter is that any conversation about Christianity and other religions must be conducted as a discussion about the address of the Gospel to men in their several homes. Therefore, though beginning with a summary of answers already given, there is no intention to continue the debate on the old terms. The hope rather is so to open up the whole question that future discussion of it will move away from the world of religions as such and become lodged in that reality of human life in which God's sovereign mercy and man's blundering faith are in mutual relation, informing that life in all its parts and affecting its every activity.

The Christian Component in the Discussion

To begin then at the point at which the discussion of this subject has arrived, the first essential is to define more closely the two components or factors whose relation is the subject of examination. First of all, what is the Christian factor? Is it the Christian Faith, or the Christian Religion, that is, Christianity, or the Christian Church or the Christian Gospel? If it is granted that the uniqueness which is affirmed about the Christian factor lies in Jesus Christ Himself (John 1: 18), who He is, what He has done, and what He is continuing to do, then we have a criterion with which to judge the adequacy and correctness of the term that we use.

If we speak about the Christian Faith, we are speaking about the body of Christian doctrine, belief, and practice. Obviously, this includes and is dependent on our affirmation about Jesus Christ; but it is our faith, that is, the faith as formulated by and enshrined within the life of the Church. This means that the term "Christian Faith" is a term which is centripetal by nature and, therefore, will cause confusion if the attempt is made to establish a relation between it and the world outside it.

If we speak about the Christian Religion, that is, Christianity, we are speaking about a historical phenomenon. We are speaking, on the one hand, about a body of people who through the centuries have maintained an identifiable continuity and, on the other hand, about their faith and life. This life has been lived in the world and has been subject to the influences and pressures of the world, so that in smaller or greater measure at different times of its history it has been conditioned by the world. In other words, the term "Christianity" partakes so much of "the world" that it is too inclusive a term to use in this discussion.

If we speak about the Christian Church, we are speaking about the Body which professes the Christian Faith and whose life constitutes the stream which is Christianity. This Church lives in the world and is related to it, but this relationship is not the relationship of two things which exist side by side so that an objective definition or description can be given of the relation between them. Rather, it is part of the nature of the Church to relate itself to the world in a particular way, so that if we take "the Christian Church" as the first term in our discussion we shall be led not so much to discuss the relation between the Church and something else as to discuss the nature of the Church itself in its relationships. In other words, to use the term "the Christian Church" for one component in this discussion is to destroy the integrity of the other component.

If we speak about the Christian Gospel, the emphasis falls on that action of God in Jesus Christ which has caused the Church, and set it in the world, and given to it its mission. The term "the Christian Gospel" emphasizes the fact that the rela-

231

tion around which the discussion centres is a relation which is caused by the Gospel itself when it is addressed to all those who are claimed by it. Thus, for example, when we speak about "the relation between the Christian Gospel and Hinduism" we are actually speaking about the relation caused by the Christian Gospel between itself and Hinduism when it is proclaimed. In other words, we may not conduct the discussion by first defining and describing each component term and then seeking to define or describe the relation between them. We must, rather, seek to find out directly how the relation itself is set up and why; and what, therefore, its nature is.

In order to designate the Christian component in this discussion, therefore, the term "the Christian Gospel" or "the Christian Message" is the one which lights up the true situation. It focuses attention on the Gospel proclaimed, it also witnesses to the connection between the Gospel and the proclaiming community. It is the peculiarity of the Christian community which points to the peculiarity of the Gospel. Christians used to speak of themselves as a third race—a *tertium gens*. They realized how peculiar they were and ought to be. Were this only foolishness or arrogance, no question need arise about the Gospel and its relation to the religions; but, rooted as it is in the teaching of the New Testament, the question is truly raised. It is made clear too that the discussion of it is not to be in the area of comparative religions or comparative religious psychology but in that of evangelism and missionary responsibility.

That "the Christian Message" is the right term to choose for this discussion is seen also in that it does justice to the other terms to which it is preferred. It affirms that there is a Message —the Gospel that, in Jesus Christ, God has acted on man's behalf and demands man's response; that there is a Messenger —the Church which the Gospel brings into being, and the Body within which the Gospel is continuously experienced; that there is a Story—the story of the Christian religion, which is the story of the Church's witness to and life in the Gospel; and that there is a Faith—the normative testimony by the historical Church to the eternal Gospel.

All this means that the discussion is not about the relation between the religion, or the religious life, of Christians and that of those who are not Christians; nor is it about the relation between the religious beliefs of Christians and the beliefs of those who are not Christians; rather, it is about the operation of the Gospel itself among those who are Christians and among those who are not. It is when the Gospel is preached that the relation which we are seeking to understand is set up. Indeed, that is why this subject is so immediately relevant to a consideration of the missionary task. Something happens when the Gospel is proclaimed, and an understanding of what happens is essential for an understanding of the nature of the proclamation.

The Non-Christian Component in the Discussion

If, then, our submission is right, that the subject of our discussion is the relation which is created when the Gospel is proclaimed, the simplest way of defining the non-Christian component or factor in our discussion is to ask, "What is the object to which the Gospel is addressed?" The answer surely is "the world". It is the world which God loved and which Jesus died to save; it is the world over which He rules and which, at the end, He will judge. This world, nevertheless, has not fully accepted His rule nor does it rejoice in it. Countless millions of people in this world do not yet know Jesus as their Saviour. To this world the Gospel is addressed.

But this world lives, and in its life exhibits much truth, beauty, and goodness; in it is found faith toward God and love toward man; it is very much a religious world. It is also a world which will not, and thinks that it need not, accept the Gospel of God in Jesus Christ. Indeed, it is this contrariness in the nature of the world which constitutes the chief problem in our discussion. Because of it there is created the double relation both of judgment and of kinship which the Christian message establishes between itself and its addressee. Because of it there arises also the Gospel's universal demand for repentance. All must repent and no one is exempted. Whether Nicodemus (John 3:

233

1-15) or Mary of Magdala (Lk. 8: 2), whether religious teacher or wayside sinner (Lk. 7: 36-48), both need repentance and both can repent. Whether Saul of Tarsus (Acts 9) or Elymas the sorcerer (Acts 13: 8-12), servant of God or servant of the devil, both must become blind before they can see. How important it is, therefore, so to define the non-Christian component in our discussion that we make clear its double nature both as being open to and contrary to the Christian message.

In the history of the discussion we are speaking about, the non-Christian factor has been variously defined as non-Christian faith, non-Christian religions, a non-Christian world.

When Jesus said of the Roman centurion, "Truly, I say to you, not even in Israel have I found such faith" (Matt. 8: 10), he was speaking about a fact to which Christians who have lived with followers of other religions can bear testimony. Again and again, when the Gospel is proclaimed, it is proclaimed to persons who already have this kind of faith, so that it is a legitimate and essential question to ask "What relation does the Gospel, when it is proclaimed, establish between itself and such faith?" But it would be foolish to assume that the answer to this question holds the key to an understanding of the relation between the Christian Gospel and the non-Christian world; for the nature of the non-Christian world is not determined by the presence in it of persons of faith; it is determined rather by those complete systems of life and belief which are able to sustain themselves without accepting the Gospel of Jesus Christ and, therefore, cannot accept it without being subverted by it.

It is these complete systems of life and belief which we speak about when we speak about non-Christian religions. But the Gospel is not addressed to these religions either; it is addressed to the world of whose life and thought these religions are a part. The world is made up of the world of nature and of persons in all their manifold relationships. This world the Gospel claims for itself and calls to repentance. Thus, our discussion cannot be about the Christian Gospel and non-Christian religions; it has to be about the Christian message in a non-

Christian world. The importance, however, of remembering the part these religious systems play in the world cannot be overstressed. From it arises the pressing need to study each of these religious traditions and the specific forms of faith which condition each man's response to the Gospel.

And yet, the basic truth remains that it is man whom the Gospel addresses. William Ernest Hocking is reported as having asked C. F. Andrews, "How do you preach the gospel to a Hindu?" to which Andrews replied, "I don't. I preach the gospel to a man." That is a profound answer. The Christian message is not addressed to other religions, it is not about other religions: the Christian message is about the world. It tells the world a truth about itself—God loved it and loves it still; and, in telling that truth, the Gospel bears witness to a relation between itself and the world. It is this relation which is the subject of our discussion.

Also, it is well to remember that the world is non-Christian only in a temporal and, in fact, a temporary sense (Rev. 11: 15). It is already in God's purpose a world for which Jesus died and over which He rules (Matt. 28: 18). When a Buddhist, for instance, denies meaning to human history, he is simply bearing evidence to the fact that it has no meaning apart from Christ. Standing apart from Christ, the Buddhist is unable to see life's meaning. The truth, however, is that the human story has already been seized by Christ and will be comprehended by Him. Of course there are many who have not accepted Him as their Lord and Saviour, and refuse so to accept Him still; but even they are within the rule and saving work of Christ. In Charles Wesley's words:

> The world He suffered to redeem;
> For all He hath the atonement made;
> For those that will not come to Him
> The ransom of His life was paid.[1]

In the final analysis, then, the "relation" which we are seeking to understand is a relation established by Jesus Himself.

[1] *Methodist Hymn Book*, 75.

There is the Gospel to be proclaimed and there are those whom the Gospel claims; and from both these facts arises the question which we seek to answer: "What is the nature of the existence of the Christian message in a non-Christian world?"

When the Gospel is Proclaimed

The commission under which the Church acts when it proclaims the Gospel is summed up in the words with which Matthew's gospel closes: "All authority in heaven and on earth has been given to me. Go therefore and make disciples of all nations" (Matt. 28: 18-19). Those to whom the Church is sent with its message are already those over whom Jesus has been set as Lord. They are His. They are those other sheep about whom He spoke when He said, "I have other sheep, that are not of this fold; I must bring them also" (John 10: 16). They are His sheep. He already has them. He must bring them into His fold. When the Gospel is proclaimed, it is to this activity of the Christ that that proclamation bears witness, and it is with this activity that it seeks to co-operate.

God is busy with man. He made man in His own image. He made man in such a way that man lives by "imaging" God. This also means, therefore, that God is always "toward" man, seeking to evoke man's glad response. It is not necessary for us to define or describe the ways in which God's busy-ness with man has been exercised; it is enough to know that that busyness has been there. The story of the Old Testament is abundant proof that Gòd wàs busy all the time not only with Israel but with all peoples. When the Gospel declares that God loved the world, it is this truth that it is declaring. The Gospel is for all men with each of whom and all of whom God is still busy. His Christ is seeking them to bring them into His fold (Lk. 15: 4). The Christian witness does not grasp the true inwardness of his work where he does not see that God is previous to him in the life of the person whom he is seeking to win for the Gospel, and also previous to him in whatever area of life he is seeking to make the Gospel effective.

What happens, then, when the Gospel is proclaimed? That is the question for which we are seeking an answer, an answer which we may now proceed to outline.

The activity of God in the world, His busy-ness, can be set out within four different frames of thought.

1. There is God in His activity to win men to live in fellowship with Him.

2. There is God in His activity to reveal to men His true nature and purpose.

3. There is God in His activity to create for Himself a people who will be His instrument in the world.

4. And there is God in His activity to bring to pass His Kingdom into which will be gathered all the treasures of the nations.

It is on this fourfold activity of God that the Church's commission to proclaim the Gospel depends. We preach the Gospel not simply as those under command to do so, but as those who, being in Christ, find ourselves involved and implicated in His continuing ministry to and in the world. God is at work and we work with Him, and the consequence of what we do is subordinate to the consequence of what He does. Our work is an offering to Him (Gen. 4: 4-5), His work is what fulfils His purposes.

God in His Activity of Salvation

Let us look, then, at the first activity of God which we mentioned—His activity to win men to live in fellowship with Him. Here the basic truth which we must affirm at the outset is one we have mentioned already; the truth that God is always busy with every man, because each man is made in God's image. While it is true that men call themselves Hindus or Muslims or Buddhists or Christians and that each of these religions has identifiable and defined beliefs, it is nevertheless also true that the religion of one man is not exactly like the religion of another man. There is a true sense in which each man's religion can be more or can be less than his religious system. Whether men are engaged in flight from God or search for God or acceptance of God (and all men are involved in all these three attitudes at the same time), they are, in all these things, reacting to the action of God upon them in His work of salvation. No man's religion and no religious system is purely a product of man. To say that they are, is to deny that man is made in God's image.

It is true that God's image in man has been distorted by sin, but the image is still there. A mirror may be a broken mirror, but as long as one stands in front of the mirror it will reflect one's image—a broken and distorted image, certainly; but one's image nevertheless. Our reflection of God's image is there as long as God has not forsaken us (Rom. 1 : 24, 26, 28). We can only break the mirror. We cannot get rid of God's busy-ness with us.

The Incarnation is the climax and fulfilment of this continued busy-ness of God with man. Jesus is not merely the fulfilment of God's work with Israel, He is the fulfilment of God's work with humanity. The Word became flesh. God became man. Jesus is more than Jew. So, with respect to Christ, too, our affirmation has to be a universal affirmation. He became a man like all men. He is busy with all men. He loves all men. He died for all men. He seeks all men. He rules over all men. He is judge of all men. Hence the Christian message is proclaimed to all men. "God so loved the world that he gave his only Son, that whoever believes in him should not perish but have eternal life" (John 3 : 16).

But what of those who already have "faith" to whom this declaration is made? Are there not those who have not consciously accepted God in Christ, but who nevertheless in some measure respond truly to God's action on them? Are there not those who, being outside the Christian faith, still do the truth? (John 3 : 21). The answer must be "yes".

But it is necessary to go on and affirm that even they are in need of the challenge of the Gospel and that their faith can be both a preparation and a hindrance to finding faith in Jesus Christ. The relation between Christian faith and non-Christian faith (both words being used in the singular) is not a relation that can be systematized. The work of the Holy Spirit in each soul cannot be described in the same way. There are those who, because of their previous faith, find themselves prepared to accept the Lordship of Jesus Christ. They also find that, once they have accepted His Lordship, their previous faith undergoes a radical transformation. There are others who, because of their faith, find themselves hindered from accepting the Lordship of Jesus Christ, but who find that, once the Holy Spirit has led them to accept Christ's Lordship, then their original faith is not something they need to throw away. It becomes part of the soil in which their faith in Christ grows and blossoms.

In other words, the actual living process of men finding faith in Jesus Christ is not a process that can be described according to one pattern. The attempt to do this is, very often, simply the result of those who are already Christians attempting to find out a way in which, when they study other religions, the knowledge of these religions relates itself to their Christian faith. Some Christians find that they can move from their Christian faith to an understanding of other religions without being conscious of a break in thought; there are others who find themselves unable to avoid this break, while there are still others who find it completely impossible to establish any relation between their Christian faith and their understanding of other religions. May it not be that the whole discussion about the relation between Christianity and other religions has been vitiated by the fact that we have been talking, not so much about what happens when the Christian Gospel is proclaimed to adherents of other religions, as about what happens when we who are of the Christian faith study other religions?

God in His Activity of Revelation

In speaking about God in His activity of salvation, we spoke primarily of the effect of that activity on all men. But there is also a central story of this activity. He, who had not left Himself without witness among any people at any time (Acts 14: 17), nevertheless made this witness to Himself the central concern of

His dealings with a particular people. He made the Jews the bearers of His revelation. The demand of God on the Jewish people was that they should be faithful to Him. In the indictment of the nations which Amos drew up, it was only with respect to Judah and Israel that the judgment turned on what God had done for them. The other nations were to be punished because their wrongdoing was a denial of their belonging to God (Amos 1-2). The words in which Isaiah accused his people of infidelity stated the central concern of God in His activity of revelation. "The ox knows its owner, and the ass its master's crib; but Israel does not know, my people does not understand" (Is. 1: 3).

This activity of God in revelation, which we trace through the Bible story, is certainly also His activity in salvation; but here it is distinguished as revelation because its intention was not only to save but also to raise a people who would be the messengers of this salvation. They would know God as Saviour. They would recognize His saving works. They would proclaim this good news of God's salvation. Through His dealings with the Jews, it was all mankind that God sought to save, and it was for this purpose that He demanded of the Jews that they understand and acknowledge Him as Saviour and themselves as His people. The sorrows that fell upon them were for the healing of the nations (Rev. 22: 2); the light lit upon Zion was in order that the nations might come to it (Rev. 21: 23-26).

This revelation reached its fulfilment in Jesus Christ. "In many and various ways God spoke of old to our fathers by the prophets; but in these last days he has spoken to us by a Son" (Heb. 1: 1-2). The story of revelation finds its culmination in Jesus, and through Jesus it becomes effective and meaningful for all men. The purpose of God in His dealings with the Jews is completed in Jesus, who was a Jew, so that by the obedience of Jesus that purpose proceeds to its realization in the life of all mankind.

The instrument in history by which this fulfilment of God's revelation in Jesus Christ is witnessed to in the world is the Church. The Church is created by that revelation; its life is what response to that revelation makes possible. The Church is continuous with Israel, it is the object and bearer of God's revelation. Thus arises the demand of the Gospel that men accept it and become witnesses to it. It was this demand that the early Church made of the Jews, and if the demand was made of the Jews, how much more decisively it is made of the Gentiles.

In other words, the form in which the question is put to men by God's activity in revelation is determined by the fact that God not only seeks to save but also seeks participants in His work of salvation. What is set before men is a demand made within the here and now of their earthly life. What must they do who, whatever their previous faith, find faith in Jesus Christ? The answer is that they must repent and be baptized (Acts 2: 38). They must become members of the Christian community. Baptism is the sign of the essential discontinuity between life outside conscious acceptance of Jesus as Lord and inside His Body which is the Church. Outside Jesus, they may have been religious men, but now they have become something quite different. They have become messengers of the Gospel. Their essential occupation has changed.

There has been in India, for some time now, a group that calls itself "the fellowship of the friends of Jesus". It is a group that has sought to express its faith in Jesus Christ without breaking away from the Hindu community. Some of its members, like the late Mr O. Kandasamy Chetty, have borne significant witness to Jesus Christ as Lord. But the effect of this group has been to blur the nature of the demand which Jesus makes on men. God in His activity of revelation is asking for a people who will be His, who will come out of the world and be separate, who will be the sign and symbol and evidence of what God has done for man in Jesus Christ. Any attempt to treat the story of Jesus simply as a part of the general story of how God has been busy with men results in making that story pointless. The significance of Jesus is bound up with His claim that all men must answer the question as to who He is (John 17: 3).

The Christian message in a non-Christian world, therefore,

not only poses the problem of man's response to God's will to redeem him, it also presents the issue of man's response to God's desire to use him. In Jesus, God's plan and purpose for the world have been revealed, and God is asking for fellow workers with Jesus. The first qualification of such a worker is that he must be known as belonging to Jesus Christ and to no one else (Acts 19: 15). It is an inescapable part of the task of Christian witness to make this call for fellow workers known and have it accepted. It can, of course, be argued that God can use any man to fulfil His purposes; but the point here is that Christian submission to God's use is also the method and measure of one's participation in the experience of salvation. When Paul claimed that for him to live was Christ (Phil. 1: 21), he was witnessing to the truth that participation in the life of Christ which is salvation was by way of living obedience to Him.

Thus, while a consideration of the questions raised by the nature of God's activity in salvation leads to answers which cannot be tied up into neat formulae, a consideration of the questions raised by the nature of God's activity in revelation demands a simple and unequivocal answer. "The times of ignorance God overlooked, but now he commands all men everywhere to repent, because he has fixed a day on which he will judge the world in righteousness by a man whom he has appointed" (Acts 17: 30-31).

God in His Activity of Mission

It is already evident that the connection between God in His activity of salvation and God in His activity of revelation lies in the fact that God has raised up for Himself a people whose primary obligation is their mission to the world. One of the essential distinctions between the Christian faith and other faiths is that the Christian faith can be proclaimed. The other faiths can only be taught. The Christian evangelist announces that something has happened which is of both immediate and ultimate significance for each man and all men. The adherents of other religions, on the other hand, expound the teachings of their own religions as the true interpretation of the meaning and responsibilities of life. The Christian evangelist is primarily concerned with evoking obedience to Jesus Christ. The teachers of other religions are concerned with winning acceptance for the truths they teach.

This fact that the Christian faith is something to be proclaimed is so important that its significance may be pointed out also in another way. So often we have heard Christians say, for instance, "The Hindus believe in rebirth, Christians believe in the resurrection," and this is said as if what each believes is what will happen to him. The Christian faith proclaims certain things as true and as true independently of human belief in them. "Jesus is man's Saviour" is the core of the preacher's proclamation and it remains proclamation. It is announced. It is true in itself. It is a truth about Him.

At first we spoke about the relation between Christian and non-Christian faith in terms of God in His activity of salvation, and we saw that that relation had to be expressed dialectically in terms of continuity and of discontinuity. Then we spoke about the relation between the Christian and non-Christian communities in terms of God in His activity of revelation, and we saw that that relation had to be expressed in terms of the distinctiveness and newness of the Christian community as the bearer of God's revelation. Now we speak of the relation between the message which the Christian community proclaims and the beliefs which the others hold. Here we see that there is true and essential discontinuity. The Christian message cannot be grafted upon other beliefs or added to them. There is only one way in which the Christian message can be accepted and that is by a radical conversion to it, so radical that the New Testament speaks of it as a new birth, the coming into being of a new creation, a dying and a living again (John 3: 3; 1 Pet. 1: 3; 2 Cor. 5: 17; Rom. 6: 5-8). The mission of the Church and the task of the missionary are directed to this end. There is no connection between one's obedience to Jesus Christ and any other attitude of mind or spirit which preceded it.

Psychologically, of course, there is always a connection, but religiously the man in Christ is a new man.

When Nicodemus came to Jesus he began his conversation with the acknowledgment that Jesus came from God. "No one can look at the things you are doing," he said, "without seeing that God is with you." The answer of Jesus was to deny that Nicodemus even saw what was happening. "No one," says Jesus, "can see the Kingdom of God unless he is born again." For the only way to see is to see from within; and only they are within who have been born of water and of the Spirit. John baptized with water demanding repentance, Jesus baptized with the Spirit demanding obedience; Nicodemus must repent and obey (John 3: 1-15).

The Christian message, in the last analysis, is concerned with creating messengers, participants in God's mission, so that the discussion as to what happens when the Christian message is set in a non-Christian world has to be pushed beyond the area of such a question as "Who will be saved?" into the area where the determining question is "What does God require?" It is essential for the discussion that we do not forget that in order to be a Christian one has to partake in the Church's mission, and that the only way to believe in the Gospel is to witness to it. I was "set apart for the Gospel," says Paul (Rom. 1: 1). He knew a "break" which had taken place in his life. That "break" always exists between what Christian obedience demands and what is demanded by every other kind of religious attitude and conviction.

God in His Activity of Fulfilment

God's work of salvation, God's work of revelation, God's call to mission—the natural climax of all this is God's final act of fulfilment. The activity of God will find its fulfilment when He brings all things under the headship of Christ (Eph. 1: 21-23). The activity of Christ will find its fulfilment when He has subdued all who contest His rule (1 Cor. 15: 24-25). The mission of the Church will find its fulfilment when it has grown to its full maturity in love (Eph. 4: 14-16). The ministry of the Holy Spirit will find its fulfilment when the witness of the Church to Christ is done (Acts 5: 32). In other words, the world at present is in the process of fulfilment so that, when we look at the process and precisely because we are looking at the process, it is impossible to describe it in any simple way. We see both the scaffolding and the building, both the work being done and the fruit of it. The very intricacy of the process lends truth to all the various types of assertions made about those relations which are the result of the Christian message being active in a non-Christian world. Professor Hocking defined the old missionary attitude to other religions as one that sought "radical displacement". A modern version of this attitude he described as that of "aloofness". He himself expressed great sympathy with the attitude of those who saw the Christian faith as the fulfilment of hopes entertained in other faiths, so that they believed comprehension and not displacement to be the goal of Christian evangelism. We can claim supremacy, they would say, for the Christian faith, but no monopoly; we can claim that it is absolute, but not exhaustive; we can claim that it is final, but not complete.

This reading of the process is legitimate within a discussion that is concerned with the process, but it becomes illegitimate when it is presented as an assessment of the nature of the Christian faith itself and its Gospel. That is why, in this whole discussion, there can be no way of arriving at agreed positions. The discussion can never be left within any one of the areas we have sought to define. These areas interpenetrate one another. If they did not, the discussion would be futile anyway; and, because they do, those involved in the discussion must necessarily speak about different things.

"The light shines in the darkness" (John 1: 15): this is a process within which it is impossible by strict definition to separate out the darkness from the light. "The light has come" (John 3: 19): this is an event which is both unique and alone, both final and complete. "The Life was the light of men" (John 1: 4): this is an activity which is particular in its origin but universal in its presence. "We have beheld his glory" (John 1 : 14): this is the experience which sets at the heart of Christian obedience the task of Christian witness.

In a discussion about the Christian message in a non-Christian world we must speak about all these things. We shall not, therefore, always agree in what we say. But we shall have helped to make clear why we are engaged in this discussion at all. We have been entrusted with a mission.

2

THE WORLD OF NATIONS
—THE SECULAR FRONTIER

"WE can hear the Gospel and obey it only in relation to the geographical, linguistic, social and general cultural realities which comprise our own world. At the secular frontier, question and answer are both shaped and reshaped by the situation in which human beings are found. Christ manifests Himself as Lord, but the attestations to that Lordship must be in the many languages of mankind.

"What do we find in the Old Testament? The temple of Yahweh is modelled upon Canaanite temple types and is built at the direction of a Phoenician architect. Kingship in Israel is an institutional latecomer, borrowed from Israel's neighbours. Yahweh is declared to be the giver of fertility to the soil. Sexual imagery is taken over from the religious traditions of the Canaanites. The forms of prophetic address are extremely close to modes employed in ancient Near Eastern religions. The situation is no different in the New Testament where the materials of Jewish sects and of Gnostic or pre-Gnostic speculation are freely used. Nor is the situation any different to-day."[1]

> The demand always is to take the world of nations and their cultures seriously, to set the Gospel in their midst in freedom, and to press into the service of the Gospel all varieties of cultural and religious forms. This also means greater boldness in rejecting those traditional forms which do not help in proclaiming the Gospel.[1]

Let another quotation underline and explicate the plea here made.

> The Church is sent because Christ came. The Gospel as such has no native country. He who goes out humbly with Christ in the world of all races will perpetually discover the multiple, but con-

[1] Professor Walter Harrelson, at the Bossey Consultation, July 1961.

stant, relevance of what he takes. It is the ruling conviction of the ecumenical movement within contemporary Christianity that it takes a whole world to understand a whole Christ. Those who take are not vulgarly universalizing their own culture: they are conveying that by the apprehension of which both they and their hearers learn. If the claims of the Gospel are valid, it could not be otherwise. For those who take only themselves may not expect to do more than teach. They who take Christ are in a state of perpetual discovery. The discoveries they make are through the discoveries they enable.[1]

The missionary call and the missionary task receive their substance from the rich variety in human living. The world of mankind in its differences is what the Gospel is meant to redeem and reconcile. In the tenth chapter of Genesis there are enumerated over seventy groups including the ancestors of the Hebrews: and the chapter closes with the affirmation:— "These are the families of the sons of Noah, according to their genealogies, in their nations; and from these the nations spread abroad on the earth after the flood" (Gen. 10: 32).

"In their lands, each with his own language, by their families, in their nations" (Gen. 10: 5)—here are those particularities of mankind from which arise the varieties of social, political, cultural and religious peculiarities which are the stuff of history. With this history God is concerned, and over it God will triumph. The differentiations between men constitute the cause of their strife and their strivings. Because of their differences they gave up building the city of man in which all men could dwell (Gen. 11: 8). But, at the end, these very differences will become part of the glory of the city of God. "I looked, and behold, a great multitude which no man could number, from every nation, from all tribes and peoples and tongues, standing before the throne and before the Lamb" (Rev. 7: 9).

The Words Used

The words used in the Hebrew which are translated interchangeably by "nations", "peoples", "heathen", and "Gen-

[1] Kenneth Cragg, *The Call of the Minaret*, Oxford University Press, p. 183.

tiles" denote either relationship based on kinship, or political and social factors, or occupation of one land. These same meanings attach to the Greek equivalents. But whatever the word used, whether in the original or the translation, only the context will show which of two ideas is intended.

Sometimes what is intended is to mark a certain group or groups as *"not-Israel"*, *"not-the Church"*.

> May God be gracious to us (Israel) and bless us, that thy way may be known among all nations (Ps. 67: 1-2).
>
> Ten men from the nations of every tongue shall take hold of the robe of a Jew, saying, Let us go with you, for we have heard that God is with you (Zech. 8: 23).
>
> In praying do not heap up empty phrases as the Gentiles do (Matt. 6: 7).
>
> Jerusalem will be trodden down by the Gentiles, until the times of the Gentiles are fulfilled (Lk. 21: 24).
>
> At one time you Gentiles in the flesh, called the uncircumcision, were alienated from the commonwealth of Israel (Eph. 2: 11-12).

But this differentiation between Israel and the nations or Gentiles is not what is always intended. Sometimes, by the use of the word "nations", the purpose is simply to speak of all men—*including Israel or the Church*—in the several forms of their communal life.

> When the Most High gave to the nations their inheritance, when he separated the sons of men. ... (Deut. 32: 8) ["sons of men" is here a parallel expression to the word "nations"].
>
> My house shall be called a house of prayer for all the nations (Mk. 11: 17).
>
> There were dwelling in Jerusalem Jews, devout men from every nation under heaven (Acts 2: 5).
>
> You shall be to me a Kingdom of priests and a holy nation (Ex. 19: 6; 1 Pet. 2: 9) [the word "nation" being used to designate Israel itself].

The actual words used, therefore, do not give any clue as to their precise meaning. The meaning is dependent on the theological context within which the words are used.

In the Old Testament

In the Old Testament treatment of the theme of the nations, emphasis falls on three facts.

(1) It is God's concern for the salvation of the nations which underlies His call of Abraham. "I will make of you a great nation ... you will be a blessing; and by you all the families of the earth will bless themselves" (Gen. 12: 2, 3). "The mountain of the house of the Lord shall be established and all the nations shall flow to it" (Is. 2: 2).

(2) It is out of the nations that Israel is formed. When God separated the sons of men and made them "peoples", He made also a people peculiar to Himself (Deut. 32: 8-9). Israel, therefore, is not a nation like other nations existing alongside them. Rather, Israel is a nation within and out of the nations and therefore addressed to them. It is significant that in Luke's gospel the genealogy of Jesus is traced back to Adam (Lk. 3: 23 f.) so that witness is borne to the fact that Israel, of which He is the fulfilment, is descended from the whole human race. To refer to but a few texts to show how Israel is formed out of the nations, there are in its ancestry Arameans, Hittites and Amorites, Egyptians, Kenites and a mixed multitude (Deut. 26: 5; Ezek. 16: 3; Gen. 41: 50; Judg. 1: 16; Ex. 12: 38).

(3) The God who chose Israel out of the nations and gave it a distinctive history remained also and always the God of the nations too. The same God who brought Israel from Egypt, brought the Philistines from Caphtor and the Syrians from Kir (Amos 9: 7). He is concerned with the life of the nations, for He is their judge (Amos 1: 3—2: 3). He uses them to carry out His will, for He is their God (Jer. 20: 4; 42: 12; Is. 10: 5).

This threefold emphasis naturally results in a conception of Israel's life and mission which gives quality not only to the history of Israel as such but to the history of the world also. First of all, Israel lives as a mission. When the Messiah fulfils Israel's destiny "His dominion shall be from sea to sea, and from the River to the ends of the earth" (Zech. 9: 10). "He will not fail or be discouraged till he has established justice in the earth; and the coastlands wait for his law" (Is. 42: 4). Secondly, because of what Israel is, it becomes the goal of the pilgrimage of the nations. "The Lord will arise upon Israel and His glory will be seen upon her. And nations shall come to her light and kings to the brightness of her rising" (Is. 60: 2, 3). "Of Zion it shall be said, This one and that one were born in her; Egypt and Babylon, Philistia and Tyre with Ethiopia—for the Most High himself will establish her" (Ps. 87: 4, 5). Thirdly, Israel becomes addressed to the nations as God's word to them. Israel makes heard among men God's plea to them; "Turn to me and be saved, all the ends of the earth! For I am God, and there is no other" (Is. 45: 22). Israel makes actual among men God's sovereignty over them. "Kings shall see and arise; princes, and they shall prostrate themselves; because of the Lord, who is faithful, the Holy One of Israel, who has chosen you" (Is. 49: 7). Israel makes available for men God's presence among them. "On this mountain the Lord of hosts will make for all peoples a feast. And he will destroy on this mountain the veil that is spread over all nations. He will swallow up death for ever, and the reproach of his people he will take away from all the earth" (Is. 25: 6-8).

Such a conception of Israel's life and mission demanded on the one hand that it guard its identity in the world, and on the other hand that it serve the world towards which its mission was set. Ezra and the priests, who composed the book of Leviticus, are the representatives of the movement which was concerned with maintaining the identity of Israel; while the writer of the book of Jonah is the last spokesman in the Old Testament for the obligation of Israel towards the nations of the world. "I am the Lord your God, who have separated you from the peoples. You shall be holy to me, you should be mine" (Lev. 20: 24, 26). "The word of the Lord came to Jonah, saying, Arise, go to Nineveh" (Jonah 1: 1, 2).

In the New Testament

As we pass from the Old Testament to the New, there takes place a basic change of perspective. Whereas in the Old Testament the life and mission of Israel is under the pressure of an obligation to be discharged, in the New Testament the life and mission of the Church is under the pressure of a movement that has been launched. The Messiah of Israel's promise has come, round Him the new Israel has been constituted, and the obligations of the Old Testament people of God have become the very means of life of the New Testament Church.

God's call of Abraham is matched by the mission of Jesus to the house of Israel. In the first instance, it is to Israel that Jesus addresses Himself in order that they may fulfil their calling to be the house of prayer for all the nations (Mk. 11: 17). Indeed, there was a sense in which Jesus came to Israel only (Matt. 15: 24). He came that in Him, as a Jew, His people may fulfil their obedience and therefore be restored to their mission to the world (Matt. 10: 6). Jesus was that mustard seed, that little remnant of faith in Israel, which when planted would grow into a tree. In Him was the promise that Israel would yet become that blessing by which the nations would bless themselves, that Israel would yet grow into the tree in which the birds of the air would nest (Matt. 13: 31).

When, at the end, the nations are gathered together by God (Matt. 25: 32), it is around Jesus Christ that this gathering will take place. He is the holy mountain (Heb. 12: 22), the new temple (John 2: 21), the true Israel (John 15: 1). The churches everywhere are the promise and prolepsis of this gathering of the nations, and precisely in being already a gathering from among the nations they are the first-fruits for God in all the world. Tenants gave the first-fruits of their land to the landlord as a token that the whole land belonged to him, so was the Church the first-fruits offered in every nation by that nation. Paul speaks of the Christian community in Achaia as the first-fruits there (Rom. 16: 5). So also does Luke emphasize, in his description of what happened on the day of Pentecost, that

252

among those who believed were devout Jews from every nation under heaven. The prophecy of Joel was that in the last days God would pour out His Spirit upon all flesh (Joel 2: 28-32). Peter, in claiming the fulfilment of this prophecy, was claiming that the little band of Christ's disciples on whom the Spirit came was the first-fruits of all humanity, even of all flesh. "If the dough offered as first fruits is holy, so is the whole lump; and if the root is holy, so are the branches" (Rom. 11: 16).

An example of the strength of this conviction that the Church is the fact and the promise of the gathering together of the nations (Acts 2: 5) is seen in the way in which Paul speaks of those to whom he takes the Gospel. We often tell those to whom we take the Gospel that Christ belongs to them; Paul told them that they belonged to the saints. The wall of partition was broken, so that men of all nations had equal access within the household of God (Eph. 2: 14). In this household all were fellow heirs, and all received the one Spirit from their common Father (Eph. 2: 18). This purpose of God is the mystery of history. Once it was hidden, but it is now disclosed to the nations (Rom. 16: 26) so that it is known among them how great the riches are of the glory of this mystery (Col. 1: 26).

This relation of *pars-pro-toto*, the part for the whole, between the Church and the nations is the sign too of the fact that the Lord of the Church is the Lord of the nations also. The great commission as found in Matthew's gospel rests on the declaration, "All authority in heaven and on earth has been given to me" (Matt. 28: 18), so that the Church goes to the nations under and as an expression of that authority. Jesus sends because He has authority to send. Wherever we go, we go to where He wields authority already. Whatever we do, we do in the name of His authority. And, having rendered our obedience, we leave the consequences of it to His authority to dispose as He will. The mission of the Church is part of the exercise of Christ's Lordship over the world.

Thus are the Old Testament emphases in its treatment of the theme of the nations carried forward into the New Testament, and thus also are postulated in the New Testament the same consequences for the life of the Church as are the consequences in the Old Testament for the life of Israel, only more so.

The Church too lives as a mission, "that repentance and forgiveness of sins should be preached in his name to all nations (Lk. 24: 47) until the Kingdom of the world has become the Kingdom of our Lord and of his Christ" (Rev. 11: 15). So does also the Church become the goal of the pilgrimage of the nations, "that through the Church the manifold wisdom of God might now be made known" (Eph. 3: 10), that wisdom of many colours by which the nations are led to become members of the same body and partakers of the promise in Christ Jesus (Eph. 3: 6). Wherefore, the Church finds itself not only gathered from among the nations but set amidst them to bring to them the word of the Gospel which they must hear before the end is accomplished (Mk. 13: 10).

The Church makes heard among men God's plea to them. "Fear God and give him glory, ye who dwell on earth, of every nation and tribe and tongue and people, for the hour of his judgment has come" (Rev. 14: 6-7). The Church makes actual among men God's sovereignty over them. "Do not be anxious," said Jesus, "when you are dragged before governors and kings for my sake to bear testimony before them and the Gentiles, for what you are to say will be given to you in that hour" (Matt. 10: 18, 19). As the seer of Patmos saw it (Rev. 11: 1-8), God will be with His witnesses so that the rage of the nations will come to nought. The Church makes available for men God's presence among them. As it is written, "I saw the holy city, new Jerusalem, coming down out of heaven from God, and I heard a great voice saying, 'Behold, the dwelling of God is with men'!" (Rev. 21: 2, 3).

In the final vision with which the Bible closes, God's will for the nations is seen as fully complete. The prophet had written, "Your gates shall be open continually; day and night they shall not be shut; that men may bring to you the wealth of the nations, with their kings led in procession" (Is. 60: 11). In the book of Revelation this prophecy is seen as having been fulfilled "In the city, the glory of God is its light, and its lamp is the Lamb. By its light shall the nations walk; and the kings of the earth shall bring their glory into it, and its gates shall never be shut—they shall bring into it the glory and the honour of the nations" (Rev. 21: 22-26).

In the Here and Now

It is inevitable that in a concise treatment of the subject of the world of nations in the Bible, many of the subtle nuances of the theme are missed; but the main lines, as they affect a discussion of the life and mission of the Church, are clear. The various types of community, which characterize human life, shift and change under the pressures of history: governments rise and fall, peoples coalesce into nation-states, nation-states split up into separate nations: for none of these processes or results should any theological validity be claimed. But in every "here and now" God shows His concern for the groupings in which men live and to which they belong, and He treats these groupings as units of human life to be challenged by His word, judged by His law, and invited to His bounty. It is because of this truth that the missionary purpose has to be addressed to the "nations" and not simply to men, for it is aimed at the life of the world and not merely to the interior life of the soul.

The biblical concern for the nations is thus seen, in the first instance, as a concern to cross with the Gospel every secular frontier between man and man—whether it be the frontier of race or class, caste or culture, tribe or language, nation or country. And, in the second instance, it is seen as the concern to create within each secular frontier such a testimony to the Gospel as will claim the life within that frontier to a service of it. The significance of nation-states in missionary strategy to-day is not a significance derived from the Bible as such. It is a significance attaching to nation-states in the "here and now" of the twentieth century. If Scripture is right in what it says, God is as interested in the forms that human community takes in the twentieth century as He was in the forms it took in the centuries in which the Bible was written.

There is no escaping the fact that to-day, in the lands of the younger churches, there is a pressure to see the Church established in each nation-state as a church that is nation-wide and as, therefore, the means by which that nation can participate in God's total will for His Church in the world. Nor is there any escaping the fact that many influences in the older churches desire to arrest this development. Where caution is expressed against attempting to identify "the nations" in the Bible with the modern nation-states, that caution must be heeded; for it is so easy to slip from a concern to build a church for the nation into a desire to build a church of the nation. But where the caution expressed is the result of apprehension in the churches of the West at the probable consequences for their life of the birth of united churches in Asia and Africa, that caution is unfortunate. It is unfortunate too that as long as there were only Western nations to reckon with, nations were not Christianly suspect, but that they have become suspect now because new nations have come to birth which are free of Western dominance. The missionary movement of the Church must reckon with nationhood in the world. Indeed, God's concern is not only with men as persons but also with them as nations, with those secular qualities of man's life which go to make up the life of the world. "God loved the world" and not just people, the Gospel is for the redemption of the world and not just for the salvation of souls.

Let two quotations suffice to underline the significance of the truth here stated. The first quotation is from a speech of John R. Mott delivered at the Edinburgh Conference of 1910, while the second quotation is from the Constitution Canons and Rules of the Church of India, Pakistan, Burma and Ceylon.[1]

A programme literally world-wide in its scope is indispensable to enrich and complete the Church. Jesus Christ must have all the races and all the nations through which to make known fully His excellences and to communicate adequately His power.

The Church, when so organized in a great region having such

[1] The C.I.P.B.C. is the province in these countries of the Anglican Church. (The Constitution, p. 18.)

a natural, political or historical unity of its own, is in these Declarations called "a regional Church". Such a Church has a life of its own with a character, conditions and needs peculiar to itself, and it also has in its measure the liberty which belongs to the Church of Christ to order its own life in continual dependence on the Spirit of God. The liberty of a regional Church has enabled, and may in any place enable, the God-given genius of great nations to find its appropriate expression in the worship and the work of the Church, and so the riches of the nations have been carried into the City of God.

In the Ministry of Jesus

Before proceeding with this argument, however, it is essential to make sure once again that the integral relation of the missionary enterprise in its specialized sense to the total dimension which belongs to the mission of the Church is never forgotten. For if it is, the consequence will be also to forget the true relation of the mission of the Church to the coming of the Kingdom. The missionary enterprise must result in the founding and strengthening of churches, but its concern is with preparation for the coming of the King.

The gospels of Matthew and Luke introduce the person of Jesus by tracing His genealogy. Matthew calls Him the son of David, the son of Abraham (Matt. 1: 1), while Luke shows Him as descended from Adam (Lk. 3: 38). This threefold reference characterized His ministry. It was, first of all, to all men (Acts 10: 38) in their several needs. Secondly, its challenge was particularly directed to the children of Abraham (John 8: 31-59), recalling them to a sense of their true mission under God. While, thirdly, its strategy was to select and train a band of disciples who would announce and demonstrate the truth that God's Kingdom had arrived (Mk. 3: 14). The missionary enterprise of the Church too carries forward this same threefold reference. It is addressed to all men within all their forms of human relationships and in all their needs. It is incessantly concerned with the renewal and revival of the Church and with its extension. It is characterized by its obligation to manifest the Church in the world as a priestly Kingdom by whose life God is mediated to men and men are presented to God.

Another feature of the Gospel story is that in it the mission of Jesus is set out in three stages. At first, it is a mission to the lost house of Israel (Matt. 10: 6). Immediately prior to the crucifixion it becomes a mission to the nations (Lk. 10: 1). And after the resurrection, it is a mission to all the world (Acts 1: 8). Paul adds a fourth stage, after the Ascension, that of the Church's mission to the cosmic powers. Israel, the nations, the world, the powers of the cosmos (Eph. 3: 10)—these categories are another way of looking at the missionary outreach of the Church.

Israel still remains a special and specialized concern. God's purpose for Israel is that "by the mercy shown to the Gentiles, they also may receive mercy" (Rom. 11: 3). That the churches among the Gentiles commend the mercy of God which they have received to the children of Israel must always remain a perpetual obligation. No wonder Paul looked upon the contribution of Gentile Christians to the Church in Jerusalem as a symbol of a permanent relationship! (Rom. 15: 21). This concentration of Jesus, in His ministry, on the house of Israel throws light also on the nature of His mission. Were He concerned only with spreading a teaching, He would not have needed to restrict Himself for any continuous period to a specific group. "The great charm of promulgating codes of conduct or sketching plans for the social, political, and economic transformation of human life is that you need set no limits to the area within which the writ of your new code shall run, and the administration of your new plan operate. But if the enterprise is a ministry operating through personal encounter between those who give and those who receive the service: then it can only be effective in the place where its servants are."[1] Christ's strategy of restriction was necessary in order to create within Israel a community which would be the bearer of His mission. "I will make you fishers of men" (Mk. 1: 17) was what He told His first disciples. They were to be engaged in catching men and

[1] T. W. Manson, *Jesus and the Non-Jews*, Athlone Press, p. 15.

not simply in teaching them. The very word for disciple which is used in the Gospels is a word which means "an apprentice at a trade" in contra-distinction to "a pupil in a school".

The second category of nations defines men in their particularities. The steel workers of Sheffield are a nation in the biblical sense, so also are the scheduled castes of India, so also are the citizens of the several nations in the world. A mission to a nation is a mission not simply to the persons who compose it, but to that which belongs to its nationality. When in Ceylon, for instance, the Buddhists and Hindus accuse their fellow citizens who are Christians of being denationalized, they are saying in effect that the Christian mission to Ceylon has not been a mission to its nationality. Or, when the cement workers of Kastel in Germany set up their own parish, on an occupational rather than a neighbourhood basis, they are saying that that is the way they know of maintaining their nationality in the Gospel.

As for the mission to the world, the missionary obedience required must be spelled out in terms of geographical reference. The Gospel must push out from land to land. As John R. Mott put it, "The missionary activities of the Church are the circulation of its blood, which would lose its vital power if it never flowed to the extremities ..."[1] Paul's missionary life had this quality of always wanting to go still further. At Caesarea his eye is on Rome (Acts 25: 11), when preparing to go to Rome his eye is on Spain (Rom. 15: 24).

And finally, there is the purpose of God that through the Church His manifold wisdom might be made known to the principalities and powers in the heavenly places (Eph. 3: 10). The mission of the Church is set within the processes of human history, but it is itself more than a historical development. It is part of the eternal purpose of God by which all creation is encompassed, and the intangibles which impinge upon this earthly life of man are made to serve that purpose.

[1] Quoted from the speech at Edinburgh referred to on p. 256.

The Missionary Calling

Within this total calling of the Church, what does it mean to speak specifically of the missionary enterprise? Can the word "missionary" be so defined as to carry a determinate meaning?

Before an answer is attempted, an explanation is necessary as to why these questions about a definition of the word "missionary" should be raised so late in the argument of this book. If there was one thing which the consultations on "missions" revealed, it was that, while there was a great deal of hesitation in setting down a definition, there was pretty general agreement as to what the discussion was about. In other words, a discussion of substance was never inhibited by the absence of an agreed definition. This meant that the way to seek a definition was to come to it after a discussion of substance. The necessity of a definition on the other hand, however much such a definition may be open to criticism, is to ensure that at least we have a pointer to the real nature of the missionary calling as a distinct and distinguishable vocation within the mission of the Church.

It is said that Confucius created a new idea of society by what he called the process of rectifying names. Socrates wrought his intellectual revolution by seeking definitions. It may be that the missionary enterprise too needs a vigorous scrutiny of the terms that it uses and the precise meaning of those terms. There is too much tendency to speak of everything that belongs to the task of the Church as mission and therefore to designate almost anything as missionary. A clarification of the problems that belong to "missions" must include a greater preciseness of language.

It is true enough that since the Gospel is for the world, a going from New York to Sierra Leone with the Gospel cannot be theologically different from taking the Gospel within New York to East Harlem. There has been too much theological romanticism connected with the simple act of a missionary going across the seas. But the fact still remains that, within this one world, there are many frontiers which demarcate the different ways in which men live and belong to one another, so that to cross these frontiers with the Gospel becomes a specific calling. "Foreign" mission may not be a separate theological category but it does denote an identifiable task.

In terms then of the meaning of the word "nation" and its significance, the first quality of the missionary calling is its direct reference to a secular frontier. The phrase *Christian witness* suggests immediately the distinction between the person witnessing and those to whom the witness is borne. The one sees what to the others must be pointed out. They are gathered around an object—the Gospel—and conversation is taking place concerning it. There is a second phrase, *Christian evangelist*, which is close in meaning to the phrase Christian witness, but which points to a different distinction. In the work of evangelism it is man and the Gospel which are distinguished from one another. God acts and the evangelist is concerned with man's true response to God's action, both his own response and the response of his fellows. The evangelist stands alongside those to whom he is the evangelist so that together they may apprehend and be apprehended by God's action to save in Jesus Christ. The distinction which the phrase *Christian missionary* suggests is the distinction between a "here" and a "there". The missionary belongs to a world secularly defined which is his world. There are those who belong to other worlds. He goes across. Why does he go across? Because he is sent, because he is invited, because he is needed. On that other side, he is going to be a Christian witness, he is also going to be a Christian evangelist. Is there anything else he is going to be? Yes, he is also going to be a Christian missionary because he will maintain the address of his vocation which is the secularity of that area of life to which he has gone. What will this mean? It will mean a concern that in that area of life there will be a Christian community which is indigenous. The secularity peculiar to that community must become the home of the Gospel.

God made the world, and man must learn to receive the world at God's hands. Those who seek to make the world and man's life in it autonomous, de-secularize it as surely as those

who seek to charge the world with spirituality. In making the
world secular, the Gospel both subordinates the world to its
Creator and destroys every religious pretension with which the
secular in any area of life has armed itself. The idols of primi-
tive tribes must go if the cultures of those tribes are to be
exorcized. So also must all other cultures be made really secular
that in them God alone may be worshipped. To make secular is
to obtain vacant possession of every home of man that in it God
and God alone may dwell.

The whole posture of the missionary, therefore, is to have eye
and ear directed to this work of Christ by which He takes
possession of men's homes. The missionary too has come to join
others in their home that in it Christ may find His dwelling
place. "Let me join you" is the missionary request; it is not
"Will you join me?" Of course, the extent of freedom to
proclaim the Gospel in any particular situation may vary, but
the missionary cause is served when the opportunity to be
present as a Christian is offered and taken. The Roman
Catholic Church was asked in one place in India whether it
would send nuns to serve in a leprosy hospital on the distinct
understanding that they would not talk about Christ to the
patients. The Church accepted the offer. The Danish mission
was offered the opportunity of founding a hospital in Southern
Arabia on the same understanding and, the opportunity was
taken. "Destroy this temple," said Jesus, "and I will raise up
My Body in its place" (John 2: 19). This Body must become
present in every home of man, and every other temple in it
must go.

Paul expressed his missionary motive as that of presenting a
Church to Christ at His coming in every nation and place; he
fulfilled his missionary career in the constant awareness of
following Christ into every place. Speaking of Paul the missionary, Karl Barth says:

> He is eye and ear in a state which expressions such as inspira-
> tion, alarm, or stirring or overwhelming emotion, do not satis-
> factorily describe. He is actually thrown out of his course by seeing
> and hearing what I for my part do not see or hear. And if ever I

come to fear lest mine is a case of self-hallucination, one glance at the secular events of those times, one glance at the widening circle of ripples in the pool of history, tells me of a certainty that a stone of unusual weight must have been dropped into deep water somewhere—tells me that, among all the hundreds of peripatetic preachers and miracle-workers from the Near East who in that day must have gone along the same Appian Way into imperial Rome, it was this one Paul, seeing and hearing what he did, who was the cause, if not of all, yet of the most important developments in that city's future.[1]

The determining fact, then, in the missionary calling is that a missionary goes to a place to belong there, and also to represent there the arrival of the Christ. So that, however much he may be identified with the Church in the place to which he has come, and however fully he may have shared in that Church's identification with its world, the missionary will always remain a person who has come from "there to here". He will be a true representation of the nature of the Gospel which comes from God to man, but remains among men a pointer to God. Missions testify to the distance of the Gospel from organized human society as well as to its essential relation to mankind.

Thus we see how in the missionary enterprise itself are symbolized some of the basic Christian affirmations. The physical act of travel from one country to another testifies both to the fact that God has acted for man's salvation in one time and place, as well as to the fact that this Gospel is for all men. There is testimony too to the ex-centric pattern of God's working. Jerusalem was the centre of Israel but the Messiah came from Nazareth, the cross of man's redemption was planted outside the city gates, the King of God's kingdom was proclaimed by an inscription on a cross. The missionary comes and remains as a sign of this ex-centricity. Looked at rightly, is not the Church itself ex-centric to the world? At least the world looks upon the Church as quite circumferential.

And lastly, what is most important of all, the missionary

[1] Karl Barth, *The Word of God and the Word of Man* (English translation, 1928), pp. 62f.

repeats in human terms the incarnation, which is the essence of God's way with men.

> He did not send technical assistance to our backward world;
> Gabriel and a company of experts with their know-how.
> Instead, He came Himself.
> He hungered in the wilderness, He was stripped naked on a cross
> But hungering with us He became our bread,
> And suffering for us He became our joy.[1]

He came Himself—that is what it means to be a missionary, and it carries with it the further implication that he who comes, comes to mediate his Lord.

> For me 'twas not the truth you taught,
> To you so clear, to me so dim,
> But when you came you brought
> A sense of Him.
> And through your eyes He beckoned me,
> And through your heart His love was shed,
> Till I lost sight of you and saw
> The Christ instead.[2]

And yet, all who come from one country to another, all who cross a secular frontier, are not missionaries. Are they? I was often told in the United States of America that I was a missionary to them from Asia. I always denied that this was so. I was too conscious of the fact that I had no intention of "belonging" to the American people. "Call me a fraternal worker, if you like," I used to say, "but don't call me a missionary." Sometimes the issues are confused by raising the question about long-term and short-term missionaries. The length of the term will not determine whether a person is fulfilling a missionary calling or not. That depends on the nature of the calling itself. The question simply is, what is the significance to one's calling of the secularity of the secular frontier which one has crossed?

To speak of a missionary is to speak in terms of the world; to speak of a fraternal worker is to speak in terms of the Church;

[1] Edith Pierce: quoted in *The Kingdom Overseas*, Dec. 1960.
[2] Author unknown.

to speak of long-terms or short-terms is simply to speak in terms of tasks.

The Earthly Reference of the Task

It is at this point that the insistence on the earthly reference of God's salvation in Christ becomes luminous. To speak about God saving the world is to speak about God's saving activity within the structures of human society. That means the primacy of the Church in every "nation" as the strategy of God for His saving work in that nation.

> The universalism of the Christian mission [says R. K. Orchard] is not the universalism of an internationalism which grows by abstracting men from out of their national settings, but rather the universalism which, enabling men to see the true centre of their living, Jesus Christ, from within their national setting, exposes their national life to the judgment and mercy of that one central word which is God's act in Christ, so that the possibility is opened of the nations bringing their glory and honour to the one city of God. If this is anywhere near the truth, it calls for some radical rethinking of the place of churches in national life, and of what functions are properly assigned to international Christian bodies and what should not be so assigned.[1]

The direct concern, then, of the missionary enterprise is the planting of the Church in every nation and with its growth and expansion in numbers as well as in obedience. Indeed, the missionary has no greater responsibility to the church which has received him than to help it to maintain its own missionary passion. The word "missionary" is used here in distinction to the word "evangelistic". It is not enough to maintain evangelistic fervour; it is essential to be missionary, which means to carry the Gospel across secular frontiers. That such frontiers exist within every nation-state is only too true, so that in order to be a missionary one does not have to go from one country to another. And yet, because this very frontier of the nation-state

[1] Quoted from an address delivered in Nov. 1959 at the Annual Meeting of Carey Hall, Birmingham.

is something so significant to-day, the missionary enterprise is not ill-defined when that frontier is used as part of that definition.

Certainly, there is a church already in practically every country, so that it is right to speak of a missionary being sent by a church and being received by a church—this sending and receiving are essential—but, in the legitimate attention that is given to the questions involved in this sending and receiving, there must be no detraction from the truth that a missionary is primarily a person sent to a world and not to a church and that therefore, in an ultimate sense, he is not so much a person sent by a church as by its Lord.

Somehow in the procedures of missionary administration a way must be found of remembering the subsidiary nature of the church to church connection within the missionary relation. The primary connection in the missionary relation is that between the Lord who sends and the world to which He sends. When a church accepts its calling to be a mission to the world, that acceptance results in its sons and daughters going into the world both in its geographical extension as well as in its national particularities. So also must it be that when a church accepts its situation in the world it is responsive to receiving missionaries from other churches situated elsewhere. There is strength both in giving and in receiving. The "younger" churches display the strength that belongs to churches which have received, the "older" churches display the strength that belongs to churches which have given. The time has arrived for the converse also to become true. To send and to receive are equal obligations of every church. They are also permanent obligations, for it is a false position to maintain that missionaries go where they are needed and withdraw when that need is met. The need which the missionary enterprise meets, both its sending and its receiving, is not a need that is ever met; it is the need for a church to be a mission. The missionary is as integral to the being of the Church as is the witness or the evangelist. All three together identify the Church as the Church in mission.

The Challenge of One World

There is one further element to be taken into account in this discussion, and that is the fact of the emergence to-day of a common way of life among all men in spite of and within the particularities of their nationhood. The development and spread of scientific technology into the remotest villages of every continent are producing a mental attitude which makes every man claim the whole world as his habitation. "The Hindu workman," says Lesslie Newbigin, "in a modern factory will smear the sign of his god upon the latest giant machine imported from America or Russia, and not feel any sense of incongruity in doing so."[1] The giant machine represents the one world, the local god represents the many nations. The missionary enterprise of the churches has the inescapable obligation to bind this one world together with the one Gospel and so substitute for the many gods the One God who is the God of all the nations as well.

This means that the missionary enterprise should not only be characterized by its concern to cross every secular frontier, but that it should also possess and exhibit a unity of movement such as is demanded by a world rapidly becoming one. The reality of the ecumenical movement is the measure of the decision of the churches to accept this obligation. Only as churches together engaged in a common mission can the churches in their missionary enterprise bear witness to what the Lord is doing in His world. The instruments forged by the World Council of Churches and the International Missionary Council and the decision now to merge these two organizations portend a development in the missionary obedience of the Church which is in itself part of that obedience. No definition of a missionary can be satisfactory which describes only his movement and his task; it must also say who he is. And no description of who he is can be allowed to pass which does not envisage him as committed to the ecumenical vision and strategy. This is part of the

[1] Quoted from his address to the North American Advisory Committee of the I.M.C., Nov. 14, 1958.

specific correlation which exists between the missionary calling and the working out of God's purposes among the nations.

There are two sides to this ecumenical vision and strategy. There is, on the one hand, the side represented by the organs of the churches and, on the other hand, the side represented by secular movements. Both must be taken equally seriously. *God's design is one humanity.* A secular side of this design is being realized in the work of the United Nations Organization and its several agencies. *God's design is a new creation.* A secular side of this design is being fulfilled through scientific research, increased technical efficiency, the application of atomic power for peaceful purposes, and similar developments. *God's design for man is abundant life.* A secular side of this design is the goal of such organizations as the World Health Organization, the Food and Agriculture Organization, and the World Bank. *God's design for man is life in community* characterized by freedom and justice, and the wealth of human association. A secular side of this design is the concerns of the Security Council and of the World Court, and the various programmes of U.N.E.S.C.O. The missionary enterprise is not an enterprise apart from or even alongside these secular movements. It is essentially also a secular movement which gives to these other movements their true place and perspective in the working out of God's total design. The missionary enterprise and the ecumenical movement must provide the means of interlocking man's eternal destiny and his present life, of interweaving the life of the people of God which is the Church with the lives of men as men which is the World. Let four illustrations suffice to show how this obligation can be and is being fulfilled.

(i) The Division of Inter-Church Aid and Refugee Service of the World Council of Churches has rejected all qualifications of need in terms of Christian denominations or the political complexion of nations. Need is human whether it is among Christians or Muslims, Armenians or Baptists, Congolese or Chinese; and human need must be met in purely human terms without religious strings attached.

(ii) The Commission of the Churches on International

Affairs brings the churches into true political participation in current events without embroiling them in party or national politics. It also points the way in which a church in any country can act as part of the Church on political questions while taking equally seriously its life and commitment within and to that country.

(iii) Missionary Societies are engaged in a policy of re-appraisal and re-statement which will make the missionary operation more truly congruent with the secular realities of the world. Since missionaries go to "nations", the life of these nations is a prime consideration in the development of missionary policies. Also, since the world is one world there is the need for greater central operations such as are coming into being through the Theological Education Fund, and the Projects Fund of the Division of World Mission and Evangelism.

(iv) The whole ecumenical movement has developed a system of consultations and conferences and studies, as an essential feature of its life, thereby emphasizing the fact that only common thought can undergird a common obedience, and that only as the churches are aware of their secular relation to the religions and ideologies which are part of the cultures in which they are set, can they bear effective witness within them.

The Promise and the Command

The world—the world of religions and of nations—that then is what the missionary movement is concerned with, and it is emasculated where it is thought of in smaller terms. The missionary represents everywhere the claims of the King and witnesses everywhere to the thrust of the Kingdom. In every situation, and in terms relevant to each, he fulfils his duty as Christ's ambassador calling upon men on behalf of Christ, "Be ye reconciled to God" (2 Cor. 5: 20).

The promise of Jesus to the Church was that the gates of hell will not prevail against it (Matt. 16: 18), but neither can those gates be battered down unless they are stormed. A church which has become a besieged fortress to be defended, or even a recognized community with a millet existence, is in no position to inherit or experience this promise of Christ. However threatened its life, the Church lives by its mission. It is itself only as its doors are open to the world and its precincts resound to the tread of many feet as they go out or come in, whoever they be.

> Throw open the doors!
> I will not have the house of prayer, the church of Christ,
> The sanctuary, turned into a fortress ...
> The Church shall be open, even to our enemies.
> Open the door![1]

"The first day of the week, the doors being shut where the disciples were, Jesus came and stood among them and said to them, 'Peace be with you. As the Father has sent me, even so I send you.' And when he had said this, he breathed on them, and said to them, 'Receive the Holy Spirit'." (John 20: 19-22).

[1] Thomas à Becket in *Murder in the Cathedral*, by T. S. Eliot, Faber and Faber Ltd., London; Harcourt, Brace and World Inc., New York.